Event → Feeling → Th... 11 → Behavior

SOCIAL ○ SELF
Stigma ↑ stigma Disciminitive:
                    Behaviors?

Thought
Rational Stigma
            Self
Stereotypics   gender identity
                    age.
                    ect

                predjudus:
                feelings/Emotions
                irational?

THE SOCIAL PSYCHOLOGY OF DISABILITY

SELF INTERNALIZATION
    • Self-Doubt
    • Insecurity
    • Participation

Meardia
Society
Family
Self   all effect all
Friends

ACADEMY OF REHABILITATION PSYCHOLOGY SERIES

Series Editors

Bruce Caplan, *Editor-in-Chief*

Timothy Elliott

Janet Farmer

Robert Frank

Barry Nierenberg

George Prigatano

Daniel Rohe

Stephen Wegener

Volumes in the Series

Ethics Field Guide: Applications in Rehabilitation Psychology
Thomas R. Kerkhoff and Stephanie L. Hanson

The Social Psychology of Disability
Dana S. Dunn

D = dissatisfation of current state
V = Vision of future
F = First Step towards future
R = Restance

$$D \times V \times F > R$$

The Social Psychology of Disability

Dana S. Dunn

sometimes don't have V
so don't move away
from D therefore not F

OXFORD
UNIVERSITY PRESS

OXFORD
UNIVERSITY PRESS

Oxford University Press is a department of the University of Oxford.
It furthers the University's objective of excellence in research, scholarship,
and education by publishing worldwide.

Oxford   New York
Auckland   Cape Town   Dar es Salaam   Hong Kong   Karachi
Kuala Lumpur   Madrid   Melbourne   Mexico City   Nairobi
New Delhi   Shanghai   Taipei   Toronto

With offices in
Argentina   Austria   Brazil   Chile   Czech Republic   France   Greece
Guatemala   Hungary   Italy   Japan   Poland   Portugal   Singapore
South Korea   Switzerland   Thailand   Turkey   Ukraine   Vietnam

Oxford is a registered trademark of Oxford University Press
in the UK and certain other countries.

Published in the United States of America by
Oxford University Press
198 Madison Avenue, New York, NY 10016

Library of Congress Cataloging-in-Publication Data
Dunn, Dana S.
The social psychology of disability / Dana S. Dunn.
pages cm. — (Academy of Rehabilitation psychology series)
Includes bibliographical references and index.
ISBN 978-0-19-998569-2
1. People with disabilities. 2. Sociology of disability. 3. Disability studies. I. Title.
HV1568.D86 2015
305.9'08—dc23
2014021507

9 8 7 6 5 4 3
Printed in the United States of America
on acid-free paper

ACCESS

$\overset{P}{\underset{R}{\text{Act}}}$

Plan

Plan

ASSessment
- Ability / Aptitude
- Knoledge / Education
- Work / Experence
- Helth / Welness
- $ - Social life

1 Personality
2 Intrests
3 Motivation
4 What Need

For Beatrice A. Wright

Compassionate researcher, teacher, and friend

World

Physical   Provider
Medical   etc
Education
Legal
Political
Food

Vocational created for World Wars
      -1919 "Smith Act"   soldiers

congressed :

      Rehabilitation law   (More about $)
         = Rehabilitation Counseling

70's forces on developmental
                    disability
            (Retardation?)

80's-90's forces Autonomy divisions
             for disabled
             & Agency

80's Public Rehab -State -Public fund
                    -Dept of Voc Rehab
      Privet Rehab   & Blind

American W/Disabilities Act
   -1990 - ADA Amendment 2008
        -access to Employment
        -access to Building Government
        -MOBILITY

Autonomy = Freedom to make own choice
Agency = Power to make choice

Contents

Foreword

HAVE YOU EVER read a book that literally changed your life? A book that provided so many insights into the most complicated aspects of human behavior that you literally could not put it down? That book for me was *Physical Disability, A Psychological Approach* by Beatrice Wright; for you it may be its "sequel" *The Social Psychology of Disability* by Dana Dunn.

What is the story? It was the early 1970s and I had just completed my undergraduate degree in psychology at the Ohio State University. I knew I wanted to pursue a doctorate in psychology but did not know much beyond this. I had the good fortune to be hired as a vocational rehabilitation counselor for the State of Ohio. My career began with interviewing clients, developing insight into how they saw their situation, and then realizing the many contradictions they faced. For example, they defined themselves by what they could do; however, they found that others in their environment seemed to define them by what they could not do. I was bewildered by the mixed social messages they were constantly bombarded with, messages that ranged from pity to being idolized. How could I help them navigate this confusing social environment, when I did not have a clue about what was happening? I found the complexity of this social interactional landscape incredibly intriguing from an intellectual and a professional standpoint. I was hungry for knowledge but found nothing in the general psychological literature that was relevant. Then I discovered "the" classic book on the psychology of disability. This book sealed my fate. I then knew I wanted to become a rehabilitation psychologist. Parenthetically, I was not alone in an "aha" moment engendered by reading Dr. Wright's book. Years ago, I was in a reflective conversation with Mitchell Rosenthal, Ph.D., a close friend and leader in the field of brain injury rehabilitation. I asked what sparked his interest in rehabilitation psychology. His reply was simple: "Beatrice Wright's book." Similarly, in the preface to this book, Dr. Dunn reflects on the profound effect Dr. Wright's book has had on how he thinks about behavior.

So, what is so compelling about this text? The answer is the author, quality writing, and the content. Dr. Dana Dunn is a respected and recognized educator and writer. He completed his Ph.D. in social psychology at the University of Virginia in 1987. He is a fellow of three divisions of the American Psychological Association including General Psychology, Society for the Teaching of Psychology, and Rehabilitation Psychology. Recently, he was awarded the Charles L. Brewer Award for Distinguished Teaching, American Psychological Foundation in 2013. He has authored 25 books, 51 referred papers, and 52 book chapters. He has been an editor or on the editorial board of 6 journals and a reviewer for 12 journals. He received the Outstanding Academic Book by the American Library Association in 2005 for his book *Measuring Up: Educational Assessment Challenges and Practices for Psychology*. In short, he knows how to write clearly and succinctly.

What about the content? The book is written in a manner that pulls the reader in. Each chapter has a similar structure. Dr. Dunn begins with thought-provoking quotes and compelling examples. He then poses questions to the reader and proceeds to answer the questions in the body of the chapter using clear and concise prose. For example, he asks, "What does it mean to adapt to a disability? Do individuals who have congenital disabilities need to adapt to their conditions? Or, is adaptation limited to those who somehow acquire a disability? Does psychosocial adjustment differ from adaptation? What does it mean to accept a disability?" He then goes on to cite the historic and contemporary research that addresses these questions. Each chapter ends with questions that prompt the reader to revisit the key ideas presented, thus helping to solidify learning. Dr. Dunn's skills in sound pedagogy are consistently apparent.

The content of *The Social Psychology of Disability* is comprehensive. Topics include coping with disability, positive psychology and disability, stigma and stereotyping, spread effects, attitudes towards persons with a disability, the fundamental negative bias, somatopsychology, and disability identity to name a few. Throughout, Dr. Dunn highlights the seminal contributions of the founders of the field of rehabilitation psychology especially the work of Kurt Lewin, Beatrice Wright, and Tamara Dembo. He emphasizes Lewin's formulation of field theory and the critical point that behavior does not reside in the person but is the joint outcome of the interaction of person's characteristics in the context of the environment.

As a rehabilitation psychologist, I was particularly heartened that Dr. Dunn specifically writes about the 20 "value-laden beliefs and principles." He discusses the first five principles in Chapter 1 and an additional seven principles in Chapter 6. These principles, which were first articulated by Beatrice Wright in 1972, are not widely known or understood by most rehabilitation psychologists. Yet, they represent the central principles from which the field of rehabilitation psychology can rightly claim its unique identity as a specialty within the larger discipline of psychology. Highlighting these principles is just one more example of why this book will become standard reading in the field of rehabilitation psychology in the coming years.

In closing, I wish to publicly thank Dr. Dunn for writing this book. Rehabilitation psychology was desperately in need of a reboot and summary of our field. Dr. Wright's second edition of her book was published in 1983. Much has happened in the fields of rehabilitation psychology and social psychology over the past 30 years. Dr. Dunn does an outstanding job melding the contemporary insights of both fields in a book that will inspire the next generation of rehabilitation psychologists. I am hopeful that you will be enlightened and challenged by the issues raised in the book and their relevance to a world in which disability and chronic illness are increasingly prevalent. You are about to read what will become the new, classic text on the psychological aspects of disability. I am hopeful that you too will have an "aha" experience after reading this seminal contribution to the rehabilitation psychology literature.

Daniel E. Rohe, Ph.D., ABPP (Rp)

Mayo Clinic, Rochester Minnesota

Past President, Division of Rehabilitation Psychology

American Psychological Association

Past President, American Board of Rehabilitation Psychology

Preface and Acknowledgments

SEVERAL YEARS AGO, Beatrice Wright and I were discussing a project that was to involve her classic book, *Physical Disability: A Psychosocial Approach* (Wright, 1983). More than any other text I've read as a psychologist, this book has had a profound influence on how I think about behavior, including, of course, the social psychology of disability. At one point in our conversation, Beatrice, who is known to have strong and decided opinions, said simply, "Dana, you should write your own book." That particular project did not advance, but I never forgot her comment, which, if you know Beatrice, represented both an encouragement and a gentle demand.

Let me come clean as an author: I am a social psychologist by training and temperament. I have no formal training in rehabilitation psychology but, over 20 years ago, I had the opportunity to collect some data from a local rehabilitation hospital for a small project on finding positive meaning in adverse circumstances. As a matter of course, I began to read the literature pertaining to disability, rehabilitation, and social-psychological concepts, and was surprised by two facts. First, I was unaware that there was research on the social psychology of disability (I regret that statement is true of most social psychologists, living or dead). Second, I was amazed by the richness of the ideas and how, well, useful they seemed when it came to actually applying social psychology to improve people's lives. In the years since, I have been fortunate to be able to continue to think and write about research that lies along the social–clinical interface in rehabilitation psychology.

I am very grateful to my colleagues and friends, Bruce Caplan and Timothy Elliott, for encouraging me to pursue the book project and to Joan Bossert at Oxford for making it all happen. This is my sixth project with Oxford University Press and I continue to be impressed with how smoothly things proceed where book development and production are concerned (fellow authors will know this praise is not given lightly). Once the book was submitted to Oxford, Michele Rusin and Bruce Caplan reviewed the manuscript and offered detailed and thoughtful comments; I am in their professional debt. I want to thank my friends and colleagues in Division 22 (Rehabilitation Psychology) of the American Psychological Association (APA), especially Daniel Rohe, for making me feel welcome all these years and for supporting my ideas and work at so many turns. I am honored to be a part of Division 22 and, more recently, a member of the Board of Trustees of the Foundation for Rehabilitation Psychology. My collaborations with Tim Elliott and Gitendra Uswatte, too, have richly informed my approach to disability and rehabilitation matters. My friends on APA's Committee on Disability Issues in Psychology (CDIP)—Erin E. Andrews, Megan Cory Carlos, Elizabeth Mazur, Lawrence Pick, Carrie R. Pilarski, Nannette Stump, Joseph E. Rath, Ann Marie Warren, James L. Werth, Jr., Anju Khubchandani, Mara Lunaria, Patrick J. S. Waring, and Phillip Keck—have helped me think about disability more deeply of late, especially where issues of social policy are concerned. Erin Andrews graciously read and commented on each draft chapter—her insights were invaluable. Any factual faults or interpretive errors in this book, whether intentional or accidental, are mine alone.

I am very grateful to my students who worked with me on disability-related projects over the years and from whom I learned so much: Brittany Beard, Stacey Boyer, Clint Brody, Shane Burcaw, Sarah Dougherty, Susan Dutko, David Fisher, Loraine Gyauch, Alissa Lastres, Brett Stoudt, and Carolyn Vicchiullo (Shane merits special mention, as he reviewed and improved the entire first draft of the manuscript in the summer of 2013). As ever, I thank my wife, Sarah, and my children, Jake and Hannah, for allowing me the latitude to pursue my scholarship and writing. My three dogs provided pleasant and frequent respite from my computer while the book took shape.

My writing of this book was partially funded by a Summer 2013 Faculty Development and Research Award and a Summer 2013 Student Opportunities for Academic Research (SOAR) Grant, both from Moravian College.

This book is dedicated to Beatrice Wright, whose theories on disability and rehabilitation grew from collaboration with Tamara Dembo and other socially minded psychologists, and by remaining true to the ideas of Kurt Lewin.

Dana S. Dunn
Bethlehem, Pennsylvania

I do not suffer from that common failing of judging another man by me: I can easily believe that others have qualities quite distinct from my own. Just because I feel that I am pledged to my individual form, I do not bind all others to it as everyone else does: I can conceive and believe that there are thousands of different ways of living and, contrary to most men, I more readily acknowledge our differences than our similarities.
MICHELE DE MONTAIGNE (1580/1991, p. 257)

An essential core-concept of human dignity is that a person is not an object, not a thing.
BEATRICE A. WRIGHT (1987, p. 12)

... disability is only one aspect, and often a very minor aspect, of a *person*. We should always attend primarily to the person.
HAROLD E. YUKER (1988, p. xiv)

Jack was born with muscular dystrophy. He cannot walk but is mobile using a powered wheel chair.

Steve walks with a slight limp and drives a car with a modified steering wheel. He uses his left hand to steer with a knob attached to the wheel. He had a stroke a few years ago.

Sasha has a hearing impairment. She has difficulty understanding a presentation in a crowded auditorium but no trouble when chatting with friends in a quiet hallway.

1 Overview
THE SOCIAL PSYCHOLOGY OF DISABILITY

ARE ALL OF these people disabled in some way? Why or why not? How do nondisabled observers view them? How do these individuals think about themselves with respect to disability? Questions such as these are the stuff of the social psychology of disability, which entails psychological processes—perception, cognition, emotion, judgment, and behavior—on the part of people with disabilities and the individuals who interact with them in daily life (Dunn, 2010).

Why does the social psychology of disability matter? Disability means difference—or at least perceived difference, particularly among nondisabled individuals who, like all social perceivers, are inquisitive. Disability evokes curiosity in some, and uncertainty, anxiety, or even fright in others. Many people—whether bystanders, acquaintances, friends, even family members or professionals—are often unsure how to behave toward or interact with individuals who have disabilities. Should a disability be acknowledged or ignored, for example? Will a helpful act be welcomed or seen as patronizing or, worse, infantilizing? Further complicating the situation is a common tendency for observers to draw inferences about the etiology of the disability that may be unsupported.

What about the perceived—those individuals who have a disability? The social psychology of disability is primarily concerned with the experiences of people who have a disability: how they think about themselves, interacting with others who have disabilities, and their relations with those who are not (yet) disabled. As we will see, the consequences of disability are not all-or-none propositions. This reality is not always apparent in the eye of the beholder or even that of the affected individual (e.g., Sasha only has difficulty hearing in some settings). Disability is linked to the person, of course, but it is also very much a social and psychological matter.

As Olkin (1999) points out, the identification of disability should be viewed on a continuum ranging from individuals who do not have a disability (i.e., the non-disabled) to disability rights activists who see any disability—whether it is physical, psychological, emotional, communicative, or some combination thereof—as a social construct, less about the person per se and more about the world he or she inhabits. Between these two poles lie other identities, including people who possess some disability but do not identify themselves as having one; persons with functional limitations who think of themselves as disabled or as having an impairment or handicap (the distinction among these three will be clarified shortly); and individuals who view their disability as a major part of their self-concepts.

There is another way to think about disability—as part of the human condition and something that will likely affect all of us. Almost everyone will experience some temporary disability or one that endures, perhaps even becoming permanent. This observation is especially true for those who live long lives; as we age, the likelihood that we will experience functional challenges increases substantially. Disability, then, should be recognized as something that will ultimately touch almost everyone.

Clearly, however, disability is not a single state—it is multifaceted—it affects different people in different ways. How should we understand it? How should we define it?

Defining Disability

What do we mean when we use the term *disability*? What is a disability and how does it differ from a *handicap* or *impairment*? In everyday life, people are apt to use these three terms interchangeably to refer to "disability" (Livneh & Antonak, 1997). Why do distinctions among these or related terms matter?

We begin with some basic distinctions. In general, the term *disability* refers to some condition or characteristic that is linked to a particular individual and, therefore, is to some extent embodied. Disabilities are present when activities that are routinely performed by people (e.g., walking, reading, speaking) are somehow restricted or cannot be done in accustomed ways. A person who has congenital blindness has a disability. An individual who had a stroke in the right hemisphere of the brain and consequently has little mobility in his or her left leg also has a disability. What about someone who is chronically depressed due to dysregulated levels of the neurotransmitter serotonin and is therefore unable to work? That person, too, can be said to have a disability. Disabilities can also occur in combination with one another (e.g., a person who experiences both mobility and speech limitations following a stroke).

Although treated synonymously with disability in everyday language, the term *impairment* is used by professionals (as in the International Classification of Function) to refer to some disruption at the system level of a bodily organ (e.g., the brain, an arm, or a leg) that leads to some loss or an observed abnormality (i.e., some deviation from an established norm, not a defect) that is physiological, psychological, or anatomical in nature (World Health Organization, 2001). Impairments tend to be enduring, if not always permanent, problems, the products of disease or injury. The consequences of impairments are disruptions in cognitive, emotional, or physical processes (Livneh, 1987).

In contrast to disability and impairment, the term *handicap* refers to some obstacle imposed upon people by something in the environment that prevents them from fulfilling some roles (World Health Organization, 2001). The term *environment* is quite broad, as it can refer literally to some situational constraint, such as a structural feature (or the absence of one) or difficult terrain. Older buildings that have not been properly retrofitted, for example, pose accessibility barriers for individuals who use wheelchairs because they prevent them from entering and moving about freely. Thus, a wheelchair user is *handicapped*—put at a disadvantage—by the absence of a ramp or elevator. The person is not handicapped per se. Rather, the disability (whatever it may be) requires use of a wheelchair.

But "environment" is not merely a physical construct; it is also a shared, social construct, and can involve economic and sociocultural influences. People with disabilities (PWDs) are not just handicapped by physical barriers. They are also handicapped by social obstacles, such as the attitudes or beliefs held by other people (disabled or not) as well as by laws limiting the rights of PWDs. Nondisabled individuals often harbor stereotypes about PWDs and such oversimplified perspectives can be positive or negative. One positive yet problematic stereotype that some nondisabled people hold is that disability is somehow ennobling, granting virtue in perceived suffering ("God only gives you what he knows you can endure—your willingness to keep going is a testimonial for the rest of us"). A PWD can be socially handicapped by such sentiments (not everyone wants to be an object of curiosity, let alone a role model) no matter how well intentioned or sincere they might seem to the commentator or any observers. Indeed, when nondisabled people highlight such "positive" attributes of PWDs, they may be engaging in a subtle form of prejudice that subordinates the PWD to being considered incompetent, for example, or in need of protection (e.g., Anderson, 2010). The application of overly positive language can be dramatic and distorted, so that a child with a disability who learns to swim is heralded as a "hero," while a child without a disability learning to do so would be called normal.

As we will see, these terms—disability, impairment, and handicap—have a practical or heuristic value in the social psychology of disability.

The Social Psychology of Disability: An Introduction

How and why is social psychology relevant to disability? What does the social psychology of disability entail? Let's begin by defining the term *social psychology* as the scientific study of everyday social behavior. It involves carefully considering how people think and feel about, influence, and relate to the actual, imagined, or presumed presence of other people (Allport, 1985; Jones, 1998). Depending on the question being asked, social psychologists examine individual or collective accounts involving emotion, perception, cognition, and behavior. An empirical science, social psychology relies on a wide variety of research approaches to explore hypotheses about why people behave the way they do in different situations, usually in response to others (Dunn, 2013). Experimentation is often the preferred method (Wilson, 2005), as it can isolate cause from effect, but social psychologists also use a variety of nonexperimental and self-report-based approaches to elucidate how people understand, interact with, or fail to connect to other people. Social psychologists study a myriad of topics centering on the highs and lows of the human condition, including attitudes and attitude change, love and close relationships, prejudice and discrimination, stereotyping, prosocial behavior, aggression, and conformity (for a recent review, see Baumeister & Finkel, 2010).

To explore the dynamics of social encounters against these thematic backgrounds, social psychologists systematically vary the presence of personal or situational factors assumed to affect social perception, expectation, and engagement when two or more people gather together. Personal factors deal with people's physical or dispositional (personality-based) qualities, as well as their moods or emotional states, and how they act as perceivers or as the targets of others' perceptions. Situational factors are those variables or constants found outside people and in their environments. These situational factors can be tangible (e.g., friends, strangers, passersby) or intangible (e.g., social roles, cultural norms), stable (e.g., laws, organizational rules, physical boundaries) or transient (e.g., crowding, temperature).

Social psychological research dealing with disability adopts a focused view, one aimed at identifying those personal and situational factors that enhance the assessment, improvement, or treatment of those with physical, cognitive, mental, or communicative disabilities. As such, the social psychology of disability is an area of study, research, and intervention within the larger field of rehabilitation psychology (e.g., Frank, Rosenthal, & Caplan, 2010), which is dedicated to "the study and application of psychological knowledge and skills on behalf of individuals with disabilities and chronic health conditions in order to maximize health and welfare, independence and choice, functional abilities, and social role participation" (Scherer et al., 2010, p. 1). Social psychology, the social psychology of disability, and rehabilitation psychology all subscribe to the idea that the situations—whether real or imagined—in which people find themselves have a profound influence on their behavior and emotional states, a phenomenon also known as the person–environment relation.

Lewin's Person–Environment Relation

Social psychology and rehabilitation psychology share a common theoretical ancestry in the work of social-personality psychologist Kurt Lewin (1890–1947). Following the ascent of the Nazi party in Germany, Lewin, who was of Jewish descent, immigrated to the United States in 1933 (Marrow, 1977). His great intellectual contribution to the study of social relations was to argue that the multiple influences found in social situations frequently override the impact of any personal factors, including people's personalities or dispositions. In other words, how people perceive their environments (i.e., the situation) affects both their subjective experiences and how they behave. Even the most extroverted or expressive person, for example, is apt to behave in accordance with the situational rules associated with the classroom (e.g., wait to be called on before speaking, take turns speaking) or some religious services (e.g., sit, kneel, or rise when others do, pray silently).

In practical terms, how people react to social stimuli is based on the idea that neither psychological influences attributed to nature (e.g., intelligence, other inherited traits) nor psychological influences attributed to nurture (e.g., roles or expectations, learned experiences in the social world) provide a complete answer to questions about behavior. Although both personal and situational factors are important, it is actually their interaction that produces behavior. (That aforementioned extroverted student may obey classroom etiquette, but might also participate in class more frequently than the average student.) Arguing for what he called a field theory, Lewin (1935) claimed that behavior should be construed as a function of both the person and the total "life space," the psychological environment (again, real or imagined) in which the individual navigates. By this reasoning, the psychologist's goal of predicting future behavior was reduced to the quasimathematical formula $B = f(P, E)$, or behavior is a function of the person and the perceived environment [a few decades later, Bandura (1978) pointed out that the three terms influence one another equally]. How a person thinks about the world (i.e., cognition) and what strength is available to respond to it (i.e., motivation) also affect the person's resulting behavior. Thus, the focus should always be on the person *in* the situation and not just the person's qualities or those attributed to the situation.

How do Lewin's arguments play out in everyday situations, especially those involving disability? Lewin realized that observers generally ignore the influence of situations or environmental factors on behavior, preferring instead to focus on qualities attributable to the person, especially presumed dispositional (personality) characteristics (Nisbett, 1980). If a person using a wheelchair cannot enter a building (because there is no ramp or elevator access) or get inside a car (because the vehicle is too small or the seats cannot be moved sufficiently), for example, observers tend to perceive the problem as residing in the person and not the things in the environment (the building, the car) that offer no accommodation. In effect, social perceivers generally overlook or discount the impact of the situation and focus primarily on the person (Lewin, 1935; Ross & Nisbett, 1991) and, in this case, the individual's disability.

What makes this especially interesting, of course, is that people witnessing or participating in the same event often reach very different conclusions regarding what happened and why, a social phenomenon referred to in social psychology as the *actor/observer bias* (Jones & Nisbett, 1971). Actors, such as someone using a wheelchair, look to the situation and its external qualities (e.g., the physical or psychological demands of the setting, the nature of the task being performed, other people, or even luck) to explain their behavior ("I cannot get into the building because there is no ramp for me to use"). In contrast, observers watch the behavior of the other (the actor) and explain it by appealing to an internal ("He must hate being in a wheelchair") or dispositional (e.g., "He must be bitter") quality.

When observers see an actor's dispositions as more influential than the situation, they fall prey to what social psychologists refer to as the *fundamental attribution error* or the *correspondence bias* (Gilbert & Malone, 1995; Ross, 1977). The person in the wheelchair is seen as weak, helpless, or awkward, for example, just as, by contrast, a quiz show host is seen as intelligent, witty, or wise in spite of the fact that he asks rather than answers questions and relies on cue cards to guide him. Why does this happen, this fixation on the person? Primarily because people are very interesting; they grab our attention by standing out from whatever situational context or social background is present (e.g., Gilbert & Malone, 1995; Ross, Amabile, & Steinmetz, 1977). Although such explanations—what social psychologists refer to as "attributions"—are probably often incorrect or biased, they do provide perceivers with a sense of predictability and control over their social encounters (Heider, 1958). Incidentally, when observers make internal attributions about entire groups of people (all wheelchair users, all PWDs), not individuals, they are engaging in what is known as the *ultimate attribution error* (Pettigrew, 1979).

A second reason people fail to consider situational factors is that behavior is seen as "belonging to" the person (Wright, 1983); after all, when a behavior occurs (or fails to happen), the person is right there—the two (the person, the behavior) are perceived as one. But this everyday analysis can pose another judgment problem because people generally fail to distinguish between what turn out to be actual behaviors (those that people intentionally perform) and actions (mere descriptions of physical movements people display) (Vallacher & Wegner, 1987). A casual observer might assume another's spastic movement is intentional ("That's so annoying—why doesn't she stop flailing her arm?") when it is an uncontrollable action with no meaningful or purposeful behavior behind it. Alternatively, a person's inaction—say, an inability to climb stairs due to chronic back pain—while due to the situation, is erroneously treated as a behavioral shortcoming linked to some underlying disposition ("He should try harder—can't means won't!").

Person-focused judgments are most likely to occur when a behavior is identified as atypical (Kelley, 1967, 1973; Wright, 1983). Given their relative salience within many contexts, PWDs are too readily categorized as atypical and so is their behavior, which means that casual observers often look no further than the person for a satisfying (albeit premature) explanation. The environment and its other potentially contributing factors are ignored. Fortunately, there is a sometime antidote to this social perception problem. People will consider the situation as the source or cause of behavioral constraints when the person's behavior is observed in different settings. If, for example, an individual in a wheelchair is seen (or recalled) navigating other buildings with ease, then the earlier (inaccurate) behavioral explanation is readily attributed to the situation (that one inaccessible building) and less readily to the person.

The implications are clear: In a Lewinian analysis, the behavior of a PWD is a function of both the person and the environment.[1] When a person's presumed trait or other internal quality becomes the predominant focus, a careful review of the environment and the behavior of the PWD in different situations should be performed so that influential situational factors are highlighted. Clearly, there are consequences for the PWD if the power of the situation is overlooked or ignored.

Wright (1983, p. 40) provides a wonderful example illustrating why emphasis on the environment is crucial where understanding the experience of disability is concerned. Two names were suggested for a committee whose charge was to do something about some of the physical barriers found at a large university. Which of the following captures the essence of the person–environment relation and its message regarding disability?

> Committee for the Physically Handicapped
> Committee for the Architecturally Handicapped

The second choice is the best fit, as it "rightfully assigns the source of difficulty" not to people with disabilities but to the environment or the situation, here structural aspects of the campus (e.g., absence of lowered curbs) through which they must find their way (p. 40).

The person–environment relation has considerable explanatory power for understanding and interpreting reactions to disability. The concept is a keystone element in a current, comprehensive model of disability.

The WHO ICF Model

The WHO International Classification of Functioning, Disability, and Health (ICF) model (World Health Organization, 2001) is designed to be a universal classification system applicable to all levels of health, not just disability or chronic illness. This model is explicitly biopsychosocial in nature, meaning that disability is not attributable exclusively to biological processes. Instead, understanding the experience of a person with a disability entails examining the interactions among biological, psychological, and social systems factors (e.g., Rath & Elliott, 2011). The ICF model specifically treats disability as an umbrella term, thereby emphasizing the dynamic relationship existing between the person and the environment. In fact, the model explicitly incorporates the Lewinian person–environment relation.

The ICF model and classification updates conventional definitions of disability and works to individualize and apply the concept in order to advance theory, research, practice, and policy so that people with disabilities are enabled to lead full, active lives as part of mainstream society (Bruyère & Peterson, 2005; Peterson & Rosenthal, 2005). Within the model, disability is construed as lying on a continuum on which each person with a disability is presumed to react and function at a unique level due to the influence of personal and environmental factors (see Figure 1.1). These contextual influences—*environmental factors* (e.g., physical, attitudinal, cultural, social, technological, familial, institutional) and *personal factors* (e.g., gender, other health-related conditions, lifestyle, education, age, personality, coping style, profession)—are important, as they can modify or otherwise affect the other components in the model. To emphasize this fact, the term *disability* is defined as "the outcome or result of a complex

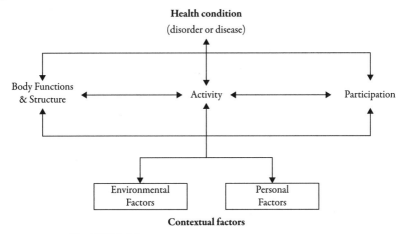

Health condition
(disorder or disease)

Body Functions & Structure

Activity

Participation

Environmental Factors

Personal Factors

Contextual factors

FIGURE I.I   The ICF Model

relationship between an individual's health condition and personal factors, and of the external factors that represent the circumstances in which the individual lives" (World Health Organization, 2001, p. 17). This definition, too, is decidedly Lewinian as well as biopsychosocial in scope.

As shown in Figure 1.1, disability is dynamic, conceptually involving interactions between *health conditions* (e.g., diseases, injuries, disorders) and those *contextual factors* linked to the person and the environment, respectively. Both a person's health condition or impairment and contextual factors affect body functions and structure, activity, and participation. *Body functions* refer to both the physiological and psychological functions of systems within the body. In turn, *body structures* are the anatomical parts of the body, including organs, limbs, and the components therein. Both represent the system levels in which impairment occurs. The term *activity* involves the individual carrying out an action or completing some behavioral task (and a person may experience *activity limitations* or difficulties executing a behavior due to a disability). *Participation* refers to the individual's involvement in some life situation in which activity occurs (e.g., going shopping, attending class, making a meal). A PWD can encounter problems in a life situation, as when some environmental constraint leads to *participation restriction*, a term designed to replace the familiar—but more pejorative and outdated—*handicap*. On the other hand, a PWD can have a significant impairment but have excellent health, and so on. Disability can occur at any of the ICF model's levels: impairments, activity limitations and/ or participation restrictions. A more detailed discussion of the ICF model can be found in Chan, da Silva Cordoso, and Chronister (2009).

Table 1.1 lists three older, more traditional models of disability that have largely been supplanted by the ICF model. The moral model is the most limiting and

TABLE I.I

TRADITIONAL MODELS OF DISABILITY

Moral model—Disability is a defect and a source of shame; it is presumed to be caused by at moral failing or sinful behavior of the PWD or family. Shame and blame spread from the PWD to the family. This model is the oldest and is still active in some cultures.

Medical model—Disability is a medical matter, therefore no sin, shame, or blame is involved; disability is linked with pathology and the presumption that a cure is possible.

Minority or social model—Disability is a social construction and PWDs are members of a minority group subjected to oppression and denial of civil rights from the larger culture. The problem posed by disability is not found in the individual, rather it is placed in the environment, which creates social, psychological, physical, and legal barriers.

socially destructive view, as it characterizes disability as a defect in the affected person and often that individual's family. The medical model removes issues of shame and blame from the moral model but remains limiting because disability is still seen as residing exclusively in the person—the emphasis is on the biological, neglecting the psychological and social components. The most recent model, the minority or social model, advances the view that disability is a social construction and that PWDs face social (e.g., prejudice, discrimination) and environmental obstacles, not challenges posed by disability per se (e.g., Chan, Da Silva Cardoso, & Chronister, 2009; Smart, 2001; Terzi, 2004, 2009). The minority model shares features of—but is less dynamic than—the ICF model.

Social perspective and point of view affect how disability and PWDs are perceived. We now turn to the power that language possesses where the social psychology of disability is concerned, as it is an important extension of the Lewinian perspective.

Person-First Language: An Antidote to Essentialism

Earlier in this chapter, the claim was made that disability is actually a multifaceted concept, one advocated by rehabilitation psychologists and therapists, as well as various medical professionals and educators, and many PWDs themselves. In daily social life, however, disability is often seen by the average person or social perceiver as an "either/or" proposition: a person either has or does not have a disability. Categorizing people this way "essentializes" disability by highlighting it over all other qualities possessed by the person (Bloom, 2010; Dunn, Fisher, & Beard, 2013).

Without careful thought, a disability—any disability—can be viewed as singularly defining, representing the essence of a person. The problem, of course, is that the disability and not much else about the person becomes the factor regulating both the interest of and interaction with nondisabled people.

An important lesson based in the social psychology of disability is that essentializing language matters. In the context of disability, language can be empowering or devaluing and it has implications for both the perceiver and the perceived (Caplan, 1995; Caplan & Shechter, 1993; Dunn & Elliott, 2005; Sapir, 1951; Wright, 1983). The working principle involved is rather simple: *To counter essentialism, people should never be equated with their disabling conditions.* In practice, the emphasis on the person must come before the disability, which means that anyone, including medical and psychological professionals, should refer to a "person with diabetes" rather than a "diabetic." By extension, people with similar disabilities should not be grouped together in everyday language just because it is easier to talk about "diabetics" rather than "people with diabetes." In the first place, one person's disability can differ substantially from another's; that is, Susan's diabetic condition might be substantially different from Stan's, so that referring to them the same way makes no sense. Thus, the focus on the person rather than the disabling condition is key and, in any case, one quality—whether positive or negative, favorable or unfavorable—should not overshadow all others.

Furthermore, no PWD should be referred to in monolithic terms (i.e., a diabetic, a tetraplegic) because doing so treats the person as a mere object, establishing the speaker's psychological distance from the individual by giving primacy to the condition in question. Use of objectifying, monolithic terms in the case of disability is no different than relying on labels that segregate along the lines of race, ethnicity, religion, or any other categorization scheme that ignores the individual differences among group members (e.g., Allport, 1954a; Wiley, Philogène, & Revenson, 2012). Doing so can lead to stereotyping, loss of individuality, and possibly even victimization (e.g., Dunn & Elliott, 2005, 2008; Wright, 1991).

As is well documented by social psychological research, such social categorizing can readily create so-called ingroups and outgroups. Ingroup members typically hold more favorable attitudes toward their presumed peers ("us") than those in some (often arbitrary) outgroup ("them") (Brewer & Brown, 1998; Tajfel, Billig, Bundy, & Flament, 1971). This sort of ingroup favoritism results even when the membership of a given group is determined spontaneously (Locksley, Ortiz, & Hepburn, 1980), a characteristic known as the minimal group effect. More to the point, ingroup members generally see outgroup members as being more similar to one another than they actually are (e.g., all people with Asperger's syndrome are alike) while viewing fellow ingroup members as distinct and unique (Oakes, 2001; see also Linville & Jones,

1980). Once perceived similarity or difference is used to establish group membership, the likelihood of prejudice and discrimination increases.

A Caveat from Disability Culture

Person-first language is not necessarily embraced by all PWDs. Pockets of opposition exist among members of the disability culture, which Gill (1995) characterized as a community response to ". . . social oppression, but also our emerging art and humor, our piecing together of our history, our evolving language and symbols, our remarkably unified worldview, beliefs and values, and our strategies for surviving and thriving" (p. 18). For example, in a critique of person-first language, some disability activists argue that separating the individual from the disability (i.e., deemphasizing it in spoken or written language) inadvertently promotes the view that disability is undesirable and that those touched by it are somehow less than human. To be sure, person-first language successfully counteracts reliance on problematic terms (e.g., "the retarded"), but perhaps this well-intentioned correction is now an overcorrection. Consider the fact that in everyday discourse, we neither say nor read about "people who are African-American" or "people with Asian ancestry."

Some critics recommend a moderate course correction in which we should alternate the use of person-first language with heretofore avoided terms such as "disabled" or even "the disabled." Gill (1995) urges writers to use the term Disabled (note the capital "D") to indicate alliance with or allegiance to disability culture in lieu of describing or identifying the impairment. Members of Deaf culture use capitalization to create and promote a sense of unity and community. Other than alternating person-first and disability culture terms, a reasonable way to resolve the dilemma posed by labels is simply to ask people what they prefer to be called (e.g., American Psychological Association, 2010). Admittedly, this approach works individually, on a case-by-case basis, but does not solve the greater issue of language for and about disability.

Labels Matter

The American Psychological Association's (APA) (1994, 2010) policies regarding how to refer to individuals and groups are quite relevant here. The APA recommends that psychologists rely on reasonable standards for determining how to refer to people, and two stand out for our purposes: contribution and sensitivity. To acknowledge their contribution, people who elect to take part in research should be referred to as *participants* rather than the outmoded, passive term *subjects*. Whereas "subjects" are "subjected to" events in research or practice contexts—that is, they are passive recipients within a situation—"participants" actively elect to take part in research or, for that matter, rehabilitative therapy. (Interestingly, the term *subjects* is now used to refer only to nonhuman organisms involved in psychological research.) Participants choose; they decide to be a part of something. Choice of terminology here denotes activity, just as it grants a certain degree of dignity.

The second standard, sensitivity, is arguably most important for person-first language. The APA advocates that people's preferences for titles or descriptions—what they like to be called—that individualize them should be followed, both responsibly and compassionately (Maggio, 1991). Thus, to be sensitive, we refer to an "elderly person" or "elderly people," not "the elderly," where individuality is lost in the group of (presumed) similar others (again, when disability is understood as multifaceted, not all disabilities are alike). When it comes to disability, we should choose language that highlights the person first, and so we say "person with a disability" or "people with disabilities" and not "the disabled." (Formulations such as "the disabled" are problematic not only due to their lack of sensitivity but also because abstract adjectives should not be used as nouns.)

Some people argue that this sort of person-first language regarding disability is awkward or cumbersome to use in scientific or daily discourse (e.g., Roediger, 2004). Admittedly, "person with a disability" or "individual who had a stroke" is more of a mouthful than "disabled person" or worse, "stroke victim." Yet therein lies the problem: Putting the disability "stroke" or the term "disabled" first emphasizes the disability and not the individual who has the disabling condition among a myriad of other qualities unrelated to it. Similar to APA's use of *participants* to acknowledge active contribution, by putting the person—not the disability—first, the individual's dignity is retained.

What are the benefits of using person-first language? In addition to the active and nonhandicapping intention of person-first language, carefully chosen words can also promote equality and inclusion. For example, rehabilitation psychologists routinely use the APA-advocated term *participants*, but never the passive *patients*, to refer to PWDs who take part in treatment or disability-related research. Wright (1960) recommended using *client* to underscore the idea that rehabilitation regimens should be "comanaged" by PWDs and rehabilitation therapists and counselors. More recently, other rehabilitation professionals recommend reliance on the term *consumers* in lieu of *clients* or *participants* (Boyce, 1998; Tate & Pledger, 2003). The term *consumers* is meant to include PWDs and their caregivers, families, and even friends, all of whom can be presumed to both use and benefit from psychosocial and rehabilitative research designed to ameliorate disability. Indeed, the consumer perspective also advocates that PWDs and those close to them work cooperatively with practitioners and researchers to develop hypotheses that can be examined empirically in the laboratory, clinic, or field to tackle the challenges posed by chronic health conditions (an approach known as *participatory action research*; e.g., Minkler & Wallerstein, 2003). When consistently referred to as participants, clients, or consumers, then, PWDs become partners and collaborators in the search for treatment options rather than recipients of aid.

Now that we have a working conception of disability based on lay and professional perspectives, as well as theory and concepts drawn from social psychology and the social psychology of disability, we should consider its prevalence in the wider world and the United States in particular.

Disability: A Demographic Snapshot

How many people in the world have a disability? A recent report of the World Health Organization (2011) finds that over one billion people or 15% of the world's population lead their lives with some form of disability. Within this larger group, close to 200 million people encounter serious and sustained challenges in functioning. Many nations, too, have aging populations in which there is a greater incidence of disability and chronic health problems (heart disease, cancer, diabetes, mental health disorders), in part because of advances in medical care. The incidence of disabilities varies from country to country due to local health and environmental conditions, as well as other influences, including natural disasters, motor vehicle accidents, conflict, substance abuse, and diet.

Prevalence in the United States

How many Americans live with disability? Disability is actually a rather common condition in the United States (all census data reported in this section are drawn from Brault, 2012). At present, there are approximately 315 million people living in the United States, and within that number, census data from 2010 reveal that around 56 million individuals reported having some disability or chronic health condition. The important point here is one that is often overlooked: Most PWDs live and work in community settings. Approximately 38 million other citizens have severe disabilities, which require them to live in institutionalized settings due to special care needs.[2] To put these adult figures in additional perspective, around 5.2 million children (age 15 or younger) also have some sort of disability.

By their nature, census figures are abstract, even dry, but they can still provide insights into how people with disabilities live their lives. Around 8.1 million people reported difficulty with sight, including those who reported being blind. Another

7.6 million people identified hearing problems, including deafness. Physical challenges posed by ambulatory activities (e.g., walking, climbing stairs, or relying on a cane, crutches, a walker, or a wheelchair), in turn, were reported by 30.6 million people.

The 2010 census data also reveal that about 12.3 million citizens aged 6 years and above require assistance with one or more activities of daily living (ADLs) or instrumental activities of daily living (IADLs). Typical ADLs include getting into or out of bed, bathing, dressing, eating, moving in and around the home, and toileting. The implication here is that someone—say, a family member or a caregiver—was often present to help with some of these everyday tasks. In contrast to ADLs, IADLs focus on assessing independent living arrangements and include things such as meal preparation, using the telephone, managing money, doing housework, taking prescription medication, and difficulty going outside the home. Many PWDs live alone but still require some assistance to maintain independence.

One final but especially important item that often colors the experience of disability is economics. Having sufficient savings or earnings is a concern for many PWDs. Compared to nondisabled individuals, a greater number of PWDs are likely to be unemployed or living in poverty for some period of time (e.g., 1 or 2 years). In 2010, for example, the median monthly income for a person with any kind of disability was $1961 whereas that for a nondisabled person was $2724. Where shared resources are concerned, the median monthly family income for people with disabilities was $2856 compared to $4771 for those with no disabilities. A conclusion here is clear: Even in America, PWDs are at greater risk than nondisabled people for unemployment and likely underemployment (i.e., being paid less than their skills, training, or education warrant; working only part-time), as well as for experiencing financial struggles.

As will be discussed in subsequent chapters, the challenges faced by PWDs, including economic pressures, are based in social psychological factors, such as stigma and attitudes toward PWDs. Dealing constructively with disability entails establishing a philosophy or set of values to guide inquiry and to ensure the rights of PWDs. In the next section, we consider an established set of beliefs and principles that can advance a positive social psychology of disability.

Value-Laden Beliefs and Principles for a Social Psychology of Disability

Though important, studying the social psychology of disability is not simply about explicating the normative processes of person perception (how nondisabled people

view PWDs and vice versa) or self-perception (how PWDs view themselves)—
this constitutes the issue of "what usually happens" in social exchanges. To move
beyond description, the social psychology of disability must also be progressive and
empowering, that is, it should emphasize "what should happen" by using research
findings to improve the lives and livelihoods of PWDs, their caregivers, and families. The message is not a new one; it emerges from the person–environment analysis
of disability and also is found in the specialty of rehabilitation psychology (Frank,
Rosenthal, & Caplan, 2010).

This affirming perspective is particularly associated with the research and writing
of Beatrice A. Wright, a rehabilitation psychologist who used social psychological
reasoning gained by working with Lewin and his other students to advance theory,
practice, and treatment of disability (for more on Wright's background, see Dunn
& Elliott, 2005; Hollingsworth, Johnson, & Cook, 1989; McCarthy, 2011). Wright
(1983, pp. x–xxvi) crafted a list of 20 "value-laden beliefs and principles" designed to
guide research with and service for PWDs (see also Wright, 1972). Five are explicitly
social psychological in scope, which means they are relevant to the analysis of disability offered in this chapter and in those that follow (rehabilitation researchers
and practitioners, as well as interested readers, are encouraged to review the remaining 15 value-laden beliefs and principles; see Chapter 6):

1. *All PWDs deserve respect and encouragement; the presence of a disability, no
   matter how severe, does not change these rights.* People should not be treated
   as objects or be in any way devalued by others. Instead, they should have the
   opportunity to develop their abilities, however great or small, and live their
   lives with a hopeful outlook. Asserting human worth and dignity is essential, so that no PWD is socially neglected or marginalized.
2. *Disability severity can be increased or reduced by environmental conditions.*
   As revealed by the person–environment relation, PWDs are apt to be challenged by environmental constraints, such as physical (architectural) or
   social (prejudicial attitudes, conventional beliefs) barriers, and not their
   given disabilities. The social psychological analysis of disability must consider the person in the situation in lieu of appealing to personal or dispositional explanations for behavior or behavioral problems.
3. *Coping or adjusting to disability is dependent upon understanding problems
   located in the social and physical environment.* The psychosocial well-being
   of PWDs can be maintained or strengthened by viewing disability challenges as being environmental, that is, as social, psychological, and physical.
   Adjustment is an ongoing, not finite, process. Positive social support from

family, friends, caregivers, and psychological and medical professionals is crucial for constructively dealing with such challenges.

4. *The assets—personal or psychological—of PWDs are important factors.* Every individual is assumed to possess some personal physical and mental qualities that can be called upon to ameliorate difficulties associated with the experience of disability and to enrich daily life. Positive, promising attributes should be supported and developed.

5. *The significance of disability is influenced by the individual's feelings about self and situation.* The self-identity of the PWD, his or her social-emotional responses, is influential when navigating life with disability. When disability is recognized by the PWD as positive and nondevaluing, the individual can flourish in daily life (e.g., McMillen & Cook, 2003).

These five statements capture the meaning of arguments about the nature of disability made earlier in this chapter. We will refer to them as helpful touchstones for the social-psychological concepts and constructs we consider in the rest of this book.

Looking Forward

This opening chapter provided a foundation for exploring the social psychology of disability by defining disability and reviewing both everyday dynamics and a comprehensive model for understanding the experience of disability. We then considered person-first language and the prevalence of disability globally and in the United States. The chapter closed by highlighting selected value-laden beliefs and principles articulated by Wright (1972, 1983) and aimed at eliminating attitudinal, social, and psychological barriers for people with disabilities while promoting their well-being and civil rights. The remaining chapters in this book will explore other key aspects of the social psychology of disability, including fundamental psychosocial concepts (Chapter 2), stigma and stereotyping (Chapter 3), attitudes toward PWDs (Chapter 4), coping and adjusting to disability (Chapter 5), disability identity (Chapter 6), a positive psychology of disability and rehabilitation (Chapter 7), and the ecology of disability (Chapter 8).

Questions

1. What is a disability and how does it differ from impairment or a handicap? Why should researchers and practitioners focus on how PWDs construe disability?

2. Define the scope of the social psychology of disability. What is the nature of the person–environment relation identified by social psychologist Kurt Lewin? Why is this relation important in the study of the social psychology of disability?

3. Why does the WHO ICF model advance our understanding of disability? How does the ICF model define disability? How does the model employ Lewin's person–environment relation? How does the ICF model differ from traditional models of disability?

4. What is essentialism? How can essentializing language be countered by person-first language? How and when can you use person-first language in your research or practice? What are some challenges associated with using language that empowers rather than devalues PWDs?

5. How will you navigate the critique of person-first language raised by members of the disability culture? Is there a reasonable way to promote the intent of person-first language while at the same time honoring the diverse membership and perspectives found in the disability community?

6. How do the five selected value-laden beliefs and principles conceived by Wright connect to the social psychology of disability? The person–environment relation?

2 Fundamental Psychosocial Concepts for Understanding Disability

THE LATE LAWYER, author, and disability rights activist Harriett McBryde Johnson (1957–2008) wrote about her rich life and experiences in a series of articles and books (e.g., Johnson, 2003a, 2003b, 2005, 2006). When not protesting the annual Muscular Dystrophy Telethon as a part of the disability rights group Not Dead Yet (among other things, she opposed Jerry Lewis's "pity-based tactics") or debating Princeton philosopher Peter Singer, who has argued that infanticide should be acceptable when infants are born with severe disabilities (Johnson, 2003a; Koch, 2004; Singer, 2011), she lived and worked in Charleston, South Carolina.

Johnson (2003a) was something of a fixture there, jetting around town in her powered wheelchair, writing that

> . . . where I live, . . . some people call me Good Luck Lady: they consider it propitious to cross my path when a hurricane is coming and to kiss my head just before voting day. But most of the reactions are decidedly negative. Strangers on the street are moved to comment:

> I admire you for being out; most people would give up.
> God bless you! I'll pray for you.
> You don't let the pain hold you back, do you?
> If I had to live like you, I think I'd kill myself.   (p. 52)

Why do bystanders sometimes feel free to make these sorts of comments to people with disabilities (PWDs), especially when their disabilities are apparent? How do PWDs feel about such comments and, more generally, how they are perceived and received by others in the course of social interactions? This chapter addresses these questions by discussing fundamental psychosocial concepts in the study of the social psychology of disability that affect both social exchanges and particular self-perception processes among PWDs. Johnson's experiences on the streets of Charleston are a starting place for the first concept, one that deals with how different points of view lead to different conclusions about the experience of disability.

The Insider–Outsider Distinction

Our discussion of Lewin's person–environment relation in Chapter 1, coupled with the actor–observer bias, revealed that people's points of view have powerful effects on how they explain their own behavior or that of others. In brief, actors explain much of their behavior by looking to the situation they are (or were) in, whereas observers focus on actors, positing that much of their behavior is caused by underlying dispositional qualities. Situational influences or constraints are readily discounted. Thus, a professor assumes the drowsy student in the back of the classroom is probably lazy or unmotivated when the student might have been up all night preparing for an important examination or holding down a late-night job to pay for college. Or, in the case of Harriet McBryde Johnson (or others like her), the presence of a wheelchair is sufficient to trigger pity or a belief in her ongoing suffering in the minds of many passersby.

Tamara Dembo (1902–1993), a student of Lewin and a colleague of Wright, introduced into the study of disability an intriguing attributional distinction related to the actor–observer bias, what is commonly referred to as the *insider–outsider distinction* (Dembo, 1964, 1970, 1982). She distinguished between people who have a disability or who have received some rehabilitation therapy (so-called *insiders*) and those nondisabled observers (*outsiders*) who endeavor to imagine what having a disability or taking part in rehabilitation must be like (Dembo, 1969; see also, Shontz, 1982; Wright, 1989, 1991). As Dembo (1964) observed:

> The role of the outsider is that of an observer, and the role of the insider is that of a participant... because the observer is an outsider, the impact of the situation affects him little. (p. 231)

This distinction matters because outsiders typically presume to know what physical or psychological disability must be like—that is, it must be awful, terrible, painful, humiliating, and disruptive to daily living. Outsiders routinely believe that the disability itself must necessarily be an on-going preoccupation for an insider, so much so that leading a "normal" or happy life is not possible. Outsiders are often overly confident about the accuracy of their personal beliefs regarding disability. When doing so, outsiders subscribe to a form of what social psychologists refer to as *naive realism*, where they see *their* view of reality as *the* reality rather than an imagined, personal interpretation (really, a form of psychological projection) of another's experience (Risen & Gilovich, 2007; Schneider, 2007).

Sometimes, too, outsider attempts to be helpful end up being condescending toward—sometimes even infantilizing—insiders. For example, Shane Burcaw (personal communication, July 7, 2013), who has spinal muscular atrophy, reports receiving many comments from outsiders regarding how "great" having a disability must be when he has the "privilege" of moving to the front of the line at concerts. Burcaw believes that they are being good-natured by trying to highlight (in their minds) what must be a positive aspect of disability while imagining all of the difficulties he must routinely face while navigating life in a wheelchair.

In reality, of course, the presence of a disability—or the absence of one, for that matter—does not predict quality of life, which is comprised of many different facets of a person's life (e.g., mental health, stress level, physical health) (Duggan & Dijkers, 2001). Most insiders are likely to consider disability but one part of who they are, particularly if the disability is congenital or they have lived with it for a substantial period of time. Thus, disability is transformed into a characteristic such as height, weight, hair color, or eye color—something that is present but not thought of moment to moment unless it is made salient for some reason. Note that this analysis is not meant to deemphasize or to trivialize how serious a disability can be; rather, the goal is to recognize that no personal characteristic, whether physical or dispositional, receives such constant attention from the person who possesses it. Our attention and self-reflection shift based upon the situations and people we encounter. In any case, as PWDs, many insiders prefer to focus on what they can accomplish; they do not think about their disabilities all the time. As discussed in Chapter 1, a focus on disability is apt to be triggered by some external, situational constraint—something in the environment, such as the lack of Braille signage or the undue curiosity or commentary of an outsider.

These divergent perspectives can have a decided impact on how insiders and outsiders relate to one another. Where disability is concerned, insiders are much more attuned to the impact of their surroundings on their behavior and how outsiders perceive them. For their part, outsiders can unknowingly offer negative social cues to insiders—they may stare, speak in a patronizing tone (e.g., "baby" talk, use overly familiar speech), address a companion rather than the PWD, or express undesired types of empathy, such as pity or unnecessary sympathy—where more positive forms of understanding (e.g., direct eye contact, normal voice modulation, a friendly demeanor, readiness to help if asked) are desired. What should be obvious but is often overlooked is the simple fact that insiders live with disability on an ongoing basis while it appears as a novel, salient quality in the minds of outsiders. Indeed, outsiders tend to view disability as an acute state ("becoming disabled") and not a chronic factor woven into the larger fabric of the lives of PWDs ("being disabled"; e.g., Kahneman, 2000). In contrast, insiders know that life with a chronic condition is not necessarily defined by the condition. Interestingly, insiders receiving medical or rehabilitative services often have a more favorable attitude about the experience than do outsiders witnessing the event (Hamera & Shontz, 1978; Mason & Muhlenkamp, 1976). Again, outsiders can engage in a form of scenario thinking ("that procedure must be painful") whereas the insider has direct knowledge ("the procedure is not that bad"); still, the former questions the validity of the latter's reported experience.

In this vein, Johnson (2003a) noted that in her view, Singer the philosopher and others simply believe that disability renders a person "worse off" than no disability:

> Are we "worse off"? I don't think so. Not in any meaningful sense. There are too many variables. For those of us with congenital conditions, disability shapes all we are. Those disabled later in life adapt. We take constraints that no one would choose and build rich and satisfying lives within them. We enjoy pleasures other people enjoy, and pleasures peculiarly our own. We have something the world needs. (p. 79)

Echoing Johnson ("disability shapes all we are"), one of my colleagues read this section and noted that "disability is our normal," which is a point of paramount importance for outsiders to consider and a point of pride for insiders (Andrews, personal communication, August 12, 2013).

One subtle but important fact must be noted about the insider–outside distinction: Insiders are in the same perceptual position as outsiders concerning the disability experience of other insiders. In other words, a person with a below-knee amputation knows his or her own experience as a person with a disability. The person cannot presume to know or explain the experience of someone else who has the same disability, let alone a different disability. By extension, asking an insider to generalize about his or her experience to all other insiders with similar disabilities is akin to asking one African-American student in an otherwise all-white college class to characterize the "black experience" (see Dunn & Hammer, 2014).

The Mine/Thine Problem: Broadening People's Beliefs about Disability

Can outsiders become more open-minded about the experience of insiders? Is there a way to help outsiders become more attuned to the person–environment relation? Wright (1975, 1983) described an exercise—the *mine/thine problem*—designed to increase sensitivity to the real nature of disability by capitalizing on the perceptual dynamic created by the divergent perspectives of insiders and outsiders (see also, Wright & Lopez, 2009). The exercise does so by helping nondisabled people take the perspective of (while at the same time acting as) *both* insider and outsider. The working assumption underlying the activity is that all people possess one or more characteristics that can be construed as a physical, mental, emotional, or other type of disability.

The exercise is very simple: A group of people—Wright (1975) had groups of students or medical and rehabilitation professionals take part—are told what constitutes a disability and reminded that "everyone is handicapped in some way" (Wright, 1983, p. 48). They are then asked to write down a disability, personal impairment, or perceived limitation on a piece of paper. The papers are then collected, and ad hoc pairs of disabilities are then created and shared with the group (written on a blackboard or projected onto a screen). Audience members are then asked to locate the first pair containing their own disability and to write the pair down on another piece of paper. They then identify their own disability in the pairing by underlining it. Next, they indicate an imagined preference: *If it were possible, would you prefer to keep your own disability or the one with which it was randomly paired?* (They then draw a star by their choice in the pair of disabilities.) Wright (1983) found that almost all respondents across a variety of different samples routinely chose to retain their own disability, thereby rejecting "thine" in favor of keeping "mine."

Why do respondents elect to retain their own disability in the exercise? For a compelling reason: They are momentarily placed in a position of being both an insider and outsider with respect to disability. Most choose to react as insiders by claiming their disability (whatever its nature) and as outsiders when presented with another's (unknown and unfamiliar) disability. Wright (1975) likely chose the word "problem" to refer to the exercise because it poses an intriguing social-psychological conflict in which people compare a known condition they have with an imagined one possessed by someone else. Thus, the disability we know—whatever it may be like—is not generally perceived to be as disruptive to our well-being as the one we do not know. By retaining their own disabilities, people are admitting that they do not understand how others live with their (again, unfamiliar) conditions. By this analysis, our own disability is not just well-known; it provides comfort and presumably contributes in some way to the individual's identity (see Chapter 6). Unknown, unfamiliar disabilities, however, are more difficult to reconcile; indeed, they elicit uncertainty and perhaps even threat.

Wright (1975) raised these points in the discussions following the exercise, noting that almost everyone can be said to have some sort of disability or will in the fullness of time, a point that must be made carefully so that the experience of disability is not trivialized. Furthermore, qualities or conditions that might be labeled by some outsiders as particularly debilitating or distressing forms of disability may well be embraced as a familiar, possibly even advantageous, condition by others (as we will learn shortly below and in greater detail in Chapter 5, disabilities often provide side benefits or enrichment, even positive meaning, to people's lives).

In fact, Wright (1983) suggested that holding onto a known disability in the exercise is explained by a variety of psychosocial factors:

- *Familiarity.* People are at ease with the disability they know and possibly have always known. The consistent mine/thine findings suggest that wanting to change a familiar aspect of oneself is challenging, even when it is only imagined.
- *Self-identity.* Concern over dealing with the unknown leads to a pull in the direction of the familiar, which means that disability is very much a part of one's self and identity. If a disability has always been present, then considering life without it seems implausible or perhaps impossible and, in any case, self-identity and disability are linked with people's personal histories (e.g., Dunn & Burcaw, 2013; Gibson, 2009; Olkin & Pledger, 2003).
- *Coping.* People know what their own condition entails—that is, they know how to live with it on a daily basis—which is not perceived to be the case with the unknown qualities of the paired disability. Uncertainty about the ability to cope with an alternative disability promotes the desire to retain our own disability.
- *Psychological spread.* Spread happens when some negative quality (e.g., a disability, a stigmatizing characteristic) channels subsequent negative associations that, while generally arbitrary, still influence subsequent social judgment. After a stroke, for example, due to aphasia, some individuals' speech becomes slow, deliberate, or slurred, behaviors that observers may assume indicate the presence of cognitive or memory deficits, which often are not present. Within the exercise, some other disability is seen as being much worse than one's own, and this negativity "spreads" to and has a pernicious impact on other abilities (note that positive spread effects are also possible; spread is discussed in detail in Chapter 3).

- *Positive aspects or secondary gains.* Many people express a desire to keep their disabilities because they believe particular advantages are linked to them (social psychologists refer to these as *secondary gains*[1]; see also the discussion of positive meaning and disability in Chapter 5). Finding positive qualities in a disability, handicap, or chronic illness (e.g., a health incident causes an individual to slow down and smell the proverbial roses in daily life) represents benefit finding, a common way of cognitively adapting to health-related conditions (e.g., Taylor, 1983; Tennen & Affleck, 2002). Because it is not adaptive and promotes inability, being excused from performing various responsibilities would *not* qualify as either a positive aspect or a secondary gain.
- *Energy-conservation motives.* Although the exercise involves imagination, people still anticipate that changes wrought by a novel disability will be taxing and disruptive to daily living. Exchanging a known disability for an unknown one is presumed to require a serious outlay of personal energy, one that is perceived to be excessive.
- *Reactance.* Psychological reactance occurs whenever individuals believe that they are being compelled to give up something valuable (as would be the case for a positive or secondary gain) and when they sense that something, particularly their behavioral freedom, is being taken away (Brehm, 1966; Brehm & Brehm, 1981). Reactance leads to resistance to persuasion or, in this context, opposition to exchanging a current state (i.e., a known disability) for another (i.e., an unknown disability).

More Than a Sensitizing Exercise

Published research on the mine/thine problem has been scant (e.g., Levinskas, 1997). Do contemporary groups of students or adults respond as consistently to this perspective problem as did Wright's samples? Dunn, Fisher, and Beard (2012) conducted two studies, a conceptual replication and an extension study, to address these questions. Following Wright (1983), participants were told that "everyone is handicapped in some way" (p. 48) and that any condition that was physical, mental, emotional, or some other quality that a respondent saw as disabling could be used. The replication study paired disabilities from a group of 52 participants (sample pairings are shown in Table 2.1). Over 78% of the participants in the first study elected to retain their own disability, a finding that replicated Wright, who found between 62% and 95% of those who took part in her studies reclaimed their own conditions. When asked to explain why they preferred their own disabilities, many participants expressed concern about navigating their lives with an unfamiliar disorder (recall the list of psychosocial explanations reviewed above).

TABLE 2.1

SOME SAMPLE PAIRINGS OF SELF-REPORTED DISABILITIES

Attention deficit hyperactivity disorder	Sprained ankle
Corrected vision/glasses	Anhedonia
Colorblindness	Bipolar disorder
Fibromyalgia	Scleroderma
Developmental dysplasia of the hip	Low visual acuity
Autoimmune disease	Shyness
Lack of time management skills	Obsessive-compulsive disorder

Source: Adapted from Dunn, Fisher, and Beard (2012, Table 1, p. 116).

The second study's aim was to determine whether the mine/thine exercise caused people's beliefs about disability to become more positive, as Wright (1983) posited. To evaluate whether positive attitude change occurred, Dunn and colleagues (2012) had participants complete the *Scale of Attitudes Towards Disabled Persons* (SADP), composed of 24 items that assess individual perceptions of people with disabilities as a group (higher scale scores indicate more favorable attitudes toward PWDs; Antonak, 1981; Antonak & Livneh, 1988). Study participants completed the SADP at three points in time: 1 week before participating in the exercise (a baseline measure completed online), immediately after the exercise (a paper-and-pencil measure given prior to the debriefing), and 2 weeks after taking part in the study (a follow-up, online measure). When they arrived to take part in the exercise, the researchers also randomly paired participants' disabilities with one independently rated as being either more or less severe than their own (a separate sample of 96 people rated 78 disabilities on a 9-point scale of severity, in which higher scores indicated a perception of greater severity). For example, blindness ($M = 8.01$) was rated as more severe than colorblindness ($M = 2.34$) or stuttering ($M = 3.28$).

As predicted, disability severity (whether more or less) had little impact on participants' decisions, as 90% elected to retain their own disability. What about the attitude measure? Did taking part in the mine/thine exercise change participants' attitudes toward PWDs? It certainly did: Participants' attitudes remained significantly more favorable immediately after the exercise ($M = 117.10$) and 2 weeks later ($M = 119.22$) compared to the pretest assessment ($M = 110.41$). In effect, Wright was right: The mine/thine exercise does sensitize people to insider (people with disabilities) and outsider (nondisabled) perspectives, which leads to more positive attitudes toward disability and PWDs.

The mine/thine exercise is relatively easy to conduct and represents an engaging way to challenge biased beliefs about disability while bringing the insider–outsider distinction to life. Naturally, individuals who take part in the exercise must be carefully and thoroughly debriefed so that they do not misinterpret the goal of the exercise by trivializing disabilities (e.g., "Well, we all face challenges because we all have some sort of disability"). Indeed, before using this or any similar exercise, readers should consult Burgstahler and Doe (2004) on how to effectively conduct disability simulations. Alternative forms for running the mine/thine exercise can be found in Wright and Lopez (2009), Levinskas (1997), and Dunn et al. (2012).

Somatopsychology

Clearly, apparent, perceived, or imagined differences related to the body capture people's interests, and we can imagine that insiders can be just as curious as outsiders regarding others' disabilities. Within the social psychology of disability, researchers refer to the *somatopsychological relation* or how physique influences a person's self-image, his or her social exchanges with others, and the choice of activities and behavioral pursuits (Barker, 1947; Barker, Wright, Meyerson, & Gonick, 1953; Wright, 1983). As Barker et al. noted:

> [The] relation between physique and behavior arises because the body is a tool with physical properties that make it possible for a person to engage in some activities and not in others. The definition of what activities are possible for a particular physique may be arbitrarily imposed by authority . . . or it may be developed through trial and error . . . (p. 3)

Conceptually linked to the person–environment relation, the somatopsychological relation is more important than any psychosomatic connection of an organic or physical disorder to the individual's psychology. How people view their disability is connected to its embodied nature and the social and psychological situations they inhabit and must navigate.

The psychological impact of the somatopsychological relation concerns how accomplishing some behavior is perceived by a PWD. Imagine a soldier who lost both legs (below the knees) in a roadside bombing in Iraq. Once an avid runner, he undergoes extensive rehabilitation and eventually obtains two prosthetic carbon blades that will enable him to sprint again. His focus is on running—he is less concerned with the metallic nature of his new legs or with attention they draw than with resuming this favored activity. Another soldier with a similar loss might decline the opportunity to learn to run again using such prosthetics because he harbors concerns about his altered physique. Coupled with his concern that the experience of running "won't be the same," he also fears the reactions (the surprise, the stares, the questions, the silences) his altered appearance will elicit from family, friends, and, perhaps especially, strangers. His concerns about his new physique and the changes wrought by it override his desire to learn to run again. In both cases, psychosocial adjustment is not solely dependent upon the nature of the disability; the individuals themselves and their perceived physical, social, and psychological environments play key roles (Lewin, 1935).

Adaptation, Adjustment, and the Acceptance of Disability: An Overview

> What needs to be stated is that disability—while never wished for—may simply not be as wholly disastrous as imagined.
>
> MICHELLE FINE AND ADRIENNE ASCH (1988, p. 11)

What does it mean to adapt to a disability? Do individuals who have congenital disabilities need to adapt to their conditions? Or is adaptation limited to those who somehow acquire a disability? Does psychosocial adjustment differ from adaptation? What does it mean to accept a disability? These are important questions that deal with how PWDs think about and cope with their circumstances. Lay and professional views on coping with disability have changed rather dramatically across time, evolving from a basic acknowledgment that a disability is real and lasting (there is no psychological denial present in those who are affected) to contemporary activism in which PWDs see themselves as a vocal minority with civil rights to protect and expand (e.g., Fine & Asch, 1988; Vash & Crewe, 2004) and whose differences contribute something unique to society (Johnson, 2003a).

Terms such as adaptation and adjustment tend to imply that a disability or some other chronic illness is not congenital—that is, the disability occurs as a result of a disease, an accident, or some other acute event in time. In contrast, individuals with congenital disabilities do not have to adjust to their disabilities per se—they have always been insiders with respect to their conditions; they know no other state of being. Still, they must often adapt or adjust to externalities, such as the reactions of others as well as to the social (e.g., attitudinal) and environmental (e.g., physical, structural) limits or constraints they encounter as they navigate the world (Olkin, 1999).

The rehabilitation literature is replete with numerous models for characterizing how people adapt to disability (for a comprehensive review, see Smedema, Bakken-Gillen, & Dalton, 2009). The remainder of this discussion focuses on somatopsychological perspectives. The onset of an acquired disability causes the affected person to begin a process of psychosocial adaptation—understanding and coming to terms with disability and how it is gradually incorporated into an individual's sense of self, identity, body image, and daily life. *Adaptation*, then, refers to the dynamic, ongoing somatopsychological process that PWDs undergo as they progress toward the idealized destination of *adjustment* (Livneh & Antonak, 1997). Psychosocial adjustment occurs when the person is satisfied with his or her own person–environment relation so that any physical losses or bodily changes are not preoccupations and the individual constructively focuses on abilities and what can be accomplished (Wright, 1983). Adjustment is marked by a strong correspondence between how the PWD views his or her subjective experience and the actual external environment (Livneh & Antonak, 1997; Roessler & Bolton, 1978) as indicated by the following:

- Independence
- Active problem-solving skills for daily living
- Awareness of existing and potential assets as well as any functional limitations
- Positive self-concept and self-esteem
- Sense of personal mastery
- Ability to navigate social and physical environments
- Routinely engaged with social, vocational, and leisure activities

Based on this model, not all PWDs will "adjust" to their conditions; some individuals will adapt better than others.

Wright (1960, 1983) argued for expanding conceptions of adapting and adjusting by focusing on the acceptance of a disability. The idea of *acceptance* involves cases in which a disability or chronic illness becomes incorporated into the person's self-concept. A key part of acceptance is that the individual views disability—to use Wright's language—as a *nondevaluing* outcome, one that does not lessen the self-worth, future potential, or psychosocial functioning of the person. Acceptance of disability is not resignation to one's fate, nor is it characterized by a pretense of normality, mimicking people who are not disabled, or an attempt to hide or cover up the condition (i.e., "passing"). If anything, acceptance can be characterized as a realistic response, one that does not preclude a person from finding a disability to be disruptive to daily life or bothersome. Instead, acceptance is marked by a realistic recognition of things as they are with respect to a disability and often a desire to continue to work to "improve the improvable" (Wright, 1983, p. 159; see also, Kerr, 1961; Vash, 1978).

Acceptance of a disability as a means of coping requires the PWD to focus on what can now be functionally achieved rather than continually revisiting, even ruminating, on what can no longer be accomplished. In effect, acceptance of a disability is the acceptance of some loss or inability (Dembo, Leviton, & Wright, 1956; Wright, 1960). To make this shift in perspective, Wright (1960, 1983) suggested that PWDs should frame their experiences as "coping with" rather than "succumbing to" the consequences of a disability (the coping versus succumbing framework is discussed in Chapter 5). Given contemporary culture's fixation on perfect physiques, appearance, intellect, and accomplishment, adopting such a change in perspective can be challenging. Individuals who surrender to negative thoughts and emotions will dwell on loss, an outcome that makes them less likely to adjust to their disability. Those who cope well with their disability try to exert direct control on their current and future lives by recalling or looking for personal accomplishments, identifying existing or potential assets, putting any setbacks into proper perspective, and working to successfully manage any social and physical barriers they encounter. Clearly, acceptance of a disability is not an all-or-nothing proposition—it is best construed as existing on a continuum in which higher degrees of acceptance are marked by more constructive coping efforts.

Investigators have developed instruments to assess whether and to what degree PWDs are able to accept their loss(es) and, therefore, disability (Groomes & Linkowski, 2007; Linkowski, 1971). Based on a sample of over 1200 adult PWDs who completed an acceptance of disability instrument and a series of other measures, Li and Moore (1998) conducted a correlational study and found that individuals with congenital disabilities tended to have higher acceptance scores than those with acquired disabilities, as did participants with one rather than multiple disabilities. Other results revealed that PWDs with higher levels of self-esteem, lower levels of perceived discrimination, no chronic pain, and who were younger were more likely to accept their disability. Li and Moore also highlighted an interesting observation: Factors such as education or income level prove to be less predictive of adjustment to a disability than do particular psychosocial factors such as self-esteem or the experience of discrimination (see also, Belgrave, 1991). The impact of self-esteem in this and related research (e.g., Heinemann & Shontz, 1982) suggests that general self-image is an important influence on acceptance.

Rath and Elliott (2011), however, suggest that findings like these are not consistent across studies, which means that results supporting acceptance of disability must be interpreted with caution. Individual differences among people, as well as their other psychological characteristics, typically predict adjustment to disability better than any condition-specific factors, including acceptance of disability. For example, one common misconception is that more physical impairment leads to poorer psychological adjustment. Thus, the level, location, number, and site of amputations should matter, and yet none of these factors have been empirically linked to adjustment (e.g., Epstein, Heinemann, & McFarland, 2010).

Wright (1960, 1983) also posited that acceptance requires PWDs to change and expand their personal values and beliefs about disability (see also, Dembo, Leviton, & Wright, 1956; Keany & Glueckauf, 1993). Such value changes are discussed in detail in Chapter 7. Certainly, one's existing interests, values, and goals cannot be discounted. Perhaps the likelihood of acceptance increases when a person has more interests or outlets. In some social-psychological research not focused on disability, Linville (1985, 1987), for example, demonstrated that greater self-complexity serves as a cognitive buffer for personal challenges and setbacks. *Self-complexity* entails possessing a relatively larger number of cognitive self-aspects while maintaining substantial distinctions among these qualities. People displaying greater self-complexity are able to avoid putting all their "cognitive eggs" in one basket; that is, when something goes wrong in one area of their mental lives (e.g., relationship problems), they have other areas on which to fall back (e.g., interesting work). Greater self-complexity is linked to less dramatic swings in both affect and self-appraisal when confronting positive or negative outcomes (Linville, 1985). Subsequent research found that higher levels of self-complexity could combat depression, perceived stress, the presence of physical symptoms, and the onset of illnesses following distressing circumstances (Linville, 1987).

The onset of disability is apt to represent a more seismic change for most people than a career setback, divorce, or other life stressor, but there is evidence that people who have fewer interests and then lose the ability to take part in them find adjustment more difficult than those who have various interests, some of which they can continue doing (Massimini & Delle Fave, 2000; Schafer, 1996; see also, Lewinsohn, Clarke, & Hops, 1990). Thus, identifying PWD's interests and abilities or helping them to find new ones—their known or realizable assets—is apt to be a fruitful way to encourage adapting, adjusting, or accepting a disability.

Identifying Assets

A fundamental psychosocial tenet is that no matter how severe a disability might be, every PWD is presumed to either possess or have the opportunity to develop some *asset or assets*. Assets entail the broad array of resources that are distinct in every person, such as one's self-concept or self-identity; personal qualities or strengths; professional, intellectual, social, or physical abilities; and work or career-related talents. Some assets are quite real, such as social support from family and friends or household income. Other assets are achieved or attainable (e.g., education, job or profession, awards), imagined (e.g., goals, hopes), and psychological, such as personality (e.g., sense of humor, extraversion) or more motivational qualities (e.g., tenacity, self-discipline). An asset can even be esoteric topical knowledge (e.g., baseball statistics, architectural history), a hobby (e.g., stamp or coin collecting, reading, writing), or other activity (e.g., community service, volunteer work, blogging). Vash and Crewe (2004) use the term *remaining resources* for any of the aforementioned traits and abilities—that is, assets—people retain in spite of disability onset. Some sample categories and accompanying assets are shown in Table 2.2, the content of which is suggestive, not exhaustive.

As shown by Table 2.2, a person's assets can be real, perceived, or potential. Their presence benefits PWDs by developing or maintaining identities or social roles because what people do for vocation or avocation often reveals who they are, both to themselves and to others. An asset can metaphorically allow an individual to stand alone (e.g., a solitary hobby or interest, an individual skill or strength) or to join in with others (e.g., a group activity, shared concern or political cause). Having an acknowledged asset promotes connections with other people who are drawn out of shared interest, camaraderie, or curiosity. The presence of an asset emphasizes that something is already being accomplished or can be done by a PWD. Assets can also signal opportunities or future possibilities for PWDs. To that end, assets can motivate PWDs to be resilient (Craig, 2012) or thrive within their particular circumstances (and family members, caregivers, and friends should encourage ongoing interests or the cultivation of new ones).

One topical area within the nascent subfield known as positive psychology (see Chapter 7) is relevant to both understanding existing and developing new psychosocial assets. Peterson and Seligman (2004) developed a detailed taxonomy for exploring what they called character strengths and virtues. Essentially positive individual traits, these strengths and virtues can be explored using the Values in Action (VIA) Classification of Strengths, which was designed to offer a constructive and balancing alternative to the various pathology-centered iterations of the *Diagnostic and Statistical Manual of Mental Disorders* (DSM). A measure developed to assess 24 strengths, the Values in Action Inventory of Strengths (VIA-IS) may be a useful assessment device for PWDs because it can help them to identify their strengths and to potentially capitalize upon them to enhance their daily lives and promote well-being (Peterson & Park, 2011). The strengths are organized into six domains: wisdom and knowledge (e.g., curiosity, love of learning), courage (e.g., integrity, persistence), humanity (e.g., love, social intelligence), justice (e.g., fairness, leadership), temperance (e.g., forgiveness, modesty), and transcendence (e.g., gratitude, hope). Two key ideas linked to character strengths, which can be

TABLE 2.2

SOME ASSET CATEGORIES AND EXAMPLES

Family
 Spouse or partner
 Meaningful role as parent, child, or sibling

Education
 Goal direction for education or degree pursuit
 Degree in hand

Work/Career
 Employment
 Income
 Expertise, training, or specialization

Social Support
 Family
 Friends
 Co-workers/colleagues
 Religious community

Finances/Income
 Stable income
 Home ownership

Personality
 Extraversion
 Optimism
 Resilience
 Character strengths and virtues
 Determination, goal setting

Recreation
 Hobbies
 Sports (as participant or fan)
 Travel
 Community service and volunteering

Spirituality
 Religious community
 Faith

construed as a type of asset, are that beneficial personal qualities can be learned (Niemiec, 2013; Peterson & Seligman, 2004) and can promote a meaningful life (Peterson & Park, 2012).

What about the loss of assets? As is almost always the case, emphasizing the loss of an asset (i.e., never being capable of doing x in the future) should be avoided by PWDs because it is dispiriting, counterproductive, and possibly untrue. Disability is not an end state; rather, it is part of a person's larger life experience and in that light, simply one frame of reference among multiple possibilities (Dunn, 2010). Admittedly, it can be difficult for PWDs to avoid comparing their preinjury self with their postinjury self; however, there is apt to be therapeutic value in encouraging particular reframing by having individuals compare their current self with their soon-after-onset self. Whether disability is acquired or congenital and regardless of its severity, the outlook of PWDs and their caregivers, lay or professional, needs to be focused on what can be done or can be learned or relearned. On occasion, framing disability in this way requires PWDs to adjust their values, goals, or priorities regarding ability and disability. Another approach is to capitalize on implications of the person-first language introduced in Chapter 1 by individuating rather than deindividuating the experience of disability.

Individuation and Deindividuation

Mainstream social psychologists characterize the psychological state known as *deindividuation* as one in which a person loses a sense of both individuality and personal responsibility. Deindividuation can compel people to obey group norms (Postmes & Spears, 1998), for example, which can be positive or negative based on the circumstances. Consider a negative case: A loss of individuality happens when a person merges with a gang or a mob, leading to a loosening of normal behavioral inhibitions. Because individuals cannot be identified within these larger groups, antisocial—even violent—behavior can result (Lea, Spears, & DeGroot, 2001). By reducing self-awareness, deindividuation—in a sense, an anonymous merging with others—encourages people to feel less accountable for their actions (Diener, 1980; Zimbardo, 1970; see also, Milgram, 1963).

One classic study found that when costumed children who were trick-or-treating were "individuated" (a homeowner asked them identifying questions, such as their names, where they lived, and who their parents were), as instructed, they took only one piece of candy from a bowl when the homeowner left the room. The anonymous or "deindividuated" group of trick-or-treaters, however, were not asked any personalizing questions and they frequently took many more pieces of candy when the host left, sometimes even the contents of the entire bowl, despite also being asked not to do so (Diener, Fraser, Beaman, & Kelem, 1976).

Within social-psychological research on disability, however, use of the term deindividuation emphasizes the consequences of being seen as simply one person in a collection of comparable others; distinctive person-specific traits are ignored. This form of deindividuation entails a loss of individuality among PWDs when they are grouped together (literally or figuratively) and then labeled by the physical, psychological, or emotional natures of their shared disabilities. The arguably primary instance of deindividuation was introduced in Chapter 1, when the power of person-first language and the problems created when it is absent were discussed. Person-first language is individuating language, whereas deindividuating language categorizes people into groups ("tetraplegics") or large categories ("the disabled") through the use of such monolithic labels.

Wright (1991) drew attention to the consequences that any group labeling has over how people, including PWDs, are perceived and treated by others. Reviewing social-psychological research on small groups and categorization, Wright noted that labeling people invariably leads to two outcomes linked to deindividuation. First, the natural act of labeling people and placing them into groups deindividuates the groups' members—with little or no cognitive effort, they are seen as similar to, not distinct from, one another (Wilder, 1978, 1986; see also Tajfel, 1978; Wiley, Philogène, & Revenson, 2012). Second, this labeling also heightens the perception that there are clear differences between ingroup members (i.e., the perceivers) and those who are labeled as outgroup members (i.e., the perceived). The psychological distinction of self from other leads to greater psychological distance, presumed difference, and the risk objectifying people, thereby raising the possibility of social misunderstanding, biased impression formation, the opportunity for prejudice and stereotyping, and even discrimination (see Chapter 3).

In short, there are potential antisocial consequences of the use of deindividuating language and thought, which reinforces perceived differences between individuals and groups, including nondisabled people and PWDs. An antidote to the problem is to eschew labels whenever possible, to rely on person-first or individuating language, and to focus on the person (the individual) and how he or she interacts with the environment, as was recommended in Chapter 1. Whenever possible, then, ways to create individuating circumstances should be identified and promoted.

One caveat is worth noting here: As a practice, individuation should not prevent PWDs from meeting peers with disabilities. Being separated from other PWDs hampers the development of social and political alliances. Many PWDs have no family members with disabilities with whom to share common experiences, and many have little contact with peers due to limited opportunity, shame, or other reasons (Gill, 1995). Thus, although important, individuation should not promote isolation from the disability community or disability culture.

Psychosocial Fundamentals

This chapter emphasizes the importance of focusing on personal strengths rather than individual deficiencies linked to the experience of disability, an approach that challenges both intuition and some professional judgment (Wright & Lopez, 2009). These psychosocial concepts are rooted in person–environment relations (Lewin, 1935) but they all point to the importance of treating PWDs as distinct individuals with particular perspectives, stories, and assets that must be considered if accurate and helpful understanding is to be achieved. As Harriet McBryde Johnson (2005, p. 3) put it:

> For me, living a real life has meant resisting. . . formulaic narratives. Instead of letting the world turn me into a disability object, I have insisted on being a subject in the grammatical sense: not the passive "me" who is acted upon, but the active "I" who does things.

These positive perspectives and concepts serve as beneficial resources for constructively confronting and responding to stigmatization and stereotyping, the topic of the next chapter.

Questions

1. What is the insider–outsider distinction? How is this distinction related to the actor–observer difference and the person–environment relation, which were introduced in Chapter 1?
2. Describe the mine–thine exercise. How does this exercise inform people about a key aspect of the experience of disability? What are some benefits associated with taking part in the exercise?
3. How could the mine–thine exercise be altered for use in clinical or counseling settings? How might it be adapted for use in the classroom or for research purposes?
4. Describe the process of adaptation to disability—how does adaptation differ from adjustment? How do these two terms relate to acceptance of disability? How can disability acceptance be achieved?

5. Within the social psychology of disability, what are assets? Provide some examples of assets and explain why assets are important to PWDs and potentially for understanding the experience of disability.

6. Define deindividuation within the context of disability. How does it differ conceptually from deindividuation as portrayed in mainstream social psychology? Why is individuation important and how can it be achieved for PWDs?

[P]rejudice is an antipathy based upon a faulty and inflexible generalization. It may be felt or expressed. It may be directed toward a group as a whole, or toward an individual because he is a member of that group.

GORDON W. ALLPORT (1954, p. 9)

There is general agreement in the literature on physical disability that the problems of the handicapped are not physical, but social and psychological.

LEE MEYERSON (1948, p. 2)

3 Challenges
STIGMA, STEREOTYPING, AND DISABILITY

A CLASSIC DEMONSTRATION in social psychology finds that the presence of one trait often leads people to assume the presence of other related traits (Asch, 1946). In the experiment, one group of participants heard about a person described as "intelligent, skillful, industrious, warm, determined, practical, cautious." A second group heard the same list of traits with one subtle change—the descriptor *cold* was substituted for *warm*. That slight change led the two groups to form distinctly different impressions of the imagined individual. The *warm* group conceived of someone who they thought of as being more generous, happy, funny, and good-natured than did the *cold* group. Solomon Asch argued that the differences in perception occurred because *warm* and *cold* are central traits that lead perceivers to infer the presence (or absence) of particular other traits and influence the content of their final impressions (see also, Kelley, 1950; Stapel & Kooman, 2000).

What happens when disability is introduced into a similar person perception task? Leek (1966) had participants rate a hypothetical person whose physical status was described first, followed by four personality traits. Physical status varied, so that participant groups learned the target was physically disabled, crippled (not then viewed derogatively), able-bodied, or robust, and Leek suggested that this single characteristic provided a guiding context for subsequent ratings. The presented personality traits were either all positive or all negative (note the opposite pairings below):

Set A (positive context)	*Set B* (negative context)
Physically disabled	Physically disabled
Industrious	Lazy
Courageous	Cowardly
Generous	Selfish
Pleasant	Unpleasant

Participants wrote sketches of the imagined person and also evaluated him using various rating scales. An interesting finding emerged: Only in the context provided by the negative traits was the target with the physical disability (or the crippled status) judged more negatively than the able-bodied (or robust) condition. When the personality traits were positive, there was a trend to rate the physically disabled person more favorably than the able-bodied target (see also Mullen & Dovidio cited in Dovidio, Pagatto, & Hebl, 2011). In other words, the presence of some disability—its specific nature was not revealed—led participants to make biased ratings in overly unfavorable or favorable directions.

What can we conclude from this simple demonstration? Context—situation, circumstance, what is known or presumed—can guide people's impressions and intensify interpersonal reactions to the presence of a disability. Put another way, responses to disability pose particular social and psychological challenges to people with disabilities (PWDs) and their allies, that is, nondisabled individuals who are personally committed to supporting members of the disability community. This chapter highlights research on disability as a stigmatizing quality, one that elicits predictable stereotypes and expectations regarding PWDs, including the requirement of mourning, halo and spread effects, the fundamental negative bias, and nondisabled people's characteristic emotional reactions to disability. We begin by defining stigma and outlining stereotyping processes.

Stigma, Stereotyping, and Disability

Social bias—prejudicial feelings or discriminatory actions—toward PWDs is often rooted in characteristics that perceivers associate with disability. The degree of visibility of an impairment and the age at which it was acquired, for example, have long been known to elicit social interest and judgment (usually negative, sometimes ambivalent, occasionally positive) (Barker, 1948; Kleck, 1969; von Hentig, 1948; see also Katz, 1981). A disability, then, is a *stigma*, an attribute or identity that is perceived by other people to have a broadly negative quality in a given context or culture (Corrigan, 2014; Crocker, Major, & Steele, 1998; Goffman, 1963; Jones et al., 1984). Disability is also *stigmatizing*, serving as a social marker delineating PWDs as distinct and somehow different from nondisabled people.

The sociologist Erving Goffman (1963) pointed to three categories of stigma: tribal identities (e.g., religion, nationality, sex, race), body abominations (e.g., physical deformities), and blemishes of individual characters (e.g., mental health problems and disorders, unemployment, addiction). Although disability can sometimes be seen in tribal-like terms ("wheelchair users," "amputees"), most disabilities probably fall into and are processed by Goffman's latter two categories. Bodily differences (which are largely visible) and character blemishes (sometimes visible, usually labeled or diagnosed) render people who have them as distinct and different from others who do not carry such stigmas (for a discussion of concealed or concealable stigmas, see Quinn, 2006). Generally, then, the individualizing or conspicuous qualities of disabilities trigger an independent rather than a group-based emotional response that is immediate and usually strong (e.g., fear, anxiety, disgust, upset) (Dovidio, Major, & Crocker, 2000; Jones, Farina, Hastorf, Markus, Miller, & Scott, 1984).

When PWDs are stigmatized by others, they serve as targets of primarily negatively stereotyped judgments because they are seen as somehow different and even deviant, worthy of devaluation or distancing by virtue of a particular characteristic (Major & Crocker, 1993). Jones et al. (1984) identified six dimensions of stigma (see Table 3.1); however, PWDs are most likely to be stigmatized by the visibility of a disability (e.g., some physical difference) or visible recognition of the presence of a disability (e.g., salient bodily movement or gait, wheelchair). Regrettably, available evidence indicates that nondisabled people routinely stigmatize PWDs (e.g.,

TABLE 3.1

SIX STIGMATIZING DIMENSIONS

Visible versus concealable—Is the stigma obvious (e.g., missing limb) or hidden (e.g., psychological or mood disorder)?

Origin/responsibility for condition—Is the stigma congenital, accidental, or self-inflicted?

Aesthetic—Is the stigma distressing or upsetting to others?

Perilous—Is the stigma viewed as dangerous or contagious to others?

Disruptiveness—Will the stigma block or otherwise prevent social interaction or communication?

Course of the mark—Will the stigma change over time, getting better or worse?

Source: Adapted from Jones et al. (1984).

Corrigan, 2014; Fichten, Amsel, Bourdon, & Creti, 1988; Fichten, Robillard, Tagalakis, & Amsel, 1991; see also Yuker, 1994).

The roots of emotional reactions to stigmas can be explained by appealing to a variety of social-psychological causes, from authoritarian-based psychopathology to low self-esteem, among other explanations (e.g., Adorno, Frenkel-Brunswik, Levinson, & Sanford, 1950; Allport, 1954; Dovidio, Pagotto, & Hebl, 2011; Fein & Spencer, 1997). As Dovidio et al. suggest, however, stigmatizing reactions that lead to prejudice and discrimination often occur as a result of normative psychological processes leading perceivers to categorize people quickly and efficiently into different groups ("like us" vs. "not like us," "foreign" vs. "familiar," "friend" vs. "foe"; e.g., Macrae & Bodenhausen, 2001), as was noted previously in Chapter 1. Ample evidence indicates that judgment, decision-making, and categorization processes are based on heuristics or quick, mental rules of thumb, and other simple cognitive principles that allow people to reduce to a manageable degree the otherwise overwhelming complexity found in daily experience (e.g., Fiske & Taylor, 2008; Gilovich, Griffin, & Kahneman, 2002; Nisbett & Ross, 1980; Kahneman, 2011).

Allport (1954a) argued that categorization is a necessary part of social life, particularly for what he called the "normality of prejudgement" (see also Fiske, 2005). Allport cited five compelling reasons that people rely on categories to prejudge those they encounter (see Table 3.2). As is the case with any outgroup, nondisabled people categorize PWDs quickly, a process that has decided consequences for subsequent social interactions (Dovidio & Gaertner, 2010). Although time and effort are saved by using group membership to guide inference (Gaertner, Dovidio, & Houlette, 2010), such categorizing is socially costly, leading to predictable and often problematic outcomes: Any differences among individuals within groups are minimized (i.e., "they are all alike") whereas distinctions between groups are amplified (i.e., "we are all different, even unique"), influencing the nature of subsequent impressions and actions. In both cases, perceived similarities in an outgroup and perceived differences within an ingroup are seen as character-based traits, which in turn create stereotypes that are applied to individual members of the respective groups.

What happens when a nondisabled person meets a PWD who defies the anticipated (outgroup-focused) stereotype? For example, a perceiver meets and has an extended conversation with someone in a wheelchair who seems to be particularly intelligent (contradicting the perceiver's general belief that people in wheelchairs must possess average or below average intellects). Instead of adjusting or broadening the stereotype, such an exception is treated as a *subtype* (Altermatt & DeWall, 2003; Richards & Hewstone, 2001). Subtypes are special categories used to understand individuals, really, misfits, who do not fit general stereotypes. Thus, the "intelligent

TABLE 3.2

CATEGORIES AS NECESSARY FOR SOCIAL LIFE

Categories help people function in daily life. Categories allow us to cope with the myriad people and things we encounter; we cannot know them all. Categories allow us to call upon prior encounters to deal with current ones.

Categories gather considerable information into idea clusters. Humans prefer to use the least effort possible to judge and decide, and categories simplify the process for us because we can call upon prior judgments.

Categories enable us to identify people and things. By placing people or objects into categories, we know what they are and are for, and stereotypes can guide our perceptions and interactions with speed and efficiency.

Categories attach emotion. We have distinct feelings of like or dislike for people, objects, and ideas once they are categorized.

Categories can be irrational. Where prejudices are concerned, categories can enable people to readily develop and maintain emotional reactions to other people and social groups. They permit us to resist and often ignore exceptions to our expectations and experiences.

Source: Adapted from Allport (1954a, pp. 20–22).

person in the wheelchair" is mentally placed in a subtype reserved for "smart people in wheelchairs."

Stereotypes, then, are associations (good or bad) or beliefs (positive or negative) that link groups of people with certain presumed traits or characteristics (e.g., Nelson, 2009). These oversimplified images organize peoples' thoughts, beliefs, expectations, and often behaviors toward groups, including PWDs. In the remainder of this chapter, we review examples of stereotypic thought and response to disability that are elicited by its stigmatizing qualities. We begin with nondisabled people's expectations of how PWDs should feel due to their disability.

*Unmet Expectations: The Requirement of Mourning and
Related Points of View*

Whether fleeting or sustained, social encounters are filled with expectations. As was introduced in Chapter 1, outsiders harbor consistent expectations about what the experience of disability must or should be like (in spite of the fact that insiders' actual perspectives may defy such outlooks). One type of expectation deals with what disability researchers have called the *requirement of mourning*. Dembo, Leviton, and

Wright (1956) argued that when outsiders of any type feel compelled to protect their own cherished values, they are likely to be adamant that individuals they identify as unfortunate must necessarily be suffering (even in the absence of any apparent distress). If this sort of required suffering is not on display, then an anticipated social script is violated; in response, the outsiders must devaluate—even derogate—the unlucky target because he or she *should be* in anguish but, for whatever reason, is not. (Note that this anticipated mourning response is present in a wide variety of social encounters, not just those involving disability or chronic illness—neither job loss nor divorce is necessarily always negative, for example—they can also represent opportunity.) Thus, a woman with a facial disfigurement would be expected by others to display shame and embarrassment—forms of suffering—for her condition but would likely be seen as unrepentant (and unsympathetic) if she expressed pride in her state. The pushback—opposition or resistance to expressions of pride or social demands—that disability culture and its activists elicit from nondisabled people is probably rooted in the requirement of mourning.

Thus, in the attributionally ordered universe of nondisabled perceivers, the PWD (e.g., someone with multiple sclerosis) must appear to be suffering or something is wrong—wrong with the situation (an expectation is not met) and, therefore, wrong with the person ("Why is she hiding the truth?", "Why would he want to fool us, anyway?"). Entertaining the possibility that the presence of disability is not always accompanied by an ongoing loss is cognitively challenging because observers, as outsiders, assume that any loss—be it physical, mental, financial, social (influence, power, opportunity), or whatever—simply must be mourned (Vash & Crewe, 2004).

Outsiders rely on the requirement of mourning anytime they insist that someone deemed unfortunate is reacting more negatively, particularly affectively, than the insider reports feeling. Wright (1983) outlined three types of required mourning reactions—empathic, self-aggrandizing, and ought. We briefly review each in turn.

Projecting personal perspectives. The *empathic requirement of mourning* is largely based on outsider self-projection: "If I became disabled, I would be upset and distressed and never get over it; therefore, anyone who has a disability must still be upset and distressed by it." Wright suggested that we often find what we seek, so that if outsiders expect to see suffering in a PWD, then chances are good that comments and behaviors will be construed so as to match such perceiver expectations ("She looks so tired and weary all the time—she says it's her hectic job but I bet her condition is wearing her down").

When the PWD appears to be functioning well and expectations are not met, the outsider can revise the script by presuming the afflicted person is putting on a brave face, acting as a role model for others, or just "masking the pain." On the surface, this sort of positive spin does not seem pejorative—after all, the PWD is viewed in a positive light ("Tom is showing real courage by acting as if nothing is wrong since the stroke—if only other people had that strength of will"). Yet the outsider continues to believe that some suffering must be present somehow or somewhere because mourning what has been lost is required. Thus, the insider's point of view is still being discounted as unreal or unreliable. Empathy for the PWD, then, can contain a degree of condescension.

If outsiders can revise their expectation so that a PWD is not seen as suffering, then the empathic requirement of mourning can be diluted or even eliminated and genuine understanding of an insider's perspective can be achieved. If not, then the empathic mourning bias will persist and the affected outsider will express either apprehension and sadness about disability or, alternatively, overblown veneration ("She is a real fighter—I just don't know how or why she keeps going"), which turns the PWD into an object of (potentially unearned and undesired) high regard.

Promoting personal status needs. In contrast, the *self-aggrandizing requirement of mourning* lacks even a misguided sense of compassion. Enhancing or exaggerating one's own self-importance serves as a platform for wanting those deemed unfortunate to suffer so that one's own place in the social hierarchy is maintained or even elevated. An important aspect of the self-aggrandizement requirement of mourning is that if the PWD is not found to suffer, then one's own (nondisabled) status is at risk because it may somehow be devalued when a comparison is made. A fit and muscled athlete relying on the self-aggrandizing requirement of mourning might look at a person with muscular dystrophy and engage in the following internal monologues:

If I couldn't lift weights and work out and had to ride around in a wheel chair like him I'd probably just kill myself. And why is that guy smiling—what does he have to smile about? He's probably just lazy; yeah, that's it. Even if I had his problem I'd still try to do something, maybe bulk up. He must be lazy. That's not me, thank God.

Or another athlete might look at the same PWD and think the following:

Wow, he is inspirational! He's a real athlete—never giving up or giving in! From now on, when I feel lazy, I'm gonna remember that guy so I am motivated to get off the couch. If he can do it, I can, too!

Some degree of cognitive dissonance or psychological tension triggered by discomfort with the disability is clearly operating here (Festinger, 1957).

In any case, the self-aggrandizing requirement of mourning has several possible outcomes that all lead to the same conclusion: A desire for or the persistence in a belief that an observed person must surely be suffering. Outsiders are satisfied when suffering is apparent and become distressed when it is not. Ironically, however, outsiders are prone to devalue the PWD in either case.

Preserving proper behavior. The third form, the *ought requirement of mourning*, is aligned with sociocultural notions of what constitutes normal or typical proscribed behavior, including how people should both feel and act when confronted with particular social events. There is a decidedly moral element here, however, as engaging in or displaying proper responses to particular social situations is deemed the "right" thing to do. Although public displays of crying are justified in both settings, we assume that it is associated with sadness or bereavement at a funeral and with happiness or joy at a wedding. To display happiness at the former event and sadness at the latter is not only unexpected, it is (behaviorally speaking) bad form. Similarly, the recently disabled person who is laughing or joking during a bout of physical therapy is likely to be seen by an outsider as clearly not trying very hard "to get better" because rehabilitation should not be a pleasant experience; without pain, there is no gain. In this context, the ought requirement of mourning is akin to sociologist Arlie Hochschild's (2012) "feeling rules," which point to what we owe others (i.e., "I need to be happy and grateful") when there are gaps between what we "ought" to feel contextually (e.g., "People are supposed to enjoy surprise parties organized by friends") and what we actually feel experientially (i.e., "I hate surprises and surprise parties in particular").

The desire to maintain decorum and meet expectations motivates outsiders who appeal to the ought requirement of mourning to strongly insist that suffering is a fitting response to the situation. As a result, outsiders are placated when they witness an individual's "appropriate" suffering. When this required distress is absent, they devalue the individual in order to uphold their own values.

Regrettably, little research explores the influence and impact of the requirement of mourning. A few studies on spinal cord injury (SCI) found that caregivers tend to see rehabilitation patients as more upset and pessimistic about their prognosis than do the patients themselves (Bodenhamer, Achterberg-Lawlis, Kevorkian, Belanus, & Cofer, 1983; Cushman & Dijkers, 1990; Dijkers & Cushman, 1990; Ernst, 1987). Another study compared the responses of hospital patients who experienced surgical "losses" (i.e., removal of a body part due to amputation, hysterectomy, colostomy, or mastectomy) or a terminal diagnosis of cancer with the observations of their caregivers (nurses, nursing assistants or students, physicians; Mason & Muhlenkamp, 1976). The caregivers consistently exaggerated the extent to which the patients were experiencing negative affect (depression, hostility, anxiety) compared to what the patients themselves reported. The discrepancy between the respective emotional perspectives was not due to patient denial over the surgical losses, suggesting that caregivers were appealing to the requirement of mourning when evaluating patient adjustment.

Another study found that the members of a burn trauma team evaluated patients' depression levels as higher and optimism lower than was the case in the patients' actual responses to a validated depression measure and self-reported rating scales (Adcock, Goldberg, Patterson, & Brown, 2000). Interestingly, nurses and physical/occupational therapists with more experience (over 2 years on a burn unit) were less accurate in assessing patient emotional distress and well-being than were less experienced professionals. One explanation for the erroneous staff judgments is the persistent belief that acute physical disability requires an adjustment stage in which depression and preoccupation with loss and impairment are not only typical, but also necessary. Such stage models of coping with disability have been discredited empirically for understanding either burn trauma (Patterson, Everett, Bombardier, Questad, Lee, & Marvin, 1993) or other forms of disability (Caplan & Shechter, 1987; Frank & Elliott, 1987; Trieshmann, 1988). How people do cope with the onset of disability or trauma appears to vary greatly, primarily due to characteristics of the individuals' lives prior to the event (see also Chapter 5). The fact that many healthcare professionals endorse the requirement of mourning suggests that suffering is assumed to occur so as to support outsider values regarding the process of coping with loss.

Meaning and Suffering

As a social-psychological factor, suffering is not limited to requirements of mourning. The idea that pain and tragedy lead to profound personal insight and meaning is a sociocultural touchstone. Some classic literature (e.g., Dostoevsky's *Crime and Punishment*) and dramatic works (e.g., Sophocles' *Oedipus Rex*) contain the message that "to suffer is to learn," and at least one therapeutic approach to psychological difficulties grew from the idea that humans search for meaning in trauma and can emerge stronger thereby (Frankl, 1985). Struggles in life are often linked with greater rewards, whether material or spiritual. And not surprisingly, there is evidence that bodily impairment and loss due to disability can trigger both suffering and a subsequent search for meaning (Dunn, 1994; Wright, 1983).

Indeed, people with acquired disabilities often report that their loss has led to some enlightenment about their own lives and even the larger human experience. The notion of *secondary gains* or positive side effects due to disability was introduced in Chapter 2, for example, and we will consider how disability can be linked to positive meaning and well-being (e.g., Dunn, 1996) in Chapter 5. For their part, many nondisabled people unquestioningly subscribe to the belief that PWDs should be honored and respected for living with (and in spite of) their conditions, a form of objectification that insiders learn to endure and outsiders view as either benign or even beneficial.

Embracing the view that suffering is necessary for spawning meaning and understanding does have some problems. First, however well-intentioned an outsider may be, putting PWDs on a pedestal based on esteem for their presumed and attributed suffering maintains and hardens social boundaries between insiders and outsiders. In fact, stigmas do not have to be negative—they can also be positive, favorable characteristics that still create social distinctions and promote social distance between groups (recall the power of labels discussed in Chapter 1; Wright, 1991).

Second, meaning is not always linked to traumatic events, whether disability is implicated or not; some people find significance in suffering whereas others see only meaninglessness in their loss (Bulman & Wortman, 1977; Lehman, Wortman, & Williams, 1987). Worse still, perhaps, is being encouraged to look for meaning where none can be found—such continued, if fruitless, searching and lack of closure can be frustrating, fatiguing, and ultimately psychologically distressing (Lehman et al., 1987). Friends, family members, and professionals should be wary of enjoining PWDs to look for meaning in their loss. Asking about secondary gains or even observing them is quite different than mandating their appearance or influence.

Perhaps a better way to construe the link between suffering and meaning is by defining the difference between what Wright (1983) called "soul-searching" experiences and "soul-torturing" experiences. The latter are clearly linked to suffering, but the former need not be. As Wright (1983, p. 191) wrote:

> Although there is good evidence that one *may* rise to great heights of emotional understanding from the depths of despair, this may not be the only or the best course . . . It is the *process* of adjusting to suffering that leads to sifting out the trivial from the important and culminates in a deeper understanding of the basic underpinnings of human values. [italics in original]

Just World Beliefs

The requirement of mourning and the virtues of suffering are not the only expectations outsiders have about PWDs. Stereotypical responses linked to negative reactions that disability elicits can often be understood by the well-known social-psychological theory called the *Just-world hypothesis* (Lerner, 1980). The theory's premise is simple: In daily social life, people expect that good things will happen to good people (i.e., virtue is rewarded) and that bad events will befall people of bad character (i.e., karmic justice exists). In this view, successful people deserve their successes and the less fortunate must somehow be responsible for their fate, a quality shared with the moral model (see Chapter 1). The theme of suffering is present here as well, but in a slightly different form than the requirement of mourning or the link to meaning—here, it is seen as being earned or deserved based on something one must have done or failed to accomplish. Still, the processes are similar: To maintain the view that the world is a consistent and logical place and to downplay the impact of random events (which remind us that much of our fate is beyond our control), people devalue or even derogate PWDs. Nondisabled observers or outsiders engage in this sort of thinking to preserve their own place or status in the world, one that is—compared to PWDs—believed to be a better one.

Consider familiar examples from daily life. We learn that a friend has been severely injured in a car accident and he is unlikely to walk again. This news is upsetting and distressing—we worry about our friend's future—but then ask whether he was wearing a seat belt. When it is revealed that he was not wearing this protective restraint, we express dismay and regret while at the same time feeling that his "preventable" circumstances are his own fault ("If only he'd worn a seatbelt, then he likely wouldn't be in such bad shape"). Perceptions of responsibility matter (Weiner, 1993, 2006) and, by extension, we quietly remind ourselves that a similar fate is not likely to befall our family members or ourselves because "we all consistently put on our seatbelts." Psychological tension is reduced and attributional balance is restored because we again see the world as a just place in which good or bad events are caused by the choices people make. It is quite easy to imagine how many negative events—including chronic diseases (e.g., diabetes), disability (e.g., SCI), cancer (e.g., smoking), accidents (e.g., DUIs)—that happen can be cognitively explained as justified due to people's choices or inactions (see also Janoff-Bulman, 1992).

By broadening the just world concept, we can circle back to the issue of the impact of physical appearance on outsider impressions. As is well-documented in social psychology, the "what is beautiful is good" stereotype encourages observers to attribute all kinds of positive characteristics and qualities to people who are physically attractive (Dion, Berscheid, & Walster, 1972). Good-looking people are routinely judged by others to be happy, successful, intelligent, well-adjusted, socially confident and smooth, as well as assertive—and frequently vain (Eagly, Ashmore, Makhijani, & Longo, 1991). Of course, physical beauty (or the lack thereof) is unrelated to objective psychosocial measures that tap into this list of qualities, which means that people's perceptions are exaggerations of reality (Feingold, 1992). What we do know is that differences in physique (e.g., facial disfigurement, a missing limb) can trigger negative perceptions and evaluations (Berscheid & Walster, 1974; Hahn, 1988). And, as will shortly be discussed with respect to the "spread" phenomenon, a single visible physical characteristic or a behavioral quality (e.g., stuttering) can be generalized more broadly by observers, leading them to presume the presence of linked deficits in other parts of the target person's body or mind (Wright, 1983).

Halo and Spread Effects

Good and bad are among the most basic categories of human cognition, and people make initial evaluations of those they encounter in a rapid manner. As previously demonstrated, a fundamental quality of social cognition is this: The presence of one quality can lead perceivers to readily anticipate the presence of other, similar qualities (e.g., Asch, 1946). When these qualities are positive or favorable, psychologists usually refer to the phenomenon as a *halo effect*. The "what is beautiful is good" stereotype qualifies as a halo effect, as does any positive judgment about a person in one category that leads us to make similar favorable judgments in other categories (e.g., people who appear to be articulate or intelligent are presumed to have leadership qualities). With halo effects, it's as if the people being judged truly have angelic halos hovering over the top of their heads that render them sympathetic and make them shine in the minds of others. As we will see, negative halo effects are also possible and have decided consequences for PWDs, but let's first discuss the implications of positive halo effects.

On occasion, PWDs experience positive halo effects from those persons they meet casually. The halo these acquaintances perceive may derive from naivete, as if disability confers certain exceptional, beneficent qualities such as politeness, happiness, and cheerfulness that somehow compensate for the disability (Image Center Blog, 2011). Insiders might refer to this as "being seen as a good crip." The problem, of course, is that perceptions of perfection, unreal goodness, or even sainthood can be as socially offputting to a PWD as the presumptive presence of negative characteristics. As the blogger mbullis, a PWD, wrote:

> . . . we're somehow above the worldly creatures of the Earth. We don't drink, smoke, or swear. We would never steal . . . The problem with this halo effect . . . is that it really limits your potential to meet people, make friends, and get jobs. (Image Center Blog, 2011)

We can imagine that his sort of halo effect is especially likely to befall children with disabilities, leading adults to act in overly solicitous ways. An otherwise robust child who wears a leg brace or powerful corrective eyeglasses, for example, might be perceived as fragile or in need of protection. Well-intentioned but overprotective parents unknowingly create problems for the child's normal social development and academic success.

Researchers have dubbed this sort of halo response the "kindness norm" when nondisabled people show apparent positivity biases in interacting with and evaluating PWDs (i.e., all else being equal, we should be "kind to the less fortunate"; Kleck, 1968). At the same time, however, perceivers' interaction with people who are, for example, somehow physically stigmatized triggers higher levels of physiological arousal and anxiety as well as inhibited nonverbal reactions (e.g., eye contact, body lean) during social interactions (e.g., Hastorf, Northcraft, & Picciotto, 1979; Kleck, Ono, & Hastorf, 1966). Wright (1988) raised an important issue regarding studies suggesting that overtly positive exchanges with PWDs are always indicative of the kindness norm by suggesting that what might actually be happening is that nondisabled people are genuinely surprised when PWDs act in nonstereotypic ways. In other words, outsiders anticipate that insiders will be depressive or overly self-conscious and inwardly focused on their disabilities. When this expectation is not confirmed, then, we should not necessarily conclude that any bias is at work—spontaneous and positive social behavior may represent surprise and relief that the interaction with a PWD will go much better than expected (however, as we will learn in Chapter 4, the possibility of ambivalent feelings is not ruled out).

To counteract the effects of being put on a perceptual pedestal, PWDs and those close to them could rely on impression management techniques to demonstrate to strangers that their first impressions, however well-intended, are off the mark. The challenge, then, for PWDs who sense that they are the subject of a positive halo effect is to engage in conversations and behaviors that establish the firm presence of ordinary or everyday qualities, not rarified or beatified ones.

There is some persuasive evidence that the interpersonal behavior displayed by PWDs can moderate such halo effects while promoting genuinely positive cognitive and affective reactions. Elliott and his colleagues found that how PWDs react to nondisabled people can reduce stigmatization and shape social exchanges in constructive ways (Elliott, MacNair, Yoder, & Byrne, 1991). College-aged participants watched a videotaped interview of a research team confederate who appeared either with or without a physical disability (sitting in a wheelchair) and who behaved in either a depressed (e.g., lethargic, sad, pessimistic, tired) or a socially appropriate (e.g., engaged, humorous, assertive) manner. Participants were told that they could elect to meet the person, had to meet the person once the tape was over, or were never told anything about meeting the person. Participants rated the disabled target favorably only in the socially appropriate behavior condition, suggesting that when PWDs create impressions that defy negative stereotypical expectations, subsequent social exchanges should be positive. Elliott and colleagues argued that the keys are how nondisabled perceivers process the information about the behaviors they witness and the situational context, and that social stereotypes can moderate their normally biased judgments about PWDs.

And yet real social life is not always as clear-cut as social-psychological experiments would suggest, as PWDs cannot always expect (or be expected) to moderate the behavior of others. Psychologist Erin Andrews (personal communication, August 12, 2013) described what may be an all-too-familiar circumstance for many PWDs:

> The other week, I was having lunch out with a colleague. He was wearing a suit, and I was dressed in business casual. We were clearly discussing professional work. A woman felt compelled just by seeing my disability to approach and try to bless me and tell me what an inspiration I was. The more I tried to normalize myself and the situation, the more insistent she became in her praise. I am not sure how I could have "passed" more or behaved better. I have these experiences constantly.

The Concept of Spread

What about negative impressions linked to the presence of disability? When halo effects are negative and specifically triggered by the presence of a single, salient characteristic, they are referred to as *spread* or *spread effects* (Dembo et al., 1956; Wright, 1964, 1983). (Again, spread effects can be positive, but for purposes of clarity, I prefer to identify judgments with a positive valence as halo effects and those with a negative one as spread effects.) In essence, some recognized cue to a person's disability status—a wheelchair, a cane, a missing limb or limbs, slow, slurred, or stuttering speech—is sufficient for leading observers to assume the presence of other qualities that are considered to be negative or off-putting. An initial, reasonable judgment would be to assume that the affected person has some deficit or decrement linked to the single observed quality but not necessarily any others. The problem is that the spread effect does just that—it taints observers' general judgments in a negative direction, leading them to infer the presence of other complications or liabilities from the outset.

When the consequences of a stroke disrupt a person's gait, for example, observers may also assume (correctly or not) that the person's memory and intelligence are also affected (i.e., the perceived impact of the stroke influences social judgment by spreading from one domain to others). If the individual's speech is slowed, halting, or otherwise affected due to aphasia in addition to the impaired movement, the spread is likely to be wider still, leading to yet more unfavorable perceptions that are possibly unfounded or even imagined. Of course, still greater difficulties occur when the target of spread perceptions—the PWD—senses that others are perceptually and therefore socially devaluing him or her. The opportunity for an open, friendly, and meaningful social encounter is hindered, derailed by misunderstandings that can lead to poor communication and confirmed stereotypes on both sides (e.g., Snyder, Tanke, & Berscheid, 1977).

The issue of perceived severity is an important one because observers, particularly strangers or passersby, are prone to view a discernible disability as much more severe than its true nature. Wright (1983) described a study in which 500 college students were asked to estimate what percentage of people with intellectual disabilities possess IQs below 50 (where the scale average is 100). The typical student guess was around 30%, while the true proportion of the population was closer to 5%. Wright (1983) noted that spread effects can involve a variety of features common to groups, such as race, religion, ethnicity, sex, and nationality.

Spread effects are the likely culprits that lead nondisabled people to infantalize PWDs. Dovidio, Pagotto, and Hebl (2011), for example, found that individuals with apparent physical disabilities are routinely treated as if they are needy and helpless children; when outsiders offer help, it tends to be of the sort that promotes dependency rather than self-sufficiency (e.g., doing everything without seeking permission rather than assisting when asked). When approaching passersby for directions on a university campus, confederates using wheelchairs elicited more overly simple and repetitive replies than did nondisabled confederates (Gouvier, Coon, Todd, & Fuller, 1994). Other research found that college students provide directions in a manner more appropriate for speaking to children or preadolescents (e.g., speaking loudly and with a high pitch, using more words than necessary) when responding to adult confederates using wheelchairs, doing so even when the adult's role as a working professional was highlighted (Liesener & Mills, 1999).

Spread is not limited to the perceptions of strangers. Caregivers and friends who know a PWD well may on occasion act in a controlling manner out of genuine, if possibly misplaced, concern. As already noted, we can imagine that undue concern or worry over the welfare of a child with a disability ("Should she be left alone to play with other children?", "Are the boys going to be too rough with him?") is likely to be more common than that for adults.

There is one other issue related to spread, that of compensatory motivation, in which some disabilities linked to individuals' physiques are seen as their guiding force (Wright, 1983). Professor Stephen Hawking is a contemporary candidate whose professional success could be seen as strategically offsetting his disability. A world-renowned theoretical physicist who has the neuromuscular disease amyotrophic lateral sclerosis (ALS), Hawking is a prolific writer who uses a power wheelchair and a computerized speaking device. His brilliance at physics could be incorrectly viewed as a response to—a compensation for—his disability when the two qualities likely have little to do with one another (i.e., Would his career be that different if he did not have a disability?). Readers can no doubt identify other celebrities with disabilities who are unfairly presumed to put considerable energy into displaying skills that offset or otherwise counterbalance their disabilities.

The Fundamental Negative Bias

Halo and spread effects are person-focused perceptions and neither adequately considers the influence of situational or environmental factors that promote undue (biased) focus on a person's disability. In Chapter 1, we discussed the fundamental attribution error, the pronounced perceptual tendency to attribute the causes of other people's behaviors to their presumed internal characteristics (e.g., personality traits, abilities, deficits) while ignoring the impact of influential situational or environmental factors (e.g., rules, barriers, other people) (Ross, 1977). Observers look at actors and not the settings within which the actors operate. Regrettably, professionals in any mental health or rehabilitation field can fall prey to the fundamental attribution error when they know little about the person they are evaluating or treating, including how the individual views—and feels about—his or her situation (Snyder, Lopez, & Pedrotti, 2011; Wright & Lopez, 2009). Neglect of environmental influences is less likely to happen when people, as actors, reflect on the likely causes of their own behavior because, in addition to introspection, they also tend to look outward to consider any influential situational factors (Nisbett, Caputo, Legant, & Maracek, 1973).

The environment is not the only influence that can be overlooked in social perception. People often overlook positive information or qualities linked to others and instead focus on—really, emphasize—negative features. Consider the case of an attractive woman using a wheelchair who is told by someone she just met that "you are too pretty to be in a wheelchair." Wright (1988) referred to this sort of reaction as the *fundamental negative bias*—that is, when some object or person's characteristic stands out (saliency), is considered for whatever reason to be negative (value), and the context in which it operates is vague, sparse, or poorly defined (i.e., context).[1] Context affects meaning or, as Wright (1991) suggested, "The context can refer to conditions external to the perceiver or to intrapsychic predispositions of various sorts" (p. 471). When these three criteria are met, the negative value of the observed object or person will influence perceptions, thoughts, and feelings to match its negative character. In effect, the fundamental negative bias amplifies the magnitude of whatever negative characteristics people recognize in the course of their social encounters.

The fundamental negative bias is one example of what is no doubt a broader phenomenon. Social psychologist Roy Baumeister argues for a general and pronounced negativity bias in which, in effect, "bad is stronger than good" so that negative qualities routinely override the influence of any positive information (Baumeister, Bratslavsky, Finkenauer, & Vohs, 2001; see also Rozin & Royzman, 2001). The available evidence is compelling. For example, negative emotions are known to have a greater impact on people than positive ones, just as unfavorable impressions and bad stereotypes develop more quickly and are more resistant to change than good ones. Without conscious, cognitive effort, any initial negative evaluation will remain at the ready in one's mental arsenal (Bargh, Chaiken, Raymond, & Hymes, 1996).

A straightforward study conducted by Whiteman and Lukoff (1965) readily illustrates the fundamental negative bias (note that this research was conducted before the advent of person-first language). Participants were asked to react to labels such as "blindness" versus "blind people" and "physical handicap" versus "physically handicapped people." If you recall the arguments made in Chapter 1 for adopting person-first language (and thought), then you will not be surprised to learn that the two negative states were rated much more negatively than were the people possessing those states. Blindness and physical disability are both salient qualities that are also usually viewed as negative. When the words are presented without a supporting context to guide judgment, the rating is even more negative. Attaching the word "people" to either state provides a needed context, thereby reducing the negative bias. Recall the related impression formation study that opened this chapter, in which a person with a disability who was described as having a disagreeable personality was rated more negatively than a nondisabled person with the same problematic character (Leek, 1966).

Stereotyping Disability Redux: Warm But Incompetent?

In this chapter, we have reviewed with respect to disability a variety of expectations resulting from perceived stigma and subsequent stereotyping processes, including the requirement of mourning, meaning in suffering, just world beliefs, spread effects, and the fundamental negative bias. Beyond those described above, are there other consequences for PWDs when they are categorized, grouped, and stereotyped? Fiske (2011) argues that stereotypes follow from how the members of various social groups including PWDs are perceived on two key dimensions of judgment: *warmth* and *competence*. Each dimension has two levels that arouse distinct emotional reactions. Thus, warm people are perceived to be friendly and trustworthy, whereas those who are cold (low warmth) are presumed to be foes that may be hostile or even exploitative. Competent people are automatically seen as having high status, whereas low-status individuals are viewed as incompetent.

The resulting four combinations portray how various societal groups are viewed in emotional terms (Fiske, 2011; Fiske, Cuddy, Glick, & Xu, 2002; see also Cuddy, Fiske, & Glick, 2007,2008; Dovidio, Pagotto, & Hebl, 2011). Those people viewed as being high in both warmth and competence are seen as allies, member of one's own ingroup. In daily life, our fellow Americans and middle-class people fit this niche. Groups that generally garner warm feelings but are also judged to be incompetent—people with disabilities and elderly people—elicit pity and sympathy. Groups stereotyped as low in warmth but high in competence include rich people, professionals, Jews, and Asians, all of whom trigger feelings of envy. Welfare recipients, substance abusers, homeless people, and those of lower socioeconomic status constitute groups regarded as being low on both warm and competence, which means they elicit feelings of disgust, resentment, and even anger.

When stereotypes are activated, they guide people's thoughts and behaviors in distinct ways based on the groups being considered. People with dominant personalities, for example, are apt to compare themselves to the members of high-status groups, leading them to express envy for the members of those groups. In contrast, individuals who feel insecure might compare themselves to those with lower-status positions—women, various minority groups, and, naturally, people with disabilities—which means feelings of scorn, contempt, or derision result (Fiske, 2011). At the same time that feelings of warmth induce approach, low competence judgments signal avoidance, which suggests a mixed or even ambivalent attitude toward such outgroups. As we will learn in the next chapter, such ambivalence is very much a part of the structure of attitudes toward people with disabilities.

Questions

1. Why is disability a stigma? What are some of the stigmatizing qualities of disability? Stereotypes are often said to be efficient and functional: Should stereotypes about disability be characterized this way?

2. How is the requirement of mourning linked to disability? Is the requirement of mourning simply a variation of the familiar insider–outsider distinction or does it provide additional insight into perceptions of disability?

3. How does the requirement of mourning appear to influence the social judgments of caregivers, friends, and even professionals regarding the experience of disability? Are there ways to debias such outsider perspectives?

4. Is the purported link between seeing meaning in suffering constructive or problematic where understanding disability is concerned?

5. How do beliefs in a "just world" influence some nondisabled individuals' views of disability? How do just world beliefs impact judgments of causal responsibility?

6. Are halo effects similar to spread effects? Can either effect ever be beneficial to PWDs or are social drawbacks inherent in such social perceptions? How does the fundamental negative bias relate to spread effects?

7. On what two key dimensions are people routinely stereotyped? Characterize the emotional content of the stereotypes elicited by PWDs.

[The attitude] concept is probably the most distinctive and indispensable concept in contemporary American social psychology.

GORDON W. ALLPORT (1954, p. 43)

[P]eople with disabilities are construed as objects of ambivalence, triggering momentary, fluctuating favorable and unfavorable feelings of compassion and sympathy but also of aversion and distaste.

HANOCH LIVNEH (1988, p. 37)

4   Attitudes Toward People with Disabilities

KNOWING HOW NONDISABLED people feel and think about disability might allow us to predict how they will react to and interact with an individual or a group of people with disabilities. But how are thoughts, feelings, and likely future behaviors assessed? Imagine rating a series of 24 statements like the following using a scale ranging from the option of *I disagree very much (−3)* to *I agree very much (+3)*:

> The opportunity for gainful employment should be provided to disabled people.
> Disabled people should live with others of similar disability.

These two items are from the Scale of Attitudes Toward Disabled Persons (SADP; Antonak, 1981, 1982), which was created for use in psychosocial research in rehabilitation and related fields. Scales such as the SADP are designed to allow investigators to study how attitudes toward people with disabilities (PWDs) are formed and structured and to what degree they correlate with other psychosocial (e.g., authoritarianism, social distance) and demographic (e.g., education, sex, socioeconomic status, income) measures. Attitude scales allow researchers, practitioners, and interested others to determine how people think, feel, and act regarding disability (Antonak & Livneh, 1988; Yuker, 1988). As we will see, attitudes toward disability and PWDs are multidimensional (Findler, Vilchinsky, & Werner, 2007) and at the heart of research on the social psychology of disability.

The attitude construct has a long and storied history in psychology, having been a popular and (as Allport noted) even indispensable research tool since the 1920s (e.g., Albarracin, Johnson, & Zanna, 2005; F. H. Allport, 1924; Banaji & Heiphetz, 2010; Eagly & Chaiken, 1993). There are at least two attitude literatures dealing with social perception and cognition, the dominant one in traditional social psychology in which attitudes are a central topic and one in rehabilitation psychology that largely deals specifically with attitudes toward PWDs (e.g., Yuker, 1988). Naturally, we will focus primarily on the latter, but before doing so, we need to define attitudes and explain why they play such an important role in psychosocial research.

Attitudes as Evaluative Constructs and Behavioral Barometers

Attitudes are global evaluations of a person, an object, an idea, or an issue that are positive, negative, or ambivalent (i.e., comprised of mixed reactions) (e.g., Eagly & Chaiken, 1993; Katz, 1981). Or as Bem (1970) succinctly claimed, "Attitudes are likes and dislikes" (p. 14). Social psychologists identify whatever or whomever is being evaluated as the *attitude object.* When people express attitudes about someone or something, the level of intensity is usually apparent (e.g., *love* is more intense than *like, detest* is less intense than *hate).* Attitudes are distinct from *beliefs,* which are facts or opinions referring to someone or something.

Beliefs are very much a part of attitudes, which are generally assumed to be comprised of cognitive, affective, and behavioral components (e.g., Breckler, 1984). The *cognitive component* contains beliefs, which may be accurate or based on personal views (e.g., "I think nondisabled people should not park in accessible spots"). Emotional reactions are contained in the *affective component* (e.g., "I get so angry when I see nondisabled people parking in accessible spots!"). And how people act (or believe they will act in the future) is linked to the *behavioral component* (e.g., "I report the license plate numbers of nondisabled people who park in spaces reserved for people with disabilities").

What role do attitudes play in people's lives? Similar to most cognitive constructs, attitudes help people navigate their social worlds in ways that manage or reduce complexity. Katz (1960) identified four primary functions—utilitarian, knowledge, ego-defensive, and value-expressive—attributable to attitudes. These functions are defined in Table 4.1.

Arguably, the main point of attitude research, the theoretical as well as empirical advantage, is that when a person's attitude is known, his or her actions in the future should be more or less predictable. Thus, knowing people's political philosophies can help determine how they will likely cast their votes in an election or whether they will donate to one political campaign or another. Social psychologists refer to the links among feelings, beliefs, and actions as attitude-behavior consistency.

TABLE 4.1

FOUR FUNCTIONS OF ATTITUDES

Utilitarian—An attitude provides individuals with direction to search for and obtain rewards (e.g., connections with others, material goods, goal pursuit) while avoiding punishments (e.g., rejection by others, loss, failure).

Knowledge—An attitude helps to impose meaning, to make some aspect of the social world more comprehensible by satisfying people's need to explain, classify, categorize, and respond to the environment and the people in it.

Ego-defensive—An attitude protects individuals from psychosocial threats, including projecting feelings of inferiority on outgroup members in order to maintain feelings of superiority or to enhance a self-image and sense of self-worth.

Value-expressive—An attitude allows people to share their core values or beliefs, thereby promoting self-satisfaction and self-affirmation while reducing openness to persuasion or attitude change.

Source: Adapted from Katz (1960).

Yet knowing someone's attitude does not always predict his or her actions (LaPiere, 1934). The reason is that attitudes do not lie on a single continuum running from the positive to the negative—that conception is too simplistic. People can have strong positive affective reactions (approach), strong negative reactions (avoidance), ambivalent reactions (a mix of good and bad feelings), or feelings of indifference or even apathy toward other people or things (Cacioppo, Gardener, & Bernston, 1997).

In fact, recent evidence points to what are known as *dual attitudes*, in which individuals maintain different, competing evaluations of the same attitude object (Wilson, Lindsey, & Schooler, 2000). Sometimes an individual will express a preference for an activity ("I love watching old movies"), but when the opportunity arises to do so, there is no behavioral follow-through ("I don't feel like watching those old films right now"). These different evaluations can indicate the presence of both an *explicit attitude* and an *implicit attitude*. Explicit attitudes are based on controlled and conscious evaluations, whereas implicit attitudes involve automatic, nonconscious evaluations. Conflicts between what we say and what we do can arise, for example, when the two attitudes are not consistent with one another (i.e., a woman genuinely believes she likes watching old movies but, at a nonconscious level, she does not enjoy the activity).

Such attitudes can be potentially unrelated to one another and serve different psychological functions. An interesting quality is that people are unaware of the mental conflict that exists between the discrepant dual attitudes—they are really only aware of the conscious attitude, the one they control and reflect on when an attitude object is encountered or recalled from memory. Where behavioral consistency is concerned, implicit attitudes should be better at predicting spontaneous acts whereas explicit attitudes are more linked to deliberate, controllable actions (Wilson et al., 2000; see also Dovidio & Fazio, 1992; Dovidio et al., 2011).

Problems arise, of course, when the attitude object for dual attitudes turns out to be another person or a group of people. Consider this: Cultural change over the past 60 years has dramatically reduced the incidence of racial and ethnic prejudice in the United States. Most people claim they believe in the equality of all societal groups but, based on careful psychological research, many of these individuals continue to display negative, automatic responses—that is, implicit attitudes—toward minority groups and members of minority groups (e.g., Greenwald & Banaji, 1995; Greenwald, McGhee, & Schwartz, 1998). Unconsciously, then, people may dislike individuals and groups they consciously claim—indeed, sincerely believe—they like. Of greater concern are the findings that such negative implicit attitudes have been linked to various prejudiced responses, including tentative verbal exchanges, making or avoiding eye contact, and absent or present smiles (Dovidio, Kawakami, Johnson, Johnson, & Howard, 1997). These dual attitudes may be one source of the ambivalent feelings that are sometimes aimed at PWDs. However, much of the rehabilitation literature suggests that predominant attitudes toward PWDs are explicit and negative.

Attitudes Toward People with Disabilities

Rehabilitation psychologists have long been concerned with the study of attitudes toward PWDs (Antonak & Livneh, 2000). The rationale for this emphasis is clear: To advance opportunities for PWDs where education, civil rights and equality, and employment are concerned, the social and psychological environment should be open and welcoming, or at the very least neutral. A clear understanding of the origins and impact of nondisabled people's attitudes toward PWDs can suggest ways to create interventions that promote positive interactions between the groups (Siller, 1984; Yuker, 1965). This need is apparent, as a considerable number of studies and research reviews indicate that although "attitudes toward disabled persons are complex and multifaceted" (Yuker, 1988, p. xiii), in the main, nondisabled people appear to hold negative attitudes toward PWDs (e.g., Brodwin & Orange, 2002; Chan, Livneh, Pruett, Wang, & Zheng, 2009a; Livneh, 1982; Smart, 2001; Vilchinsky, Findler, & Werner, 2010; Yuker, 1988, 1994). The resulting problem, of course, is that negative attitudes influence social interaction and integration (or the lack thereof), and even the rehabilitative process (Chan, Tarvydas, Blalock, Strauser, & Atkins, 2009b). Chapter 3 indicated that stigma and stereotyping processes, including spread effects and the fundamental negative bias, serve as explanatory sources for this negativity. Another contender is the nature of information (or the lack thereof) that nondisabled people have about disability and PWDs. Nondisabled people's prior contact with PWDs is often limited or nonexistent; thus their education about disability can be sparse and any knowledge they do possess might be limited to the mass media (e.g., Byrd & Elliott, 1988) or a few salient celebrities with disabilities (e.g., Michael J. Fox, the late Christopher Reeve).

Livneh (1982, 1988; see also, Chan et al., 2009a) identified various additional sources for negative attitudes toward disability, including the following:

Anxiety due to unstructured social encounters. Ambiguity about the nature and implications of disability affects nondisabled people, especially when they are uncertain about how to behave toward PWDs or how their overtures will be received (Hebl & Kleck, 2000). Lack of familiarity and experience with PWDs can lead to anxiety and negative feelings and awkward reactions in the presence of disability.

Shared responses to minority groups. PWDs are frequently marginalized similar to the members of other minority groups due to particular qualities (e.g., race, ethnicity, religion, sexuality); thus they evoke stereotypes, prejudice, and even discriminatory behavior from majority group members. These reactions are related to categorization processes (Chapter 3) and ingroup–outgroup distinctions (Chapter 1).

Social and cultural conditioning. Negative attitudes emerge toward disability because nondisabled people are swayed by dominant cultural and societal norms of physical attractiveness and beauty ("what is beautiful is good"; recall Chapter 3), physical "wholeness" and fitness biases, as well as an overemphasis on health and well-being (recall the *aesthetic* dimension of stigma presented in Table 3.1). Reactions to disability are relatively automatic due to its connotations as a stigma (see Chapter 3).

Fear of death thoughts. Loss of mobility, physical function, or even a body part (e.g., amputation) can stir up symbolic associations with death. In effect, nondisabled people can be affectively troubled by disability because it reminds them of their own mortality, an argument consistent with the existential tenets of Terror Management Theory (TMT; Hirschberger, Florian, & Mikulincer, 2005; Solomon, Greenberg, & Pyszczynski, 2004). TMT explores the psychological conflicts between people's desire to live and their anxious awareness that mortality and their own death are very real and threatening concepts.

Prejudice-eliciting actions. Through no fault of their own, the particular behaviors of some PWDs (e.g., hostility, dependence, insecurity, and need for assistance) can maintain or heighten prejudicial feelings in nondisabled persons ("Why can't he take care of himself?"). Thus, for example, appearing to be dependent on others opens the door for devaluation by observers.

Demographic and personality factors. Women may generally display more favorable attitudes toward PWDs than men, although the results here are mixed. An exception is in the case of dating and marriage, in which nondisabled women are more likely than their male counterparts to partner with an opposite-sex PWD (see Chen, Brodwin, Cardoso, & Chan, 2002). People with higher education and a higher socioeconomic status (SES) tend to display more positive attitudes toward PWDs than those with less education or who have a lower SES. Particular personality factors, such as low levels of authoritarianism (Adorno et al., 1950) and greater ability to tolerate ambiguity, too, can lead to more open-mindedness regarding disability.

Hierarchical attitudes toward disability. Nondisabled people appear to consider some disabilities as more acceptable than others; physical disability is viewed more favorably generally than mental disabilities, and in turn, intellectual disability is characterized more favorably than a psychiatric disability (e.g., Chan, Lee, Yuen, & Chan, 2002; Chan et al., 2009; Tsang, Chan, & Chan, 2004), particularly if individuals with the latter are viewed as being responsible for their conditions (Corrigan & Watson, 2002; Corrigan et al., 2000; see also Weiner, 1995). The main point is that attitudes become increasingly negative moving on the continuum from physical to more cognitive and mental health-related disabilities.

Moral beliefs about disability. In the minds of many outsiders, disability is associated with punishment for sins or other wrongdoing, either that of the PWD or his or her family (recall the *moral model* introduced in Table 1.1). Fear of difference due to presumed past transgressions can lead to fear of disability and rejection of PWDs.

Various other disability-related factors. Attitudes toward disability can become more or less negative depending upon the presence of other factors, such as the perceived severity of the disability (i.e., subjectively, less severe disabilities are perceived more favorably), visibility (i.e., more visible disabilities are rated more negatively), contagiousness (i.e., conditions apt to affect or be passed on to others are rated more negatively; recall the dimensions of stigma presented in Table 3.1), and predictability (i.e., disabilities that run their course and are curable are deemed more favorable than permanent ones).

Attitudes Toward Disability: Three Spheres of Influence

Attitudes expressed toward PWDs occur in three social spheres that, although individually distinct, frequently connect or even overlap one another (Altman, 1981). First, the primary expression of attitudes is found in the circle inhabited by the PWD's family, friends, peers, and associates. The attitudes found in this sphere help to develop the PWD's self-concept and identity (see Chapter 6), and contribute to his or her socialization in the immediate community.

The second sphere of attitudinal influence entails the PWD's relationships with rehabilitation, medical, and related professionals (e.g., doctors, psychologists, physical or occupational therapists, nurses, social workers, counselors, teachers). The attitudes displayed by these professionals are likely to have a profound impact on the PWD's psychosocial processes of adjustment. This may be especially true for individuals with acquired disabilities, as it is with the clinicians with whom the newly disabled have their first interpersonal interactions in their altered state. In turn, these professional attitudes can also shape those held by family members and close others in the first sphere, as well as to a lesser degree the strangers who inhabit the third sphere.

Members of the general public, then, comprise the third and largest sphere of attitudinal influence. The attitudes herein are likely to be based on limited knowledge and experience with PWDs specifically or the concept of disability more broadly. Attitudinal expressions in this third sphere tend to be negative, sometimes ambivalent, and are often based on stereotypes, related minority or outgroup processes, and outsider presumptions about the nature and experience of disability. With the exception of ambivalent attitudes regarding disability, we previously discussed these other processes in some detail.

Ambivalent Attitudes and Disability: Possible Explanations

As already acknowledged, not all attitudes toward PWDs have a negative valence; some appear to be a mix of positive and negative sentiments, which renders the resulting evaluation as ambivalent (e.g., Barker, Wright, Myerson, & Gonick, 1953). Classic experimental research by Kleck and his colleagues (Kleck, 1968; Kleck, Ono, & Hastorf, 1966) reveals the often conflicted attitudes and actions of nondisabled people in their interactions with PWDs. In face-to-face encounters, nondisabled participants extended more efforts (amplified responses) to be socially agreeable when a researcher's confederate was seated in a wheelchair than when standing; later, participants rated the personality of an individual using a wheelchair more positively than the standing person. At the same time, however, participants interacting with the wheelchair user displayed more discomfort and inhibited behaviors, ending conversations more abruptly, suggesting the presence and influence of ambivalent feelings.

To explain why ambivalent attitudes suggest that social perceivers are of two minds, Irwin Katz (1981; Katz, Hass, & Bailey, 1988; Katz, Wackenhut, & Hass, 1986) developed what is known as the ambivalence-amplification theory, according to which individuals are found to hold negative (e.g., disgust) and positive (e.g., empathy) reactions to stigmatized groups, including PWDs, virtually simultaneously. These reactions can fluctuate in the moment, as when a nondisabled person encounters a PWD and has feelings of distaste that switch to compassion and back again (Livneh, 1988).

Katz (1981) suggested that when the mixed valence attitudes are in conflict, the resulting psychological tension amplifies psychological reactions to outgroup members, so that energy from one impulse is transferred to the other with some predictable results. Ingroup members are more likely to react either favorably or more negatively to members of stigmatized rather than nonstigmatized groups, based on whether the observed behavior is identified as positive or negative. As Katz observed:

> The stronger the positive and negative dispositions and the more nearly equal their respective strengths, the greater the amount of ambivalence. Common observation suggests that ambivalence creates a tendency toward behavioral instability, in which extremely positive or negative responses may occur toward the object of ambivalence, depending on how the specific situation is structured. (p. 23)

Thus, the nondisabled perceiver's conflicted attitudes create a threat to his or her self-image as someone who acts reasonably and responsibly toward others. This feeling of psychological threat triggers threat-reducing reactions that appear as the aforementioned extreme actions, either positive or negative, toward the PWD.

Consider a study confirming this hypothesis performed by Katz, Glass, Lucidio, and Farber (1979, Experiment 2). Participants were required to deliver very unpleasant noise or a mild noise whenever a confederate (who either used a wheelchair or was a nondisabled person) made a mistake on a task. To learn how people respond to requests for help, when the study was supposedly over, the participants received a message from the confederate requesting assistance in a handwriting study she was running. The participants were asked to write a specimen sentence ("The quick brown fox jumped over the fence") as many times as they could for use in her study. Those participants who unintentionally caused the confederate in the wheelchair condition harm by delivering the loud, unpleasant noise agreed to write twice as many sentences as did participants in the other experimental conditions (in point of fact, they agreed to write around three times as many sentences when they administered the unpleasant noise to the confederate with the disability than to the nondisabled confederate). Katz and colleagues confirmed the hypothesis that amplified positive reactions to the members of a stigmatized group occur when the latter are unintentionally hurt (similar results were found in Experiment 1, which compared actions toward a black or white confederate).

What about amplified negative responses? Katz, Glass, Lucidio, and Farber (1977) previously conducted an experiment that was almost identical to Katz et al.'s (1979) Experiment 2, but with one exception: Participants did not have an opportunity to subsequently aid the researcher's confederate who was (or was not) in a wheelchair—instead, they were given the opportunity to denigrate the confederate in a postexperimental questionnaire. As Katz and colleagues predicted, the highest (most severe) denigration ratings were made by participants who delivered the unpleasant noise to the confederate in the wheelchair.

Katz's ambivalent attitude research has in turn informed social psychology's attitude literature on prejudice and racism. Gaertner and Dovidio (1986; Dovidio & Gaertner, 2004) developed the construct known as *aversive racism*, wherein racist tendencies operate unconsciously, subtly, and indirectly. Aversive racists sincerely believe that they are not prejudiced, but they nonetheless maintain negative feelings and beliefs about minority group members. The role of ambivalent feelings seems clear here. In effect, aversive racists will engage in overt behavior that is nonprejudicial, even positive, but due to their unacknowledged biases, will discriminate against minorities in subtle, private ways when they have the opportunity to do so (e.g., in surveys, when voting, when hiring, when speaking privately to others who hold similar attitudes). Deal (2007) has argued for a corresponding construct called *aversive disablism,* in which unintentional and unrecognized biases are enacted toward PWDs, biases that are routinely denied by their perpetrators. Like aversive racists, aversive disablists are unaware of their own prejudices, as they express the overt view that discrimination or oppression of PWDs is wrong.

Both ambivalent attitudes and negative attitudes are important for understanding reactions to disability and PWDs. Dual attitudes, which contain a conscious explicit component and a nonconscious implicit component, too, also account for inconsistent beliefs and behaviors toward PWDs. In the next section, we explore the available evidence concerning implicit attitudes toward disability.

Assessing Implicit Attitudes: The Implicit Association Test and Disability

The study of implicit attitudes—the automatic, nonconscious reactions people have to objects, ideas, or other people—is important because of the challenges posed by the traditional examination of explicit, that is, consciously controllable, attitudes (Rudman, 2011; Wittenbrink & Schwartz, 2007). In the first place, people may decline to share their true attitudes with others for various reasons, including embarrassment, evaluation apprehension, or the realization that their views fall outside the mainstream and may trouble others. Failure to disclose genuine attitudes is especially a concern in the study of prejudice and discrimination: How can researchers determine if an expressed attitude is sincere or false? In the second place, respondents may be unable to adequately access their own actual attitudes to learn and subsequently report what they are (Nisbett & Wilson, 1977; Wilson, 2002; Wilson & Dunn, 2004). As noted earlier in this chapter, people may express a favorable attitude toward a person, idea, or thing, yet their unregulated, nonverbal behaviors suggest the presence of a competing, and likely contrary, attitude. In such cases, the implicit attitude can point to implicit prejudice (Greenwald & Banaji, 1995).

Many investigators of implicit, prejudiced attitudes rely on a measure known as the Implicit Association Test (IAT; Greenwald, McGhee, & Schwartz, 1998; Greenwald, Poehlman, Uhlmann, & Banaji, 2009). The IAT is a covert measure of unconscious attitudes that assesses the extent to which two concepts are associated with one another by having participants rapidly determine whether word or image pairings are either positive or negative. The working assumption underlying the IAT is that people's reaction times (i.e., response latencies) to particular stimuli reveal how they actually feel about some target or target group (e.g., race, nationality, ethnic group, religion, sport). When studying implicit racism toward African-Americans, for example, researchers examine how quickly participants respond to *black-bad/white-good* word pairings (e.g., *black-failure, white-joy*) relative to *black-good/white-bad* pairings (e.g., *black-wonderful, white-evil*) delivered on a computer screen. Images (e.g., white or black faces), too, are paired with descriptive words as part of the IAT (there are several stages involved in completing the measure). Where race is concerned, people tend to make decisions about the former pairings much more quickly than the latter, revealing that they tend not to mentally connect pairings of *black-good* and *white-bad*. In other words, quicker response times reveal actual (implicit) attitudes: If a target associated with positive terms elicits a faster response than a target associated with negative ones, then the implicit attitude is presumed to be positive. If the reverse is true, then the attitude is deemed to be negative.

The IAT has been used to examine implicit attitudes toward men and women, young and old people, and, as we will see, people with or without disabilities. Despite criticisms about its validity and the amount of time it takes to complete the testing tasks (e.g., Brendl, Markman, & Messner, 2001; cf. Nosek, Greenwald, & Banaji, 2007), as well as the notion of implicit prejudice (Arkes & Tetlock, 2004), the IAT is an extremely popular and versatile research tool. Well over 500 scientific studies attest to its empirical and investigative utility (Smith & Nosek, 2010). Among these studies are a few that deal with assessing implicit attitudes toward PWDs (Pruett & Chan, 2006; Robey, Beckley, & Kirschner, 2006; Thomas, Vaughn, & Doyle, 2007; Vaughn, Thomas, & Doyle, 2011).

Pruett and Chan (2006), for example, developed an IAT designed to assess disability attitudes (the DA-IAT). The researchers found that a sample of over 200 students from a rehabilitation counseling program reported congruent associations of negatively valenced words with disability-related symbols (e.g., the familiar wheelchair figure or handicapped symbol) and positively valenced words with nondisabled symbols (e.g., the familiar roadside symbol for school children) as compared to the reverse or incongruent associations (i.e., positive words with disability symbols and negative words with nondisability symbols). As anticipated, however, there was no correlation between the assessed implicit attitudes and the participants' responses to the Attitude Toward Disabled Persons (ATDP) Scale, an explicit attitude measure (e.g., Yuker & Block, 1986; see also, Antonak & Livneh, 1988). In other words, the participants' implicit attitudes toward disability were predominantly negative whereas little evidence of bias or prejudiced feelings regarding disability was found by the explicit measure, which mirrors routine results from studies of racial attitudes (Dovidio et al., 2011). A related study concerning implicit attitudes toward—and explicit romantic ratings of—opposite-sexed peers with disabilities also found similar results (Rojahn, Komelasky, & Man, 2008).

A study by Robey, Beckley, and Kirschner (2006) reveals that physical disability is not only linked to implicit negative attitudes but also to particular pejorative qualities. Using a version of the IAT designed to assess connections between disability-related words and childhood, Robey et al. found that staff members in a facility serving individuals with multiple disabilities were prone to implicitly associate disability with infantilizing attitudes and child-like characteristics. Once again, the staff members' explicit attitudes did not suggest any infantilizing biases toward people with physical disabilities (recall that biases aimed at PWDs by professionals who work with them are regrettably common; Benham, 1988; Brodwin & Orange, 2002; Reeve, 2000). An earlier study by Park, Faulkner, and Schaller (2003) demonstrated implicit associations between disability and disease, a connection that was enhanced when a contextual cue concerning contagion was included in the IAT exercise.

Although use of implicit measures such as IATs for disability is on the rise, the majority of attitude measures toward disability and PWDs are more explicit in nature. In the next section, we examine somewhat more deliberative measures of thought, feeling, and behavior regarding disability.

Measuring Attitudes Toward Persons with Disabilities

Antonak and Livneh (2000) wrote an extensive and focused review of available measures of attitudes toward PWDs (for general discussions of dependent measures used in social psychological research, including attitude research, see Dunn, 2013; Wilson, Aronson, & Carlsmith, 2010). The available measures can be categorized as either direct or indirect methods for assessing reactions to disability. *Direct measures* of attitudes toward disability usually disclose their purpose to respondents (e.g., "We are interested in your thoughts and feelings about disability") before assessing their responses. Typical direct measures include opinion surveys and questionnaires (open-ended or free response, close-ended or forced choice; e.g., Comer & Piliavin, 1972), interviews (i.e., face to face, over the phone; e.g., Philips, 1975), adjective check lists (e.g., Gottlieb, Corman, & Curci, 1984), ranking methods (e.g., Abroms & Kodera, 1979), Q-sorts (e.g., Shaver & Scheibe, 1967), sociometric approaches (i.e., social distance; e.g., MacMillan & Morrison, 1984), semantic differential scales (e.g., Kravetz, Katz, & Albez, 1994), and simple rating scale questions (e.g., Antonak, 1979). The drawback to most of these direct attitude assessment methods is the possible distorting impact of socially desirable responding (i.e., answering in ways designed to curry favor with others, including underreporting negative behaviors and overreporting positive behaviors) and an unwillingness to disclose actual, if private, attitudes. Furthermore, some respondents may not have established attitudes toward disability; when asked about the topic, they develop an ad hoc or transient attitude to placate the researcher, save face, or avoid embarrassment for not having an opinion. Other threats to validity for direct methods are discussed in Antonak and Livneh (2000).

Indirect methods for assessing attitudes toward disability can overcome many validity threats and empirical confounds because they are designed to measure respondent attitudes unobtrusively (for a classic discussion of nonreactive measures, see Webb, Campbell, Schwartz, Sechrest, & Grove, 1981). Antonak and Livneh (2000) identified four categories of indirect methods: unobtrusive behavioral observations in public or private settings (trained coders are often used; Samerott & Harris, 1976), assessments that mask their actual intent (e.g., projective techniques using ambiguous stimuli; Ford, Liske, & Ort, 1962; Thurstone, 1959), deception studies (e.g., disguised measures employed in experiments, such as the classic bogus pipeline; Jones & Sigall, 1971), and physiological methods (e.g., autonomic activation via electrical conductiveness of the skin; Kleck, Ono, & Hastorf, 1966). The IAT could also be classified as an indirect method of attitude assessment (recall, for example, Pruett & Chan, 2006).

When designing any study employing attitude measures, researchers should keep in mind the aforementioned observed inconsistencies often found between written or verbally expressed attitudes about disability and PWDs and those that are assessed using behavioral and other indirect methods. Such inconsistencies may reflect a conflict between conscious (explicit) and nonconscious (implicit) attitudes. Where possible, researchers should plan their studies to incorporate both direct and indirect assessment methods. When doing so is not feasible, a compelling explanation for the absence of one or the other type of attitude measure should be provided (e.g., participant reactivity, compromising mundane realism).

A Recommendation Regarding Attitude Measures

Antonak and Livneh (2000) made an important observation that investigators interested in the study of disability attitudes should consider. From their review, these researchers identified over 40 distinct scales designed to assess attitudes toward disability, people with disabilities in general, and people with specific kinds of disability. A challenge that users face is that some scales use dated or nonperson first language (e.g., "the disabled," "the handicapped"), and many were created prior to the landmark Americans with Disabilities Act (1990). In lieu of creating new attitude scales, Antonak and Livneh advocate that researchers should review, revise, refine, update, extend, and, in particular, revalidate existing measures. Such efforts will save researchers' time, reduce unnecessary duplication and replication of similar tools, extend the life and utility of the available scales, and build upon existing scholarship. These authors also edited a helpful resource, a volume containing over 20 scales for assessing attitudes toward disability (Antonak & Livneh, 1988). Some scales measure general attitudes; others focus on particular disabilities (e.g., blindness, deafness), including psychiatric conditions, intellectual disabilities, and societal responsibilities toward people with disabilities (e.g., attitudes towards mainstreaming PWDs).

How can a working knowledge of disability attitudes and available measures be leveraged to promote more positive attitudes toward disability and PWDs? In other words, how can attitude change be accomplished?

Changing Minds: The Contact Hypothesis

What routes of persuasion can be used to change negative or largely ambivalent attitudes toward PWDs into a more positive direction? Allport (1954a) suggested simply and elegantly that increasing contact between people who are somehow different from one another will lead to more harmonious feelings, beliefs, and behavior. Allport wrote the following:

> Prejudice (unless deeply rooted in the character structure of the individual) may be reduced by equal status contact between majority and minority groups in the pursuit of common goals. The effect is greatly enhanced if this contact is sanctioned by institutional supports (i.e., by law, custom, or local atmosphere), and provided it is of a sort that leads to the perception of common interests and common humanity between members of the two groups. (p. 281)

Dubbed the *contact hypothesis* in the social-psychological literature, over 500 empirical studies now attest to the benefits of promoting meaningful contact between diverse groups of people (Pettigrew & Troop, 2006, 2008; see also, Dovidio, Glick, & Rudman, 2005; Kenworthy, Turner, Hewstone, & Voci, 2005; Tropp & Mallett, 2011). Research on *intergroup contact theory* reveals favorable attitude change regarding race, ethnicity, individuals with mental illness, elderly people, people with AIDS, gays and lesbians, and, as we will shortly learn, people with disabilities (Pettigrew & Tropp, 2011). Most studies employ a variety of techniques in both controlled laboratory settings and out in the field. Some studies rely on archival data to illustrate prejudice reduction.

Table 4.2 lists four conditions of intergroup contact that can lead to improved relations between different groups of people. In some sense, these four conditions point to optimal circumstances, but meeting all four or even one may not be

TABLE 4.2

CONDITIONS PROMOTING CONSTRUCTIVE INTERGROUP CONTACT

Personal interaction—Contact should be one-on-one so that individuals from each group engage one another.

Equal status—Contact should happen so that individuals representing each group are seen as having equal rank or standing.

Social norms—Expected behavior in a given situation, which might be defined or regulated by a third party or authority, should promote intergroup contact.

Cooperative activities—Individuals from each group should work together to realize shared, specific goals.

Source: Adapted from Pettigrew and Tropp (2000, 2006, 2008).

necessary (Crisp & Turner, 2009), as the benefits associated with contact are quite robust (Pettigrew & Tropp, 2006).

What dynamics drive the beneficial results of intergroup contact? Pettigrew and Tropp (2008) suggest that contact leads to lower levels of prejudice for three reasons. First, meaningful and sustained contact between ingroup and outgroup members leads to enhanced knowledge about those in the outgroup. Second, contact promotes empathy and understanding, as well as the ability to adopt the others' perspectives (recall, for example, the mine–thine research discussed in Chapter 2). Finally, intergroup contact reduces ingroup anxiety about what people in an outgroup are really like. Note that intergroup contact will not necessarily eliminate prejudicial feelings, but it appears to substantially reduce the magnitude of negative attitudes, leading to more openness, the potential for increased cooperation, and less misunderstanding.

Disability and the Contact Hypothesis: A Selective Review

What about contact between nondisabled persons and PWDs? How and why does it work? Currently, there is no comprehensive review of research on the contact hypothesis and disability available. Certainly, though, we should expect the conditions identified by Allport (1954a), Pettigrew and Tropp (2006, 2008), and other researchers to decrease the prejudiced feelings that nondisabled persons may harbor toward PWDs. As Mason and colleagues (2004) put it, "It makes sense that repeated contacts lead to the able-bodied person learning more information about the person with the disability (family, values, aspirations, joyful experiences, sense of humor, etc.) as a 'whole' person" (p. 81).

Following this reasoning, Amsel and Fichten (1988) examined the thoughts and attitudes of nondisabled college students who had previous contact with college-aged people with physical disabilities. The investigators found that students with prior contact reported being comfortable and relaxed when interacting with peers with disabilities. In addition, nondisabled students with prior contact experience reported a higher ratio of positive to negative thoughts compared to peers who had no contact with PWDs. This ratio was true for thoughts about the self and others, but was most pronounced concerning thoughts about persons with a disability. Amsel and Fichten suggested that the benefit of contact with a PWD is that such interaction changes thoughts about future contact (i.e., reducing concerns or anxieties about meeting) with PWDs. The drawback of this study is the absence of any actual interaction component, as the student participants provided the investigators with retrospective reports about past interactions and then completed a series of paper and pencil measures. This research was also conducted before implicit attitude measures of disability were available. Still, the findings are consistent with the contact hypothesis.

Clunies-Ross and O'Meara (1989) conducted a more interactive and longer-term study as part of an evaluation of a program aimed at improving attitudes toward peers with disabilities among some Australian elementary school students. Half a group of fourth-graders were randomly assigned to participate in recreational activities with same-aged children with intellectual disabilities and the other half were not (control group members spent the same amount of time engaged in social study activities). Compared to the fourth-graders in the control group as well as their own pretest scores, those children who took part in the recreational activities with the disabled peers showed a positive attitude change. Moreover, the favorable attitude change persisted for (at least) 3 months beyond the program's end. Other research concerning nondisabled children's attitudes toward persons with disabilities finds similar results in support of the contact hypothesis (e.g., Ballard, Corman, Gottlieb, & Kaufman, 1977; Fenrick & Peterson, 1984; Maras & Brown, 1996; Ronning & Nabuzoka, 1993).

We will close the discussion of the contact hypothesis with one promising study concerning attitudes toward the employability of PWDs. Levy and colleagues studied over 300 executives employed at "Fortune 500" companies who were responsible for hiring decisions, asking them to complete a survey (Levy, Jessop, Rimmerman, & Levy, 1993). Respondents were to disclose their attitudes toward persons with severe disabilities, including whether they had prior experiences hiring such individuals. Those executives who reported previous experiences working with PWDs showed favorable attitudes toward disability generally and expressed greater belief in the employability of people with severe disabilities than did those executives with no prior contact with PWDs in the workplace.

A Future Frontier? Reducing Prejudice through Imagined Contact

For the contact hypothesis to work, must there be actual contact between a nondisabled person and a PWD? In other words, are there other ways that majority group members can develop more favorable attitudes toward minority group members? An emerging and intriguing set of studies indicates that having people imagine social interactions with outgroup members can actually produce positive perceptions while reducing prejudicial feelings. Crisp and Turner (2009) argue that having people mentally simulate positive contact with outgroup members promotes more favorable attitudes toward those outgroups while reducing the propensity to engage in stereotyping. In addition, *imagined intergroup contact* reduces the anxiety that majority group members often feel while simultaneously allowing their social perceptions of outgroup members to become more positive (for more detail, see Crisp & Turner, 2013).

What makes this approach compelling is its inherent simplicity and applicability. Imagined intergroup contact can be used to prepare people for future encounters (a first step toward actual contact and prejudice reduction) as one of several approaches to reducing prejudice or as a basic way to reduce people's inhibitions about others who are different from themselves. As Crisp and Turner claim, ". . . we assert the value in imagined contact is in its ability to encourage people to engage outgroups with an open mind" (p. 231).

The typical instructions for imagined intergroup contact are quite minimal. Here is a standard set from Crisp and Turner (2009, p. 234) revised (by me) to account for disability:

> We would like you to take a minute to imagine yourself meeting a stranger who has a disability for the first time. Imagine that the interaction is positive, relaxed, and comfortable.

Crisp and Turner note that two critical features are required in such instructions: The encouragement to engage in a mental simulation (just thinking of an outgroup person is not sufficient—imagined interaction must occur; Turner, Crisp, & Lambert, 2007, Study 2). Beyond that, the affective tone of the instructions must be positive, just as an actual interaction between people from different groups must be positive (Stathi & Crisp, 2008, Study 1). Moreover, the impact of the imagined intervention can affect both explicit and implicit attitudes, as Turner and Crisp (2010) found when they had young people imagine speaking to an older stranger. Participants who did so reported more favorable, explicit attitudes toward older people generally, but also had more positive implicit attitudes as assessed on a "younger–older" version of the IAT.

Cameron, Rutland, Turner, Holman-Nicolas, and Powell (2011) examined whether having nondisabled children aged 5 to 10 years imagine interacting with a disabled child reduced intergroup bias. Compared to peers in a control condition, the mental simulation group of children did indeed show less bias in their general attitudes as well as higher ratings of competence and warmth concerning disability. The youngest children (ages 5 to 6 years) in the simulation condition also reported having more positive intended friendships with children with disabilities than did their control group peers (this result was not found in children ages 7 and older). The researchers suggested that the findings offer reasonable support for their hypothesis that younger children are apt to reap considerable benefit from imagined contact with outgroups precisely because they have little or no experience with them and therefore have not formed stereotypes.

A related line of research deals with what is known as the *extended contact hypothesis* (Wright, Aron, McLaughlin-Volpe, & Ropp, 1997), in which the beneficial results of intergroup contact develop by way of vicarious learning opportunities. For example, we may never have personally interacted with individuals from a particular outgroup, but perhaps someone we know well—a friend or neighbor or even a relative—has done so. Wright and colleagues (1997) found that individuals who had such extended contact (again, through people they knew) were found to have lower levels of racial prejudice than members of a control group who did not have any friends with extended outgroup connections.

What about extended contact and disability? Research by Cameron and Rutland (2006) explored the impact of the extended contact hypothesis among a group of nondisabled children who participated in a 6-week intervention in which they read stories about friendships between children with and without disabilities (i.e., extended contact was operationalized by reading and hearing about other children—all positive characters—who interacted with peers with disabilities). This form of extended contact led to more positive attitudes toward PWDs, particularly in one condition in which the children heard the category membership of the characters (i.e., nondisabled child or a child with a disability) emphasized (for more on the extended contact hypothesis, see Crisp & Turner, 2009; Vonofakou, Hewstone, & Voci, 2007).

Changing Attitudes, Changing Behavior?

Clearly, under certain conditions or circumstances, intergroup contact between individuals and groups of people with and without disabilities can lead to more favorable attitudes as well as reduced feelings of prejudice and avoidance. Interpersonal contact between nondisabled and PWDs leads to personal connection and reduced feelings of anxiety, which in turn can help to overturn negative stereotypes (Dovidio, Paggato, & Hebl, 2011). More research on this critical topic within the social psychology of disability is needed, particularly in light of other evidence regarding dual (explicit versus implicit) and ambivalent attitudes. Fortunately, there is evidence that when people recognize the possible presence of nonconscious stereotypes, ambivalence, and spontaneous negative reactions that defy personal standards, they can also consciously work to monitor, regulate, and ultimately control some of their own implicit biases (Monteith, Arthur, & Flynn, 2010), thereby helping to reduce social barriers that PWDs must struggle to overcome.

Questions

1. Define attitudes. Why is the attitude construct so enduring and so central to social psychology and rehabilitation psychology, respectively?

2. What is a dual attitude? How can someone hold two inconsistent attitudes about disability or a PWD? What are some likely consequences of dual attitudes for PWDs and nondisabled people?

3. Characterize attitudes toward disability and PWDs—are they generally negative in both cases? Why? Do the reasons for (sources of) negative affect imply that positive attitude change is possible?

4. Explain the nature of ambivalent attitudes. What are some possible explanations for ambivalent attitudes toward disability and PWDs? Why is it argued that ambivalent attitudes sometimes serve as evidence of implicit attitudes?

5. Describe some of the direct and indirect methods used to assess attitudes toward disability and PWDs. What is the distinction between direct and indirect methods? Why are indirect methods sometimes superior to direct methods?

6. Define the contact hypothesis, explain the logic underlying it, and explain how it might be used to promote favorable attitudes toward disability and PWDs. Quickly sketch out a study designed to test how the contact hypothesis can reduce prejudiced or ambivalent feelings toward disability.

7. How do imagined contact and extended contact relate to the contact hypothesis? How might these variations of the contact hypothesis be used to develop constructive interventions aimed at reducing the biases, prejudice, and stereotyping often directed at PWDs?

I just want people to know that you can come out of a situation that might seem like the end of the world and come out stronger.

ADRIENNE HASLET-DAVIS (quoted in Knowles, 2013)

5   Coping with and Adjusting to Disability

THIS CHAPTER WAS written a few weeks after the bombing at the 2013 Boston Marathon, in which three people were killed and hundreds were wounded, some severely. An injured woman, Adrianne Haslet-Davis, was a dance instructor who lost her left foot in one of the explosions. She reported experiencing many "dark moments" since the event, but within days began to display solid determination to tackle the demands of physical therapy, seek a prosthetic foot, and dance again (Knowles, 2013). She even vowed to run in the 2014 Boston Marathon, although she had never run such a race before. It is too soon to characterize her recovery, but not too soon to portray her psychosocial demeanor: She is optimistic, committed, energetic, and purposeful. In short, she is constructively coping with a tragic, unexpected event that left her with a disability.

Why do some individuals seem to respond to negative events, including disabling circumstances, with fortitude and resolve whereas others appear to be undone emotionally by them? Of course, reactions to disabling events cannot simply be categorized dichotomously as "coping well" or "not coping," as there is a continuum of ongoing and fluctuating reactions between the two poles. This chapter deals with people with disabilities (PWDs) and their ability to cope with and adjust to disability. As we will see, a considerable amount of research illustrates successful coping with and integration of disability into people's lives. As was discussed in Chapter 2 (i.e., the insider–outsider distinction), however, nondisabled people routinely predict that PWDs will report experiencing a lower quality of life, although this is not the case (Ubel, Loewenstein, & Jepson, 2003), a finding from studies of individuals who have rheumatoid arthritis (Hurst et al., 1994), have colostomies (Boyd,

Sutherland, Heasman, Tritchler, & Cummings, 1990), or receive dialysis (Riis et al., 2005; Sackett & Torrance, 1978). Much of the chapter explores the experiences of nondisabled individuals who became disabled; thus, there will be less focus on congenital disabilities.

This chapter also examines how many PWDs often view themselves as being fortunate in spite of chronic disabilities and find meaning and positive byproducts in their conditions, as well as happiness and hedonic adaptation to disability (see, for example, Park et al., 2009). Affective forecasting—predictions of future feelings linked to positive and negative events—is also considered in the context of disability. The chapter closes with a recommendation for how best to understand and construe coping and adjustment to disability. We begin by considering how the mental frameworks people adopt regarding disability (their own or others) have a decided impact on their psychosocial outlook, adjustment, and well-being.

Coping versus Succumbing Frameworks

> [F]or there is nothing either good or bad, but that thinking makes it so.
> HAMLET (Act II, scene II)

How should people's efforts to make sense of disability—based on their own experience as a PWD or based on observing the behavior of PWDs—be described? There is no clear single or inevitable response to disability; rather there are apt to be many responses, some more helpful and adaptive for the affected individuals and others less so.

Wright (1983) defined the continuum of positive to negative responses to disability onset as *coping versus succumbing frameworks*. Wright was quick to note that the onset of disability typically elicits both types of responses in people; individuals vacillate between coping with and succumbing to disability before orienting themselves toward one perspective as they adapt and adjust to the changes wrought by their situations. These frameworks guide ways of thinking about, seeing, and reacting to disability. Affected persons and their families, caregivers, professionals, friends, peers, and casual observers routinely adopt these interpretive perspectives. In effect, the frameworks serve both as an insider mode of self-reflection for the PWD and as guidelines for outsiders to characterize the behavior of PWDs.

Succumbing is characterized by a predominant focus on the negative aspects of a disabling event and its consequences. The individual does not consider the possibility of eventually adjusting to the disability or give much thought to the challenges posed by the physical, social, emotional, psychological, and/or other changes. The losses linked to the disability dominate the individual's attention—what *cannot be done* anymore in lieu of *what can be done* or *can be learned* or *relearned*. Individuals who adopt a succumbing framework are essentially "pulled under" by the negative force of the disabling event and its consequences. As Wright (1978) wrote, ". . . the succumbing framework concentrates upon the difficulties and the heartbreak of being disabled and not the challenges for meaningful adaptation and change" (p. 177).

In contrast, by following a *coping framework* the newly injured person focuses less on the consequences and difficulties posed by disability and more on intrinsic values and retained or potential assets (recall Chapter 2). Disability is treated therein as one quality among many others comprising the individual's life and experiences.[1] Suffering is deemphasized in favor of searching for everyday and long-term sources of satisfaction and resolutions to disability-related problems (e.g., mobility, access, employment). A coping framework encourages the individual to adopt and maintain an active rather than passive outlook, one aimed at altering social (e.g., prejudice, discrimination, educational limitations), legal (e.g., employment opportunities), and environmental (e.g., architectural barriers in the home or community, problems with public transportations) obstacles to postdischarge life. Wright (1983) noted that coping frameworks also promote medical interventions designed to ameliorate impairments and encourage training or education for the development of new abilities; they also promote the adoption of new values or the revision of existing ones (see Chapter 7). Particular qualities associated with coping versus succumbing are listed in Table 5.1.

Note that active reliance on coping responses such as those found in the top of Table 5.1 by no means guarantees that the challenges of daily living (see Chapter 1) are readily accomplished or, alternatively, that they are overlooked or ignored. Instead, as already noted, PWDs may swing back and forth between coping and succumbing responses depending on the issue, the time (i.e., close to or distant from the onset of the disability), the current medical or physical condition (e.g., sleep disturbance, pressure sores), or the particular situation. Yet when nondisabled people see PWDs using their assets and personal resources to respond to their circumstances, the latter are viewed positively for taking charge of their lives. As noted previously (recall Chapter 3), some outsiders will attribute highly favorable, even heroic, qualities to PWDs. On the other hand, when individuals behave consistently within a succumbing framework, observers are likely to assess them negatively by feeling pity or even scorn because they appear to be surrendering to their situations. In a simple experiment (Shurka, Siller, & Dvonch, 1982), nondisabled participants watched a videotaped interview of a person in a wheelchair who appeared to either cope with or succumb to challenges posed by disability. The succumbing target was rated much less favorably than the coping target on three measures (a semantic differential scale, a rating scale, and emotional content expressed in a written evaluation); indeed,

TABLE 5.1

QUALITIES ASSOCIATED WITH COPING WITH OR SUCCUMBING TO DISABILITY

Coping

Active and independent

Emphasize participation and engagement

Focus on assets and intrinsic qualities

No devaluation of self, skills, or limits

Work to alter or eliminate physical and social barriers

Negative aspects of daily life are deemed manageable

Understanding and accepting of limitations

Seek helpful medical procedures, assistive devices (e.g., prostheses, cane) or helpers
   (e.g., guide dogs, personal aids)

Promote meaning and life satisfaction

Succumbing

Passive and dependent

Focus on shortcomings, drawbacks, and things that cannot be accomplished

Assess development or progress against nondisabled ("normal") standards

Deemphasize areas in which participation is possible by dwelling on loss

View self as victim or passive in the face of disability and linked changes

Resign self to condition *or* act as if no disability exists

Pity self or others with a disability and devalue life and future potential

See prevention or cure, not adaptation or adjustment, as the only reasonable solutions
   to disability

Source: Adapted from Wright (1983, p. 195, Figure 9.1).

coping behaviors led observers to perceive positive social exchanges between the portrayed PWD and a nondisabled interviewer, whereas succumbing responses did not.

The larger issue of whether reactions to disability are perceived by observers as
either a coping-focused or succumbing-laden reaction is an important one. As
PWDs and disability rights groups draw public awareness and interest to disability
issues as matters of civil rights, fund-raising appeals might unknowingly shape (or
worse, perpetuate) the common public impression that PWDs adhere to succumbing frameworks and are therefore especially needy (Harris & Harris, 1977; see also,
Johnson, 2005). Adler, Wright, and Ulicny (1991), for example, demonstrated that

a filmed fundraising appeal with a voiceover that either emphasized how a PWD protagonist succumbed to his condition or effectively coped with it shaped audience opinion and attitudes toward PWDs. Here are the first and last sections of the 2-minute succumbing and coping messages, respectively:

[*Succumbing*] At the age of 22 with a college degree and a bright future ahead of him, Fred Northway was in a terrible car accident that left him permanently brain-injured and physically disabled. Fred's American Dream came to a screeching halt . . .

Fred and his family have had to turn to professionals to deal with the demands Fred now places on them. Our organization helps people like Fred and his family. They need your help. Won't you please assist us in our efforts? Thank you.

[*Coping*] At the age of 22, Fred Northway graduated from college. Soon after, a car accident caused a brain injury and a physical disability. Fred had a lot to adjust to. During the many months he spent in the hospital, he vacillated between feeling depressed at how much he had changed and being encouraged at the progress he made. When he returned home, Fred worked hard at the challenges he faced along the difficult road of his continuing rehabilitation . . .

Our organization stands ready to help people with disabilities and their families use personal and community resources to the fullest in meeting the challenges of difficult problems. Won't you please assist us in our efforts? Thank you.

Participants who saw the coping appeal reported having more favorable attitudes toward PWDs than those who saw the succumbing appeal. Interestingly, however, there were no differences between the groups in terms of how much money they were willing to donate. The lack of difference here could be an indication of ambivalent attitudes (recall Chapter 4).

Awareness of the social influence of coping and succumbing frameworks should also be an important consideration in efforts designed to enlighten nondisabled people, such as role-playing disabilities. Wright (1978) warned that well-intentioned role-playing efforts designed to help nondisabled people appreciate and understand the experience of disability can unknowingly create or confirm succumbing-related expectations and stereotypes about disability. Disability simulations must be designed and executed with care so that they do not lead to erroneous (outsider) projections or extreme conclusions about disability ("After I spent two hours confined to a wheelchair I really learned what it means to be disabled, helpless, and overlooked in our society!"). Participants in constructive role-playing opportunities need to have their attention and understanding directed toward improving the situations (i.e., person–environment relations) in which they find themselves (e.g., Bachelder, 1989; Pastalan, 1974; Wright, 1978).

Successful coping with disability is not limited to concrete actions and positive attitudes. An important part of the coping process actually entails reliance on self-serving thoughts.

Self-Enhancement Biases: (Good) Fortune Phenomena

Social psychology is replete with instances demonstrating that normal, well-adjusted people routinely display a variety of judgmental biases, including self-enhancement biases (e.g., Gilovich, 1991). Self-enhancement refers to an inclination to hold positive beliefs and feelings about the self. Drives toward self-enhancement are linked to several traits and actions including personality, underlying motives, psychosocial processes, and observed behaviors (Sedikides & Gregg, 2008). The *better-than-average effect*, in which people rate one or more of their personal qualities as being above a hypothetical mean, is a familiar example (Buckingham & Alicke, 2002; Kuyper & Dijkstra, 2009). Individually or collectively, this mild distortion—seeing ourselves in a more favorable light than we likely deserve or through our own "rose-colored glasses"—is said to be a hallmark of mental health (Taylor & Brown, 1988, 1994). A survey of high school seniors who completed a familiar standardized college admissions test serves as a classic example: 100% of the students rated their "ability to get along with others" as being above average, a statistical impossibility (Myers, 1980; see also Svenson, 1981). On top of that, 25% of the students expressed the belief that they belonged in the top 1% of cooperative students! Veridical self-assessment is not a strength or skill most people possess (Dunning, Heath, & Suls, 2004; Wilson, 2002), but unless your relative standing on some dimension or quality is known, giving an answer of "average" is a reasonable and usually wise choice.

Yet Taylor and Brown (1988) argue that such modest self-enhancement biases represent constructive "positive illusions" that serve adaptive ends, whether the issue entails everyday life or coping with an unexpected trauma. Specifically, a positive illusion such as seeing yourself as "better off" than real or imagined (average) others on some dimension allows an individual to achieve three key outcomes: maintaining idealistically positive views of the self, a sense of illusory control over events, and unrealistic optimism regarding the future (Taylor & Brown, 1988). These outcomes foster mental health by motivating individual productivity and creativity, promoting happiness, and encouraging people to care for others. One of Taylor and Brown's main points in this line of argument is that, ironically, accurate contact with reality may *not* qualify as an indicator of mental health (see also, Alloy, Albright, Abramson, & Dykman, 1990; cf. Jahoda, 1958).

Do PWDs rely on illusions, such as the better-than-average effect, to cope with their experiences? Apparently, they do. Dembo, Leviton, and Wright (1975) used the term *fortune phenomenon* to describe an example of the better-than-average effect displayed by insiders in the face of real or potential devaluation (see also Wright, 1983). The fortune phenomenon occurs when individuals tend to rate themselves as at least average, and very often above average, in terms of how fortunate they are in general or on some specific dimension. This positive rating occurs even when they belong to a group that is perceived to be unfortunate or to have experienced some particular misfortune. Dembo et al. observed the following:

> It would seem that there must be a "terrible misfortune," and even this may not suffice to lead one to put himself below the average. One feels also that should somebody judge him to be unfortunate and place him low on the scale he would resist accepting such a judgment. Yet very easily does the non-injured make such a judgment regarding the injured. (p. 28)

In support of these observations, which are reminiscent of the mine–thine problem (see Chapter 2), Wright and Muth (1965, as cited in Wright, 1983) found that rehabilitation clients in a center rated themselves as above average in terms of being fortunate, whereas outsiders evaluated rehabilitation clients generally as having below average levels of good fortune, an outcome likely linked to the requirement of mourning (see Chapter 3).

A related study by Wright and Howe (1969, as cited in Wright, 1983) invited women from two socially devalued groups (welfare clients and mental hospital patients) and from two higher status groups (college students and middle-class housewives) to evaluate themselves, their own group, and the other three groups. Using 11-point scales ranging from "very fortunate" to "very unfortunate," members from the four groups evaluated welfare clients *in general* and mental hospital patients *in general* as being below average in how fortunate they were, but the women from the two stigmatized groups rated themselves (as individuals) *at least average* where being fortunate was concerned. The lesson of the fortune phenomenon seems apparent: Despite circumstance or outsider opinion, people tend to view their own situation as average or often better compared to the (hypothetical) general population. As is usually the case for disability, then, well-being is contextual and must be considered from the insider's perspective.

What about social comparisons that are more focused and less reliant on some imagined larger group of people? A substantial body of research from social comparison theory (Festinger, 1954) implies that PWDs can retain feelings of well-being by making strategic comparisons of their social, cognitive, or physical states with those of real or imagined individuals in similar circumstances. In well-known investigations on adjustment to breast cancer, Taylor (Taylor, 1983; Wood, Taylor, & Lichtman, 1985) demonstrated that women undergoing treatment for breast cancer frequently engaged in *downward social comparisons*—they identified someone appearing to be worse off than themselves—as a way to fend off despair, anxiety, and depression. When confronting real or potential threats, people will typically make such self-enhancing comparisons to less fortunate others in order to heighten self-esteem (Wills, 1981, 1983). This mental maneuver of "my own situation could be worse" does not represent psychological denial but instead serves as a constructive act of coping that likely happens regularly in acute care and rehabilitative settings.

Taylor and Lobel (1989), in turn, argued that *upward social comparisons*, which occur when individuals seek information about or an opportunity to affiliate with more fortunate others, also play an important role in coping with perceived threats, including disability. Indeed, people are apt to compare themselves to those who appear to be slightly better off than they are, perhaps to acquire reassurance and guidance (Wheeler, 1966). Taylor and Lobel suggest that the search for upward contacts can serve as an effective problem-solving activity, one aimed at gathering helpful information on how another succeeded (i.e., overcame misfortune). Whether real (an actual role-model is available) or apparent (a successful role model is imagined), the upward comparison satisfies emotional needs while also providing individuals with motivation to continue, inspiration, and hope for the future. Surely, having access to actual or imagined peers who effectively navigated the onset and aftermath of disability, including the rehabilitative process, is both encouraging in a practical sense as well as psychologically beneficial.

Self-enhancement biases are tied to another broader strategy linked to coping with and adjusting to negative events: the search for positive meaning.

Finding Positive Meaning in Disability

> Most observers have overlooked the potentially valuable experience of acquiring a physical disability. Writers have given only scant attention to positive growth and optimal living with chronic health problems, as well as the related searchers for meaning, purpose, and fulfillment.
> TIMOTHY R. ELLIOTT, MONICA KURYLO, AND PATRICIA RIVERA (2002, p. 687)

In the seemingly innate human endeavor to make sense out of our ongoing experiences, we search for meaning (Baumeister & Vohs, 2002). Life experiences such as loss, trauma, and disability trigger a particular search for meaning, one linked to misfortune and its consequences (e.g., Dunn, 1994; Frankl, 1985; Janoff-Bulman, 1992; Taylor, 1983; Wong & Weiner, 1981). Various studies demonstrate that more complete and positive adaptation to emotional and/or physical trauma occurs when people find some meaning in the event after it occurs (e.g., Keany & Glueckauf, 1993; Schulz & Decker, 1985; Taylor, Lichtman, & Wood, 1984; Thompson & Janigian, 1988; Vash & Crewe, 2004). Searching for such "silver linings," or the positive aspects of otherwise negative events, permits those affected to maintain a sense of coherence about their experiences (e.g., Antonovsky, 1987), no matter how upsetting or troubling they might be. In effect, the unfolding of events is construed as happening for some reason (Janoff-Bulman, 1992; Thompson, 1985). Note that use of the word "reason" here does not just refer to an actual cause (which is usually, but not always, apparent), such as a serious fall or a car accident; it also entails attaching significance to and seeing implications in the event. Some research also concludes that finding positive meaning in a negative experience helps people cope with physical and emotional transformations and can be indicative of successful adjustment (e.g., Collins, Taylor, & Skokan, 1990; Tait & Silver, 1989).

Within the available literature concerning disability, investigators examine whether and how PWDs derive meaning from the cause and consequences of their conditions (Bulman & Wortman, 1977; Dunn, 1994, 1996; Heinemann, Bulka, & Smetak, 1988; Schulz & Decker, 1985). Many people who acquire spinal cord injuries (SCI), for example, are prone to ask "why me?" (Bulman & Wortman, 1977; see Heinemann et al. (1988) for a conceptual replication), especially if the accident was not their fault. The explanations they offer (e.g., "God had a reason for allowing my accident to happen") support the need to find meaning following disability onset. Bulman and Wortman (1977) suggested that these *defensive attributions* occurred once the affected individuals reevaluated the spinal injuries as positive. Shontz (1982) critiqued the use of the term *reevaluation* in this context, arguing it implied that the PWDs were rationalizing rather than conveying accurate portrayals of their situations—that they did indeed identify positive qualities in their injuries (see also, Elliott, 2002). Other problematic terms linked to establishing meaning in the social-psychological literature include *victim* and *victimization* (e.g., Janoff-Bulman & Frieze, 1983); rehabilitation researchers eschew these pejorative terms because they suggest that PWDs are helpless, lacking control and perspective regarding their fates (Fine & Asch, 1988; Shontz, 1982; Wright, 1983). "Survivor" has come to be a preferred term.

The overarching message in the struggle to find meaning after disability onset is that subjective human experience matters (Wegner & Gilbert, 2000) and that self-reports of positive coping and adjustment should be given due credence in the classroom, clinic, and laboratory (Dunn, 1994). Dunn (1996), for example, examined psychosocial well-being following amputation among a group of 138 amputee golf-ers (the average length of time since limb loss in the sample was just over 20 years). Most of the amputations resulted from trauma or a combination of trauma and dis-ease; a few were congenital. The participants completed standard depression and self-esteem measures and were specifically asked about positive meaning linked to and perceived control over their disability, and had their level of dispositional optimism (Scheier, Carver, & Bridges, 1994) assessed. Those individuals who found meaning after amputations reported lower levels of depressive symptoms than those who did not; categorized examples of the meanings found by participants are shown in Table 5.2 (see also McMillen & Cook, 2003). In addition to engaging in social comparison (Taylor & Lobel, 1989), prior research found that individuals make meaning by finding side benefits (e.g., social support), framing the event as positive, imagining worse outcomes, or forgetting negative aspects of the situation (Taylor, 1983; Thompson, 1985). No particular type or category of attribution predicts better adjustment than another (see Table 5.2); rather it is finding *some* positive meaning through the disability that enhances well-being (e.g., Taylor, 1983). Dunn also found that participants who were optimistic and perceived greater control over their dis-ability in the course of daily life also reported lower scores on the depression mea-sure and had higher levels of self-esteem.

Wright (1983) referred to various physical, social, and emotional gains associ-ated with disability, including found meaning, as *secondary gains* (see also, Elliott,

TABLE 5.2

EXAMPLES OF POSITIVE MEANING FOLLOWING AMPUTATION BY

ATTRIBUTION TYPE

Engaged in social comparison

I have one leg. What about the person who has no legs?

Found side benefits

I changed to a different occupation [where] I became very successful.

Forgot negative aspects

I found that I can still do about everything I did before—only it takes longer to do it.

Imagines worse situations

I survived. I have a second chance at life. I love it.

Reframed event positively

All good has come out of it. I found God through it. It has given me purpose. It makes me special.

Source: Adapted from Dunn (1996, p. 291, Table 1).

Kurylo, & Rivera, 2002). Wright was quick to point out that this term sometimes has a negative connotation in the clinical and rehabilitation literatures, pointing to situations in which individuals take advantage of their conditions as a form of malingering or symptom magnification (e.g., absolving self of responsibility, intentionally becoming dependent on others, "working" the healthcare system) and very much a part of succumbing frameworks. When applied to constructive outlooks and outcomes in coping frameworks, however, secondary gains as construed here allow PWDs to ". . . capitalize on opportunities that become available because of their disability and derive satisfaction from the gratification they afford" (Wright, 1983, p. 204).

The particular benefit or areas of growth people identify following adverse events tend to be personal and distinctive, but generally highlight relationships with others, development or new awareness of personal strengths, appreciation for life, religious or spiritual changes, and identification of new horizons for living (Tedeschi & Calhoun, 1995). Lechner, Tennen, and Affleck (2009) note that finding this benefit and growth is relatively common in studies examining people's reactions to adversity—between 40% and 90% of participants share such positive changes (e.g., Bower, Kemeny, Taylor, & Fahey, 1998; McMillen, Smith, & Fisher, 1997). The ability to call upon these positive changes is presumed to enhance the long-term quality of life and adjustment but, as Lechner et al. (2009) suggest, definitive evidence outlining the processes and demonstrable consequences is still needed.

The available research on positive meaning, secondary gains, and benefit finding among PWDs points to larger questions concerning adjustment to disability. How does disability affect people's emotional reactions and adjustment, particularly their feelings of happiness? How does disability affect happiness in the short term and across time? We turn now to work on happiness, adaptation to experiences, and the consequences of predicting future emotions.

Happiness, Hedonic Adjustment, and Affective Forecasting

Happy people, those individuals who report experiencing positive affect most of the time and negative emotions only infrequently, tend to be highly satisfied with their lives (Diener, 1984; Diener & Biswas-Diener, 2008; Diener, Suh, Lucas, & Smith, 1999). In actuality, most people report that they are happy: They flourish in their daily lives and enjoy positive outcomes within a variety of domains of daily living (e.g., friendship, marriage, employment, income, psychological well-being, mental health) (for reviews see Diener & Biswas-Diener, 2008; Gilbert, 2006; Haidt, 2005; Lyubomirsky, 2008, 2013; Myers & Diener, 1995).

One way to characterize the findings reviewed thus far in this chapter is that across time PWDs adjust to their circumstances, including their disabilities, relatively well. In effect, they generally appear to be happy. Two researchers were even moved to label this state of affairs "the disability paradox" (Albrecht & Devlieger, 1999). Various studies demonstrate that many PWDs display relatively high levels of subjective well-being (SWB) or positive, evaluative emotions and thoughts about their lives (e.g., Diener, Oishi, & Lucas, 2003). SWB consists of happiness as well as life satisfaction, fulfillment, and a sense of peace (researchers often use "happiness" and "SWB" interchangeably, though the latter is a conceptually broader term). PWDs report being generally happy and find pleasure in work, recreation, social interactions with family members and friends, and simple daily living (e.g., de N Abrantes-Pais, Friedman, Lovallo, & Ross, 2007; Elliott & Kurylo, 2000; Wright, 1983). Other studies indicate that PWD's perceived quality of life is often elevated despite changes to their physiques or the presence of physical limitations (e.g., Albrecht, 1996; Delle Fave, 2006; Weinberg, 1988). In other words, PWD's reports of psychosocial well-being suggest that there is no paradox.

Research from positive psychology (see Chapter 7) and social psychology indicates that some but not all aspects of people's "chronic" level of happiness can be changed by self-initiated steps or outside interventions. Lyubomirsky, Sheldon, and Schkade (2005) argue that ongoing happiness is influenced by three interrelated factors: *circumstances*, which include personal qualities (e.g., age, gender, life history), key events (e.g., graduation, marriage, unemployment), and situations (e.g., culture, nation, location); *intentional actions* or the concrete behaviors and choices people execute in daily life (e.g., exercise, personal pleasures, recreational activities); and the *set point of happiness*, which is presumed to be a genetic, relatively fixed, and stable value idiosyncratic to each person (see also Lyubomirsky, 2008). Some people are constitutionally happier than others; thus each individual has a tendency to possess and remain at a certain level of happiness—in other words, we all have our own set points of happiness. Where enhancing happiness levels are concerned—changing their set points—people can really do so only through the intentional actions and choices they take.

Psychologists have wondered to what extent the onset of disability changes PWD's reported levels of happiness when circumstances, actions, and set point are concerned. For example, do PWDs experience a happiness "set back" after acquiring a disability (say, an acute event, such as an accident), one that resolves itself later when they adapt hedonically? Or can disability lead to an actual and sustained change (i.e., decrement) in their individual happiness set points? These questions became pressing ones due to a classic study conducted by Brickman, Coates, and Janoff-Bulman (1978), in which people with acquired spinal cord injuries (SCIs) were reported to show happiness levels close to those of nondisabled individuals (the article also discussed the intriguing finding that lottery winners are generally not much happier than nonwinners, a result that dovetails with related research on the short-lived impact of material gains; Kasser, 2002).

The SCI findings were interpreted as evidence for a "hedonic treadmill" in which people's reactions to good and bad events were cast as temporary (see also Helson, 1964; Brickman & Campbell, 1971). Across time, come what may, people apparently adjust to both positive and negative outcomes so that they eventually return to their original (natural) set point of happiness. If true, the downside of this process is that any favorable "bump" in happiness is transitory; people eventually adjust to it, just as a desired material gain (e.g., a new car, stylish clothing, a computer upgrade) gradually loses its luster by becoming just another possession (e.g., Kasser, 2002). But there is a potentially interesting and beneficial upside regarding mental and physical health: Perhaps people who experience especially adverse events, such as a disabling injury, bounce back to their earlier state of being (i.e., the psychological and emotional impact of bad events also dissipates with time).

Diener (2008), whose research explores SWB, highlights the Brickman et al. (1978) study as an example of a persistent myth associated with happiness research (see also Biswas-Diener, 2013; Lucas, Dyrenforth, & Diener, 2008). In a thoughtful review of the classic study, Diener, Lucas, and Scollon (2006) showed that the positive adaptation of the individuals with SCI was actually significantly lower than that found in the study's control group. Why then did so many people misinterpret the hedonic adaption results? Perhaps because the readers, including well-intentioned and sympathetic researchers, misread a table containing self-reported future predicted happiness of the SCI group, which was just that— a *future* (hoped for) *projection* and not longitudinally gathered evidence of (re) adjustment (Biswas-Diener, 2013). What we can surmise is that depressive symptoms, which are a common secondary complication associated with SCI, led to the actual and lower mean levels of happiness in the SCI group (Elliott & Kennedy, 2004). Other studies, too, indicate that when compared to the general population, people with SCI typically report lower levels of relative happiness, particularly as a result of the severity of their disability (Dijkers, 1997, 2005; Hammell, 2004; Lucas, 2007a, 2007b).

Thus, available evidence suggests that people's happiness set points can be permanently altered in the face of negative life events such as disability. Is there still reason to explore the question of adjustment to disability independent of set point theory? Perhaps. A study by Loewenstein and colleagues found that, paradoxically, people adapt better to permanent rather than temporary disabilities (i.e., those who are arguably better off objectively actually feel worse off subjectively; Smith, Loewenstein, Jankovic, & Ubel, 2009). And as Diener and colleagues (2006, p. 307) note, "although people with paraplegia and other individuals with disabilities are not subjectively miserable, happiness levels do seem to be strongly affected by this important life circumstance." It may well be that the happiness set points of PWDs are lowered even in the absence of depressive symptoms or other psychological disorders (Dunn, Uswatte, & Elliott, 2009). It is worth remembering, too, that the set point results do not counter the findings associated with self-enhancement biases or positive meaning discussed earlier, as set point theory and hedonic adaptation are but one factor that can influence SWB. Another tack is to consider people's projections for their future emotional states in spite of negative events.

Forecasting Future Feelings following Disability

A sizable literature in psychology and decision making finds that healthy people routinely predict that their quality of life with one of a variety of disabilities would be lower than the quality of life actually found among people who in fact have the particular disabilities in question (Ubel, Lowenstein, & Jepson, 2003). In other words, there is a "happiness gap" between expectation and reality where predicting feelings about health and disability are concerned (e.g., Ubel, Lowenstein, & Jepson, 2005). The presence of such biased expectations should not be surprising given the robust findings linked with the mine/thine research (see Chapter 2).

Dunn, Uswatte, and Elliott (2009) recommended that disability and rehabilitation researchers examine expectations for future well-being expressed by PWDs in order to ensure their self-reports are not unduly biased in a negative direction. They relied on findings concerning *affective forecasting*, an area of social-psychological research demonstrating that when predicting emotional reactions for future events (e.g., health, retirement, career), individuals routinely overestimate the magnitude and durability of their affective responses—whether good or bad (Wilson & Gilbert, 2003, 2005). Where the potential for bias in response to an aversive event is concerned, such bad events (e.g., loss, failure) are often projected to have much worse and lasting consequences than is the case in the fullness of time. According to Wilson and Gilbert, this forecasting error, the so-called "impact bias," is likely caused by overfocusing (or *focalism*) on the event or outcome in question while neglecting to incorporate the role of many other, competing factors that color people's emotional lives (Wilson, Wheatley, Meyers, Gilbert, & Axsom, 2000). Several studies illustrate peoples' tendency to overestimate unhappiness resulting from unwanted results on pregnancy or HIV tests, as well as job loss, among other negative events (Loewenstein, O'Donoghue, & Rabin, 2003; Mellers & McGraw, 2001; Sieff, Dawes, & Loewenstein, 1999; Wilson & Gilbert, 2003).

This sort of affective forecasting error might be important to understanding the experience of disability due to people's "psychological immune systems," which, through use of self-enhancement biases (e.g., positive illusions, the better-than-average effect, the fortune phenomenon), act as barriers against various threats to emotional health and happiness (Wilson & Gilbert, 2003). As previously noted, these mild but useful psychological defenses are automatic, nonconscious, and used regularly. The concern expressed by Dunn et al. (2009) is that when a PWD projects how she or he will feel a year or two in the future after a tragic accident or an acute health event (e.g., stroke, heart attack), the individual with the still-recent disability will *not* be influenced by these subtle psychological defenses when estimating future emotional states. Instead, the impact bias might deplete expectations, pushing them in a negative direction and leading to reduced initiative or motivation for continuing treatment or rehabilitative therapy, or making constructive lifestyle changes.

The severity of a disabling event might also affect PWD's affective forecasts. For example, there is evidence that the emotional pull of major events is greater than minor ones, so that people are more motivated to reflect on and make sense out of large upheavals. The problem is that—perhaps ironically—the emotional turmoil associated with minor events persists for a longer time than that for major events (Gilbert, Lieberman, Morewedge, & Wilson, 2004); it's the cumulative effects of hassles, then, that wear people down (Lazarus & Folkman, 1984). More to the point, people remain largely unaware of the inner drive to make sense of events that trigger negative emotions, just as they overlook their innate capacities (i.e., the psychological immune system) to deal with life's vagaries (Gilbert, Pinel, Wilson, Blumberg, & Wheatley, 1998; Kahneman, 2000). Currently, however, there is no empirical evidence indicating whether similar results apply to affective forecasts in cases of acquired disability—the relevant research needs to be conducted. Perhaps, for example, different degrees of disability are associated with briefer or more sustained, even permanent, periods of emotional adjustment (Dunn, Uswatte, & Elliott, 2009).

People's affective forecasts are both ubiquitous and significant because they often guide choices and decisions (Wilson & Gilbert, 2005). In everyday life, for example, misjudging anticipated feelings is disruptive to the pursuit of happiness. Where disability onset and aftermath are concerned, any overestimation of a disabling event's lasting impact could cause unwarranted stress and worry about the future. PWDs (as well as their caregivers and careproviders) could elect to follow inappropriate or less-than-optimal treatments by underestimating their own resilience (see

Chapter 7) or by inflating the emotional and physical demands that rehabilitative therapy could entail (Wilson & Gilbert, 2005).

Conclusion: Coping and Adjustment as Negotiated Reality

My first act of free will shall be to believe in free will.
WILLIAM JAMES (cited in Perry, 1935, p. 322)

James was a pragmatist and, in a real sense, so are many people who psychosocially adapt to negative life events such as disability. The presence of disability does not preclude well-being or happiness, which means that chronic disability should not be characterized as either "permanent illness" or a "complete loss." Multiple sources of evidence from social, rehabilitation, and health psychology reveal that these sorts of characterizations are false (e.g., Brickman, Coates, & Janoff-Bulman, 1978; Bulman & Wortman, 1977; Dunn, 1996; Fine & Asch, 1988; Heinemann et al., 1988) and that genuine benefit-finding and psychosocial growth following negative events, including disability, are possible (Calhoun & Tedeschi, 2006; Lechner et al., 2009).

How, then, should PWD's subjective reports of positive coping and adjustment be understood? In the first place, PWDs should not be encouraged or be counseled to display self-enhancement biases or to look for positive meaning in their situations. People either engage in these social-cognitive activities naturally and idiosyncratically or they don't. Urging people to find some good when they cannot or have not is ill-advised (Holland & Lewis, 2000; Lechner et al., 2009). Indeed, timing could be a crucial factor—a PWD might not make or find meaning at an early postonset point but could be more receptive later. Second, what framework, whether practical or theoretical, best characterizes processes of coping and adjustment? Dunn (1994, 2005; Dunn et al., 2009) urged that researchers and lay people alike consider how PWDs negotiate their individual experiences and realities. *Reality negotiation* refers to functional, self-generated coping responses to adverse circumstances, those situations in which people search for and adapt positive perspectives on themselves while recognizing acquired limitations (Higgins & Gallagher, 2009; Snyder, 1989; Snyder & Higgins, 1988, 1997). Various self-referent strategies—including the self-enhancing examples reviewed in this chapter—represent how individuals negotiate their own realities by the methods they use to construe and subsequently manage unfavorable outcomes (positive outcomes are also susceptible to this psychological control). In effect, people—including PWDs—"bargain" with their unique situations and by doing so, try to identify pragmatic psychosocial compromises that look toward a positive future while promoting or maintaining a favorable self-image. These constructive construals of meaning and well-being act as helpful buffers against extreme reactions to fate and fortune, whether good or bad (Dunn, 2005; Higgins & Gallagher, 2009).

We can speculate that PWDs for whom disability is seen as an integral part of who they are—in other words, disability is part of their identity—should display good coping and adjustment. We explore the matter of disability identity in the next chapter.

Questions

1. Characterize coping versus succumbing frameworks: Are these best treated as "either/or" responses or as being on a continuum? Why?
2. What are self-enhancing biases? What are the psychosocial functions of such biases? Do such biases imply positive or negative coping, and why? Provide an example of self-enhancing bias linked to disability.
3. What is the fortune phenomenon? Why could it be considered an extension of the insider–outsider distinction?
4. Why is social comparison an important facet of self-enhancement-related coping? How do downward and upward social comparisons help PWDs? Provide a disability-related example for each form of social comparison.
5. Characterize the search for positive meaning following the onset of disability. Does any particular sort of "found meaning" appear to be more or less predictive of psychosocial adjustment? Why or why not?
6. Explain the so-called "hedonic treadmill" theory. Are the happiness set points of PWDs apt to remain changed following a disabling event? If so, what are some implications of permanent change for the coping and adjustment of PWDs?
7. How does affective forecasting relate to disability? Why should PWDs and their caregivers be cautious about affective forecasts related to disability or disabling events?
8. Define and explain the notion of reality negotiation in the context of disability.

Disability identity is a frequently used but imprecisely defined concept... [but] there is general agreement that people experiencing disability often feel affinity, or even solidarity, with others who also experience disability...

MICHELLE PUTNAM (2005, p. 188)

6   Towards an Understanding of Disability Identity

SIMI LINTON IS very much a product of the counterculture of 1960s America. In her early 20s, she was in a serious car accident on her way to a protest organized against the Viet Nam War. The accident damaged her spine, resulting in paraplegia. The onset of disability changed her outlook and, with time, Linton became a disability researcher, a psychologist, an activist, and later an authority on disability and the arts. Part of her journey involved transitioning from being an outsider to the disability community to becoming very much an insider.

In her 2007 memoir, Linton critically evaluated her growth experience and the development of her disability identity, writing the following:

> I saw ... how big disability is, not the condition I or others have, but the elaborately constructed network of ideas and practices that keep disabled people in place ... I have gotten to this place not by denying my disability or, implausibly, "overcoming" it, but by sailing headlong into it. Making sense of it had become the most meaningful thing I could do. (p. 120)

Identity is an essential, even core, topic in psychology. As Wright (1983) observed, the "... self-picture is an intricate one, consisting of a variety of particular characteristics that define for the person his or her *identity*, as well as a global self-evaluation of personal worth" (p. 210, italics in original). Erik Erikson (1963, 1968) famously wrote about stages of psychosocial development that ascribed a central role to the importance of developing a lasting and coherent identity, one providing the individual with a psychological sense of continuity. Although processes of identity formation occur across the lifespan, identity emerges as a prominent theme in the fifth of Erikson's eight stages, which is generally labeled *identity versus role confusion* and occurs between ages 12 and 18 years. As part of the process of forming social relationships, Erikson claimed that adolescents are challenged by a need to develop a clear sense of self and personal identity. Successful navigation of the shoals of adolescence allows individuals to remain true to their developing selves, whereas failure leads to role confusion—uncertainty about their direction in life—and a weaker sense of self.

Erikson's (1963, 1968) stages six (young adulthood) and seven (middle adulthood) assume the importance of a defined identity in their respective psychosocial dynamics. Young adults (ages 19 to 40) look to establish meaningful, often intimate and loving, relationships with others. Failure to do so leads to loneliness and isolation. Middle-aged adults (ages 40 to 65), feeling the pull of passing time, want to establish a legacy; thus, they work to develop or nurture things that will outlast them, such as having children or initiating positive changes in the world that will benefit others. To use Erikson's term, such *generativity* or "giving back" is certainly connected to a firmly established identity. Psychosocial success later in life highlights fruitful endeavors and usefulness that connect to and benefit others, whereas disappointment is marked by superficial community involvement. Depending upon the circumstances, these elements all have greater or lesser influence on the development of people's psychosocial identities.

This chapter deals with issues surrounding disability identity, which is characterized by a positive sense of self and feelings of connection to other people with disabilities (e.g., Darling, 2013; Dunn & Burcaw, 2013; Gill, 1997; Putnam, 2005; Siebers, 2011; see also Bogart, 2014, on disability self-concept). The chapter reviews narrative approaches—the reflective, written stories persons with disabilities (PWDs) tell themselves and others (both PWDs and non-disabled individuals) about their experiences—for exploring disability and identity issues. These stories appear in books, articles, and blogs, anywhere PWDs have opportunities to reflect on themselves or their lives with an eye to disability issues. Following this discussion of disability narratives, the consequences for thought and behavior of activating particular aspects of people's disability identities are then considered. The chapter closes by considering how Wright's (1972, 1983) value-laden beliefs and principles aid the development of constructive disability identities. We begin by defining disability identity in greater detail.

Defining Disability Identity

> The kind of person you think you are becomes endowed with remarkable powers. It influences, and often decisively, the way one perceives the intentions of others, the choice of associates, the goals set for oneself, and much more.
> BEATRICE A. WRIGHT (1983, p. 217)

Identities—those characteristics that make people distinct and denote individuality—allow people to make sense of themselves (Oyserman, Elmore, &

Smith, 2012). As a psychological construct, *identity* entails ways of conceiving the self and connections to particular others (e.g., family, friends, peers), including groups (e.g., college graduates, neighbors, co-workers). Our identities are defining and personal, composed of personality traits, roles, and social bonds. Identities can be focused on an individual's past (e.g., childhood, adolescence), present (e.g., career, divorce, family life), or future sense of self where hopes, fears, and expectations are concerned (Oyserman et al., 2012). Psychological research frequently explores identity development as an outgrowth of minority status and/or group connection. Many studies examine identity within the context provided by gender, race, ethnicity, and sexual orientation, for example. Disability, in turn, serves as an identity context because it ties PWDs to a minority group that sometimes encounters stigmatization, prejudice, and even discrimination (Gill, 1997; see also Chapter 4). Like members of any minority group, PWDs must decide whether and how much to assimilate into the dominant, nondisabled culture while also weighing the possible consequences (e.g., exclusion, inequity) of aligning with the disability culture and expressing pride in one's disability identity (Gill, 1997). Increasingly, too, disability is recognized and accepted as a form of diversity (e.g., Dunn, Fisher, & Beard, 2013; Dunn & Hammer, 2014).

Disability identity refers to possessing favorable or beneficial self-beliefs regarding one's own disability as well as having positive ties to other members of the disability community (Dunn & Burcaw, 2013; Gill, 1997; Olkin & Pledger, 2003; Scotch, 1988). PWDs will have more or less well-developed disability identities depending upon where they think of themselves on the disability continuum (Olkin, 1999). For example, some people possess a disability in an objective sense, but they either are unaware of it or rarely recognize it (e.g., unilateral deafness), which means they do not view themselves as PWDs (*no or very low disability identity*). Others think of themselves as being PWDs but can "pass" as being nondisabled (i.e., they possess mild, almost invisible disabilities). Though technically disabled, these individuals may or may not identify with the disability community (*low disability identity*). Another group sees disability as very much a part of their self-concepts and they feel quite connected to the larger disability community (*moderate* to *high disability identity*). The final group is composed of activists who champion the welfare and civil rights of PWDs, treating disability as a social construct in their advocacy work (*high disability identity*).

Given the range of this disability continuum, will disability identities necessarily contain content that is primarily positive? Or is negative content (e.g., familiarity with stigma, prejudice, and discrimination) also a part of disability identity? Perhaps both types of content—or, put another way, both positive and negative identity elements—reside in the minds of PWDs. "To call disability an identity is to recognize that it is not a biological or natural property," wrote Siebers (2011), "but an elastic social category both subject to social control and capable of effecting social change" (p. 4).

Gill (1997) suggested that positive disability identity formation follows a four-stage process, one that mirrors the experiences and trajectory of members of other marginalized minority groups. Working through each stage of the model represents a deeper integration of disability identity within a PWD's psychology, one that "ends with the individual finding personal integrity, a proud identification with the group, and a readiness to construct improved relations in the mainstream" (Gill, 1997, p. 45). The first stage, *belongingness,* entails coming to feel and recognize that in spite of disability, you remain a member of the larger society with both rights and roles. Stage two, which Gill described as *coming home,* entails becoming integrated into the disability community and recognizing experiences shared with other PWDs. The third stage deals with *coming together*, in which a PWD integrates similarities with nondisabled people (shared sameness) into his or her own differences and distinct qualities emerging from disability. The process of *coming together* also marks the recognition that you are simultaneously part of both a disability culture and the larger, dominant culture. The final state of integration is labeled *coming out*, reflecting a merger of the private self with the individual's ideal self-image and public presence in ways that express confidence and clarity in your identity as a PWD. Commenting on Gill's model, Andrews and colleagues (2013) highlight a process of development in which

> . . . disabled people may initially seek societal acceptance, subsequently move away from dominant cultural values while connecting with disabled peers and developing an appreciation for the disabled self, then shift back toward the mainstream society with a fully integrated disability identity. (p. 238)

Thus, a positive, working disability identity will contain information, experiences, and goals ultimately linked to favorable views of disability. This type of identity will guide PWDs, helping them to know what to do and how to respond in various situations in which disability is or becomes a salient feature. A disability identity can also contain knowledge of stereotypes and attitudinal prejudice against PWDs; that is, at times, the identity can be negatively valenced or even ambivalent (e.g., when a person is concerned with acquiring additional disabilities or experiencing a worsening of an existing condition; Siebers, 2011). Members of minority groups need not experience prejudice first hand to have a working knowledge of the bogus and skewed views that support prejudiced thinking.

Consider the social-psychological literature on *stereotype threat,* the psychosocial vulnerability associated with being evaluated by stereotypes, which demonstrates that members of various groups experience behavioral decrements (e.g., academic or athletic ability, social competence) when their performance is linked to prevailing oversimplifications or biased opinions (Steele, 1997, 2011). Women can be threatened by the dominant cultural belief that men are far superior at math-related tasks (Spencer, Steele, & Quinn, 1999), for example, just as white men can be vulnerable to the stereotype that people of Asian descent are more skilled at quantitative reasoning (Aronson et al., 1999). Lower test scores result in these respective cases when the relevant stereotypes are activated by how testing instructions are phrased (e.g., "This test assesses innate quantitative abilities . . ."). When stereotype threats are not present (i.e., neutral directions; "This is a measure of general knowledge . . ."), no performance decrements occur. Where disability is concerned, we should expect that PWDs might experience self-consciousness (e.g., when being stared at in public settings) that could disrupt their behavior in some situations (e.g., entering or exiting a building with limited accommodations) in which their disability status elicits stereotyped responses from others (e.g., "Handicapped people cannot care for themselves"). This form of stereotype threat could trigger succumbing rather than coping thoughts and behaviors (see Chapter 5) or, at the very least, lead insiders to speculate about what negative notions are aroused in outsiders.

Depending upon the situation, then, disability identity could trigger positive or negative thoughts so that PWD's resulting behaviors could be either self-affirming or disrupted and unintended. Yet, disability identity is only *one* aspect of a person's overall identity, which means that in most PWDs, it does not always supersede other identities such as parent, employer, spouse, neighbor, friend, employee, and writer. People's identities, then, are complex and multiply determined (e.g., Campbell, Assanand, & DiPaula, 2000), so that only a small sample of self-beliefs is likely to be accessible at a given point in time (Baumeister, 2011; Markus & Wurf, 1987). Disability-related thoughts are apt to come to mind for PWDs in situations in which they stand out by being unusual, uncommon, or otherwise salient (Langer, Fiske, Taylor, & Chanowitz, 1976; McGuire, McGuire, Child, & Fujioka, 1978). Thus, disability identity is likely to be activated when a PWD tries to locate an accessible restroom or socializes with disabled peers, but not when writing a sales report for a supervisor or making an online purchase. As we are routinely reminded, the person and the situation matter where interpretation and outcome are concerned.

At present, defining disability identity and outlining its functional utility are easier than pointing to concrete examples in the literature in which it clearly affects behavior or regulates well-being. Researchers agree that disability identity, especially due to its emphasis on the importance of community, should be a valuable and salutary construct (e.g., Olkin & Pledger, 2003), but at present there is a paucity of available evidence to confirm, refute, or revise these speculations. One promising area for exploring disability identity, however, is the study of psychosocial narratives concerning the experience of disability.

Narrative Approaches to Understanding Disability Identity

Storytelling is a ubiquitous and essential human activity. People's stories reveal a great deal about their personal histories, as well as their social and psychological development and characteristics. Psychologists refer to the critical analysis and evaluation of people's stories as the study of narrative psychology or, simply, *narrative*. In contrast to most areas of inquiry in contemporary psychology, the study of narrative is largely a qualitative enterprise (e.g., Frost, 2011; Lincoln & Guba, 1985). Hevern (2008, p. 218) argues that exploring human stories and storytelling help people to achieve the following goals:

- Attach meaning to ongoing experiences
- Predict how actors (themselves, others) will behave in the future
- Negotiate various social worlds

And most important for present purposes:

- Establish personal identities for themselves and for other people

Personality psychologist Dan McAdams and others have used the term *narrative identity* to characterize the private, unfolding story of the self each person both knowingly and unconsciously crafts to merge the various aspects of the self (McAdams, 2006; McAdams, Josselson, & Lieblich, 2006; McAdams & McLean, 2013; Singer, 2004). Identity narratives deal with internal, subjective experiences of external events (What happened? Why? How? Why am I involved?), and they have been used to explore the psychology of women (e.g., Geyla, 2000), life in minority communities (e.g., Josselson & Harway, 2012), and gay culture (e.g., Cohler, 2007), among other psychocultural arenas. Although they represent a form of biography, people's identity stories also serve the particular subjective needs of their authors. The issue of what aspects of people's stories are "true" is less important than the beliefs the storytellers create and use subsequently to makes sense out of life experiences (McAdams, 1993). As McAdams (2001) claimed:

> [Identity] stories are based on biographical facts, but go considerably beyond the facts as people selectively appropriate aspects of their experience and

imaginatively construe both past and future to construct stories that make sense to them and to their audiences, that vivify and integrate life and make it more or less meaningful. (p. 101)

Narratives about disability marry biography to social experience, both the good and the bad; thus they are apt to reveal important qualities of disability identity (e.g., Darling, 2013; Dunn & Burcaw, 2013). Such narratives can also serve as a resource for studying and learning about the social psychology of disability. PWDs, their families, caregivers, and friends, as well as researchers and therapists, can acquire helpful insights about the experience of disability from them (cf. American Psychological Association, 2012a).

Dunn and Burcaw (2013) examined some published narratives written by PWDs about their disability experiences. Using a thematic model of inquiry (e.g., Riessman, 2008), their goal was to categorize the narratives according to key themes previously identified by disability and rehabilitation researchers. Table 6.1 lists and defines six key themes concerning disability identity examined by Dunn and Burcaw. Two themes, *communal attachment* and *affirmation of disability*, are based on the idea that some aspects of disability identity are born out of social activism and pro-test (Gill, 1997; Hahn & Belt, 2004; see also Swain & French, 2000). As part of a PWD's identity, for example, these themes can help the person cope with social discrimination while accepting, even reveling in his or her difference, and being part of the disability culture. The next three themes, *self-worth, pride,* and *discrimination,* were drawn from research on disability politics, which is linked to issues of activism (Putnam, 2005; see also Darling, 2013). These themes serve as counterweights in disability identity, as they are aimed at resisting or deflecting the prevailing negative attitudes and beliefs often held by some nondisabled people (recall Chapter 4). The search for meaning, particularly positive meaning, was previously considered as a way to constructively cope with the onset of disability (see Chapter 5). In the present context, *personal meaning* represents a form of personal acceptance of disability (Dunn & Burcaw, 2013; Wright, 1983).

In a preliminary investigation, Dunn and Burcaw (2013) gathered six sample nar-ratives illustrating one or more of the six key identity themes shown in Table 6.1. The work of Simi Linton's (2007), an excerpt from whose memoir opened this chapter, illustrated communal attachment. As evidence of a growing sense of connection to the disability community, she outlines a process whereby she gradually thought of herself as a PWD and a woman who claimed disability as an important aspect of her identity. An autobiography written by the late Harriett McBryde-Johnson (2005) demonstrated the affirmation of disability (Swain & French, 2000). Johnson recounts bristling at what she describes as the "telethon mentality" (wherein PWDs

TABLE 6.1

SOME KEY THEMES IN DISABILITY IDENTITY

Communal attachment—desire and feeling to affiliate with other PWDs

Affirmation of disability—private thoughts and feelings of inclusion in the larger society, including the same rights and responsibilities as other citizens

Self-worth—valuing oneself with disability; equal to nondisabled individuals

Pride—being proud of one's identity while recognizing and possessing a devalued quality, disability

Discrimination—awareness of self and other PWDs as targets of prejudiced behavior in daily life

Personal meaning—finding significance, making sense, and identifying benefits associated with disability

Source: Adapted from Dunn and Burcaw (2013).

are viewed as dependent on the kindness and generosity of strangers), which she viewed as being at odds with her own disability perspective, one in which PWDs make unique contributions to their community and humanity more generally. In a book on living with spinal cord injuries (Cole, 2004), the story of Graham focused on self-worth. In lieu of focusing on activities that he could no longer perform, Graham turned to those he could accomplish, including pursuing a degree and seeking employment. Pride in disability was explored through an advocate for deaf culture, Mark Drolsbaugh (1996), who comments on the singular importance of meeting and being with other deaf people like himself, as well as seeing them succeed in their chosen pursuits. Jesse Saperstein's (2010) struggle with Asperger's syndrome disclosed struggles with discrimination at home, school, and in his early career. With dark humor and some frustration, Saperstein recounts social problems and adjustment challenges, including being bullied. Personal meaning in disability was linked with overcoming imperfection in the story of Jennifer Tollifson (1997). Realizing that the search for perfection in an imperfect world was misguided, Tollifson embraced living with only one arm, seeing her state as genuine, not false or inauthentic.

Exactly when in the course of people's lifespan disability occurs is apt to be influential in coloring their feelings about it, and point of onset should be examined within narratives whenever possible. Heckert and Darling (2010, cited in Darling, 2013) identified the age of disability onset as a relatively reliable predictor of whether PWDs view disability in positive terms. Individuals with lifelong disabilities (congenital disabilities or those acquired in early childhood), for example, were much more likely to express pride in their conditions. Heckert and Darling observed that people who acquired the disabilities later in life possessed more negative views about their situations, perhaps because of well-established identities as nondisabled individuals (e.g., Freedman, 2012; Murphy, 1990). Another possible explanation is that these individuals had a greater length of time prior to the onset of disability to solidify their negative assumptions about what the experience of disability must be like (i.e., as outsiders).

Based on their narrative samples, Dunn and Burcaw (2013) argued that disability identity represents an important and authentic part of the social psychology of disability, one that can educate others. These researchers took care to emphasize that other disability identity themes and representative narratives should be sought for use in social-psychological research and for clinical purposes. Indeed, Dunn and Burcaw (2013) found that a given narrative is likely to contain more than one disability identity theme (e.g., the presence of self-worth often occurs with pride). The careful study of disability identity can inform rehabilitation and clinical practices by helping counselors and therapists decide whether and how to share published narratives with their clients. Practitioners could, for example, encourage a PWD to read a given narrative in order to draw attention to a particular theme relevant to the client's own disability experience (e.g., acute onset following an accident). Alternatively, perhaps disability identity narratives might be used to illustrate coping rather than succumbing frameworks (e.g., endorsing community rather than isolation) during counseling efforts with clients who appear to be in a psychological rut. Caregivers and family members, too, could benefit from developing a broader perspective on disability by reading the narrative experiences of other PWDs (e.g., disability is a common aspect of human experience, one that many people navigate successfully).

A logical extension of reading narratives is to recommend that PWDs write their own disability identity stories in order to think about disability in a deeper, more personal way. Social-psychological research, for example, finds a constructive role for such self-narratives when coping with negative life events (Pennebaker, 1997, 2004) or acquiring and then maintaining positive outlooks and actions (Wilson, 2011). Certainly, too, listening for the presence of a particular theme (e.g., self-worth, affirmation of disability) might afford clinicians the opportunity to match techniques to client needs at appropriate moments during the course of therapy. Perhaps, then, narratives concerning disability identity can serve as a "hidden resource" and a useful adjunct to conventional educational materials (Wright & Fletcher, 1982) for both PWDs and professionals.

More research needs to be conducted concerning the link between narratives and the nature of people's disability identities. For example, there is ample

opportunity for interested investigators to identify additional identity themes illustrating positive and negative adaptation to disability within other narratives. As
knowledge grows, perhaps disability identities can be examined in connection to more
objective measures (e.g., personality traits, health, well-being, depression). A working assumption, of course, is that disability identity should manifest some psychosocial consequences.

Psychosocial Consequences of Disability Identity

Thus far, our examination of disability identity has concerned whether and how
disability experience informs how PWDs think about themselves and their connection to the disability community, heretofore primarily in positive ways. Certainly,
disability is made more or less salient in the minds of PWDs depending upon
the situations and people they encounter. Socializing with friends or family, for
example, is unlikely to trigger thoughts about disability identity, but meeting nondisabled strangers who are unsure about how to behave around a PWD could be
expected to bring disability identity swiftly into consciousness. This likelihood
raises some interesting questions: How do PWDs respond when different aspects
of their identity are brought to mind? How does awareness of disability identity
influence behavior?

Despite changes in societal opportunities and accommodations, prevailing attitudes toward PWDs tend to portray them as dependent rather than as autonomous
or agentic individuals (recall Chapter 4). In spite of the substantial literature dealing with disability and stigma from the perspective of nondisabled people, little is
known about how PWDs react as targets of prejudice, especially where identity
and awareness of stigma are concerned. To explore these issues, Wang and Dovidio
(2011) recruited college students with disabilities and then "primed" their identities
as either a PWD or a student.

The term *priming* refers to increased sensitivity to particular stimuli due to some
earlier event or prior experience. When you buy a new car, for example, you suddenly notice other people driving the same brand and model and can be surprised by
how many others *seem* to have *your* car (i.e., you are suddenly primed to hone in on
your car type over all others). Students in Wang and Dovidio's (2011) student-prime
group were asked to share information about their student identity and involvement
in their campus community (i.e., to answer questions, reflecting on their *identities
as students* was necessary), whereas those in the disability-prime group answered a
series of questions about their disability (e.g., type, onset, whether it was visible) and
any association with the disability community (i.e., they reflected on their *disability*

identities). Wang and Dovidio (2011) argued that the student priming would activate more autonomous thoughts and fewer dependence-related thoughts than the disability priming. Autonomy is an important construct for disability, as a high level of self-perceived autonomy can indicate a stronger appraised problem-solving ability, which is linked to more robust psychological functioning among PWDs (Elliott, Herrick, & Witty, 1992). A second prediction dealt with an individual difference variable, *stigma consciousness*, the students' sensitivity to prejudice and discrimination (here, being stigmatized as a PWD). The researchers believed that identity priming would have a stronger effect among those with higher levels of awareness of being stigmatized due to their disability.

After the priming manipulation, all students completed a word fragment completion task designed to measure implicit activation of identity as being autonomous (e.g., "str-ng" for "strong" as opposed to "string") or dependent (e.g., "clin—" for "clingy" rather than "clinic"; see Gilbert & Hixon, 1991; for more on implicit measures, see Rudman, 2011; Wittenbrink & Schwarz, 2007). They then took part in a separate, challenging quantitative task to assess whether they would ask for assistance from another person to do it (thereby expressing behavioral dependence, not autonomy) and, afterward, completed a version of the Stigma Consciousness Questionnaire (Pinel, 1999), which assesses the degree to which individuals anticipate being stereotyped by others.

As anticipated, students in the disability-prime group activated fewer autonomy-related thoughts on the implicit measures than those who were primed by their student identity. More generally, greater activation of autonomy-related thoughts was linked with a lower likelihood of asking for help on the challenging quantitative task. Note that these results imply only that disability is associated with *dependent thoughts*, not that PWDs themselves are necessarily dependent or that they act in needy ways. The results point to the fact that greater activation of autonomous thoughts (regardless of priming group) led to fewer requests for help. There was no corresponding effect for dependence.

Wang and Dovidio (2011) suggest that these findings point to the resilience of PWDs (e.g., Dunn, Uswatte, & Elliott, 2009; see also Chapter 7), who are less likely to think of themselves in stereotypic, stigma-related terms when they are exercising available social and public opportunities for autonomy (e.g., being a student, acting as an expert with a skill, displaying leadership qualities). The increasing ubiquity of "person first" language (recall Chapter 1) in American culture and media may have helped in this regard. As the authors note, "Our findings show that distinguishing the person from the disability affects not only how others treat people with disabilities but also how people with disabilities think and act" (Wang & Dovidio, 2011, p. 126). Clearly, however, more research needs to be conducted on the impact and implications of disability identity on the thoughts and behaviors of PWDs, with a clear goal being the development of positive disability identities.

Toward Developing Disability Identity: Value-Laden Beliefs and Principles Revisited

> Although it might be hypothesized that disability identity and feeling a part of the disability community are buffers against the stresses of being an oppressed minority, this has not been directly examined... Is identity a buffer against... disability-specific hassles?
> RHODA OLKIN AND CONSTANCE PLEDGER (2003, p. 302)

Our understanding of disability identity must be broadened. Many questions remain: How can positive disability identities be developed? Is disability identity a quality that necessarily emerges across time? Should families, caregivers, and rehabilitation professionals look for opportunities to promote disability identity, or should PWDs be allowed to develop identities at their own pace? Can disability identity serve as a buffer against the hassles of daily living? How do PWD's other identities interact with their disability identities? As noted by Olkin and Pledger (2003), important questions regarding the presumed psychosocial benefits of disability identity remain to be explored.

Yet, there are concrete actions PWDs and those who work with and care for them can take, steps that actually point to a constructive philosophy of living with disability. As noted in Chapter 1, Wright (1972, 1983) proposed a set of value-laden beliefs and principles designed to promote PWD's independence and well-being and to maintain their individuality. Five social psychologically oriented principles were noted in chapter 1. We now consider seven of the remaining 15 principles as potentially relevant to the development of positive disability identities [readers are encouraged to review the principles presented in Chapter 1 and to consult the other eight found in Wright (1983)].

Active involvement of the client in the rehabilitation process is necessary (Principle 6). Respect for clients is a way to clarify their right to make choices about the near and far term while emphasizing self-respect, responsibility, and decision-making capacity, and encouraging initiatives. A positive disability identity should affirm the client's right to determine his or her fate, to make choices that others might dispute, or even to take risks.

Clients are usually part of a larger group (e.g., family), which means they should not be treated in isolation (Principle 7). A client's daily life and destiny are usually tied to others—a spouse, close friends, parents, and/or children—which means that significant others should be a part of planning and treatment. Disability identity entails connections to important others, including groups, which provide social connection and often balanced perspectives.

The personality and circumstances of PWDs are unique, so recognizing the need for flexibility is an important concern (Principle 8). PWDs should not be grouped or characterized exclusively by their disability category (e.g., cerebral palsy, traumatic brain injury) so as to avoid making stereotyped generalizations about a given person's probable needs or likely prognosis. Disability identity is more likely to emerge from individuating approaches, those that emphasize the strengths, assets, and interests of the person, rather than deindividuating situations (recall Chapter 2).

Self-help organizations are allies in rehabilitation work (Principle 12). Social support from others beyond the family and immediate caregivers can be beneficial to establishing disability identity, bolstering PWD's self-esteem as they learn from and with others who may have "rolled a mile in their chairs." PWDs can receive counsel from such organizations, but they may also be able to give back by volunteering to guide or advise others.

Client involvement and participation in the general life of the community, as well as the opportunity to contribute to it, is a fundamental principle linked to daily life (Principles 15 and 16). Whether they live with their families or in an institutional setting, PWDs benefit from taking an active part in community life and public activities, including sharing their skills and talents toward its betterment. Our discussion of disability identity emphasized the importance of close connections to the disability community, a factor that remains a very important consideration. Here, the interaction between the person and the wider (nondisabled) community also serves as a source of identity development. People can "give back" within as well as beyond the disability community.

PWDs should be invited to act as co-planners, co-evaluators, and consultants regarding disability and rehabilitation issues (Principle 20). PWDs have intimate knowledge of the person–environment relation and their own disabilities, so that their insider status can be invaluable when it comes to revising or expanding social, educational, political, psychological, environmental (e.g., accessibility), and legal matters relevant to disability. Indeed, the disability rights movement relies on a constructive slogan ("Nothing about us without us") that clearly emphasizes disability identity. Research on the social psychology of disability, too, should involve PWDs as co-investigators or as members of research teams (we revisit this issue in greater detail in Chapter 8).

Wright (1972, 1983) suggested that the values and beliefs embedded in the principles should be reviewed periodically in light of cultural changes and new information about disability. These recommendations also work well in the context of disability identity, particularly as more research on the viability and utility of the construct emerges. If nothing else has been accomplished, the examination of disability identity points to the importance of maintaining positive perspectives within the social psychology of disability. In the next chapter, we will explore the nascent area of inquiry known as positive psychology and consider its implications for understanding the social experiences of disability. As part of that discussion, we will revisit the issue of values by considering how the values held by PWDs can change in beneficial ways following the onset of disability.

Questions

1. What exactly is disability identity? Why is disability identity potentially important to PWDs?
2. Is the content (e.g., thoughts, beliefs, experiences) of most disability identities likely to be positive? Or can a disability identity also contain negative information?
3. Define and explain the study of narrative, in particular, disability narratives. What is a narrative identity? Are narrative identities true, that is, do they reflect people's actual experiences or their idealized, interpretive experiences? Does this distinction matter and, if so, why?
4. List and define several themes associated with disability identity. Are other themes waiting to be discerned? How could they be found?
5. Can narratives of disability identity serve as a hidden resource for PWDs and the professionals who work with them? How so?
6. What does it mean to prime disability identity? How can priming disability identity be accomplished and what are the potential benefits and liabilities of doing so?
7. How can the value-laden beliefs and principles championed by Wright (1972, 1983) be helpful in encouraging the development of positive disability identities? Select one presented at the end of the chapter and explain why it is relevant to issues of disability identity.
8. Design a research project aimed at exploring the benefits of a positive disability identity.

A person's healthy, physical and mental attributes can become a basis for alleviating difficulties as well as providing a source of gratification and enrichment of life. Special care must be taken to avoid overemphasis on the pathologic that leaves one inadequately sensitized to stabilizing and maturity inducing factors. Those attributes of the person that are healthy and promising must be supported and developed.

BEATRICE A. WRIGHT (1972, p. 39)

7   A Positive Psychology of Disability and Rehabilitation

IN THIS EXCERPT, Beatrice Wright wrote about the importance of attending to people's assets during the course of rehabilitation (see Chapter 2), but she might as well have been writing about the intent and direction of one of psychology's newest subfields: positive psychology. *Positive psychological science* aims to identify, understand, and apply human strengths to help people psychologically and physically (e.g., Aspinwall & Staudinger, 2003; Keyes & Haidt, 2003; Peterson & Seligman, 2004; Seligman & Csikszentmihalyi, 2000). Instead of relying on the dominant, pathology-oriented model found in much of the discipline and in psychiatry, positive psychology focuses on what factors maintain healthy, positive outlooks and behaviors in people's psychosocial arsenals.

Wright and many of her rehabilitation colleagues were forward-thinking regarding the importance of emphasizing the positive over the negative, of focusing on existing or potential assets rather than lost qualities or those that could never be achieved. This perspective is captured in the rehabilitation rallying cry: "Ability, not disability." The core strengths of rehabilitation psychology align well with objectives of positive psychology (Dunn & Dougherty, 2005). Thus, rehabilitation psychology and rehabilitation psychologists who adhere to a Lewinian analysis have always concentrated on positive approaches to dealing with disability (Dunn & Dougherty, 2005; Elliott, Kurylo, & Rivera, 2002; McCarthy, 2014; see also Ehde, 2010); other areas of the larger discipline remained less interested in affirmative approaches to dealing with life challenges. To their credit, positive psychologists are encouraging researchers and therapists in all areas of psychology to attend more carefully to the roles that positive emotions, attitudes, actions, and traits play in people's psychological and physical health and personal fulfillment.

In this chapter, we apply three positive levels of analysis to disability and the rehabilitative process and then discuss psychological resilience as a positive factor in coping with disability. Positive psychology promotes reliance on its observations and constructs as a way to lead the proverbial "good life." We will consider the nature of a good life following an acquired disability. The final section of this chapter explores ways that people with disabilities (PWDs) can develop broader, more constructive views of disability by adopting selective changes in their values. We begin our discussion by examining the shared perspectives of positive psychology and rehabilitation psychology.

Some Shared Perspectives between Positive and Rehabilitation Psychology

Social psychology and rehabilitation psychology share a Lewinian foundation and theoretical perspective, yet this connection is often forgotten (Dunn, 2011; see also Chapter 1). In a similar way, some shared perspectives of positive psychology and rehabilitation psychology, too, can be overlooked, so they are worth noting here. These shared perspectives recognize the following:

People actively create their personal and social worlds. The ways in which people construe their circumstances have an impact on their health, their well-being, and the freedom they feel to take action and to make choices about the course of their lives. Whether the focus is on issues of daily living or disability, how people explain their experiences and look to the future matters. Optimistic outlooks, for example, are apt to lead to better outcomes in the short and long term than pessimistic ones (Carver, Scheier, Miller, & Fulford, 2009).

People are creations of the physical and social world. Humans are bound up with their biology and physical selves and are influenced by constraints imposed by the environment. Yet they are more than their physiology, physiques, or behavioral responses to circumstance. As already acknowledged, what people can accomplish or can try to achieve should be of greater psychological concern than activities or actions that cannot be performed because of personal or environmental limitations. How people learn from and adapt to their situations can shape their future behavior and, in turn, some personality-related factors. Instead of focusing on what leads to failure or succumbing behaviors, the emphasis should be on what can be learned from psychosocial success or coping processes.

A focus on the development of human strengths and assets is integral to psychosocial well-being. Individuals are presumed to possess positive characteristics or the ability to acquire them, just as most generally want to improve themselves. Thus, empowering people to enhance the good they already possess or can acquire will be more helpful to them than highlighting the adverse elements present in their lives (Chou, Lee, Catalano, Ditchman, & Wilson, 2009). Peterson and Seligman (2004) identified and defined 24 character strengths that they organized under six human virtues (see Table 7.1). These strengths and virtues are universal and applicable to the development of theories, interventions, and assessments for PWDs and nondisabled individuals alike. The character strengths listed in Table 7.1 have two key advantages: They can be evaluated using validated measures (e.g., Lopez & Snyder, 2003; Peterson & Seligman, 2004) and they can be cultivated (Peterson & Seligman, 2004)—that is, when motivated to do so, people can add interpersonal strengths to their behavioral repertoires.

Positive perspectives are not new but their pride of place may be. The current emphasis on the good things in life seems to be new to academic psychology, but the study of positive thoughts and actions, as well as their salutary effects, is rooted in eastern and western philosophy (e.g., Snyder, Lopez, & Pedrotti, 2011) as well as humanistic psychology and cognitive–behavioral approaches (e.g., self-efficacy, resilience, agency), among other areas of the discipline. As already acknowledged, social-psychological approaches to disability and rehabilitation have long maintained that positive,

TABLE 7.1

SIX VIRTUES AND THEIR REPRESENTATIVE CHARACTER STRENGTHS

Wisdom	*Courage*	*Humanity*
Creativity	Bravery	Love
Curiosity	Integrity	Kindness
Open-mindedness	Persistence	Social intelligence
Love of learning	Vitality	
Perspective		

Justice	*Temperance*	*Transcendence*
Forgiveness	Forgiveness and mercy	Appreciation of beauty and excellence
Leadership	Prudence	Gratitude
Citizenship	Self-regulation	Hope
	Humility	Humor
		Spirituality

Note: Virtues appear in italics; character strengths linked to the virtues are listed beneath each one.

Source: Adapted from Peterson and Seligman (2004).

not negative, approaches are apt to be most helpful for PWDs. As a new arena for empirical work, positive psychology has successfully garnered scientific interest and enthusiasm by emphasizing "what goes right in life" (Peterson, 2006, p. 4) and applying empirical insights and observations to improve people's lives.

Keeping these shared perspectives in mind will be helpful when considering how positive levels of analysis can be used to promote a better quality of life for PWDs and to enhance rehabilitation processes more generally.

Positive Levels of Analysis: Subjectivity, Individuality, and the Group

At present, positive psychology relies on three levels of analysis for examining issues of prevention and treatment, as well as improving daily living—the subjective, the individual, and the group (e.g., Gillham & Seligman, 1999; Seligman, 2002a; Seligman & Csikszentmihalyi, 2000). The levels are designed to reduce the focus on disorders and psychological suffering by shifting toward the study of favorable outcomes in spite of challenges. Each one serves a descriptive function by helping researchers and practitioners target ways to promote people's strengths while managing their weaknesses.

Subjective level of analysis. The subjective level of analysis explores people's personal construals of their lives. Subjective experiences involve people's perspectives about their futures (e.g., optimism, hope; Carver et al., 2009; Rand & Cheavens, 2009), their present lives (e.g., happiness, "flow," positive emotions; Csikszentmihalyi, 1990; Diener & Biswas-Diener, 2008; Fredrickson, 1998), or their past (e.g., perceived well-being, life satisfaction; Diener, 1984; Diener & Suh, 2000; Ryff & Keyes, 1995). These personal appraisals enjoy a fair degree of consistency; however, they can change based on major life events and critical incidents, including the onset of disability. The subjective appraisals PWDs adopt are presumed to be significant influences where regaining strength and psychological wherewithal following disability is concerned (Elliott, Kurylo, & Rivera, 2002; see also Lazarus & Folkman, 1984). Those individuals possessing positive subjective outlooks are usually better able to stave off depression and hopelessness (Eid & Larsen, 2008; Seligman & Csikszentmihalyi, 2000). The study of PWD's narratives as a tool to learn about their disability identities (see Chapter 6) also represents a potential positive source of a subjective level of analysis.

Individual level of analysis. The second level of analysis deals with the stability represented by positive personality traits. These traits include the aforementioned virtues and strengths of character, such as courage, persistence, gratitude, and kindness (see Table 7.1; Aspinwall & Staudinger, 2003; Peterson & Seligman, 2004). When working with PWDs, rehabilitation researchers and practitioners should identify and encourage them to maintain and capitalize upon their existing strengths (Wright

& Fletcher, 1982; Wright & Lopez, 2009) and/or to develop new ones in order to enhance psychological and physical recovery. Practitioners should consider how the assessment of positive strengths (see Table 7.1; Lopez & Snyder, 2003; Peterson & Seligman, 2004) could be used in constructive concert with traditional depression and coping measures (Dunn & Dougherty, 2005) to obtain a richer, more balanced, and therapeutically useful view of the individual's personality and emotional state.

Group level of analysis. The third and most promising, if heretofore least studied, level of analysis deals with groups and their internal processes that allow people to thrive. Relevant topics here include examining the benefits of positive public virtues (e.g., patriotism, justice), civic mindedness (e.g., developing shared community resources, such as libraries and parks), and positive workplaces (e.g., Luthans & Youssef, 2009), and recognizing the essential psychologically related contributions performed by institutions (e.g., schools, local governments, charities, public works). For individuals to truly thrive, the communities in which they reside must flourish, which means that people must act responsibly toward others by being civil, nurturing, altruistic, and tolerant (see Seligman & Csikszentmihalyi, 2000). Positive institutions also provide groups (i.e., their members or employees, clients) with various benefits, usually by demonstrating institutional virtues including fairness, humanity, purpose, dignity, and safety (Peterson, 2006). Where disability and PWDs are concerned, the group level of analysis points to benefits associated with the disability rights movement (e.g., Charlton, 1998), the 1990 Americans with Disabilities Act (ADA), and the Individuals with Disabilities Education Act of 1990 (see also Bruyere & O'Keefe, 1994; Pelka, 1997). Clearly, institutional as well as personal virtues are embodied within both disability-related advocacy and legislation.

Dunn and Dougherty (2005) recommended that the subjective, individual, and group levels of analysis be used for research on disability and rehabilitation practices. Presented in Table 7.2 are sample research and practices issues for positive psychological approaches to disability. Some table entries are established topics (e.g., characterizing appraisal processes when confronting threats) whereas others have received little attention in the rehabilitation literature (e.g., tracing the development of disability identity across time; recall Chapter 6). As Dunn and Dougherty (2005) suggested, positive psychological approaches to disability should go beyond issues of treatment or adaptation so that people's psychosocial strengths can be shown to benefit their psychological and physical well-being.

Let's consider a recent, concrete example in which one of the three levels of analysis—the individual level—was used to predict a positive outcome. Using a longitudinal research design, Kortte and colleagues (2012) followed 174 adults through in-patient rehabilitation for acute spinal cord dysfunction, stroke, an amputation, or recovery from some other orthopedic surgery. The researchers were interested in whether hope, defined as the expectation that desired goals (here,

TABLE 7.2

THREE LEVELS OF ANALYSIS AND REPRESENTATIVE SAMPLE ISSUES FOR A
POSITIVE PSYCHOLOGICAL APPROACH TO DISABILITY AND REHABILITATION

Subjective

Study self-reported positive emotions (e.g., joy, interest) during rehabilitation

Characterize appraisal processes and outcomes (e.g., benefit finding, positive meaning) linked to disability

Assess optimism associated with rehabilitation and future life

Individual

Trace the development of PWD's disability identities across time

Evaluate the impact of goal setting during rehabilitation on long-term progress

Identify, enhance, or develop positive strengths (e.g., humor) and virtues (e.g., transcendence)

Examine PWD's assets during and after rehabilitation efforts

Group

Advocate for the elimination of physical, social, legal, and economic barriers affecting PWDs

Share the history and culture of disability

Collaborate with PWDs as partners in the design and conduct of rehabilitation research

Promote institutions and sociocultural norms that foster well-being in PWDs

Source: Adapted from Dunn and Dougherty (2005, Table 1, p. 307).

rehabilitation-related ones) could be achieved in the future (Snyder, 1994), would positively affect functional outcomes after treatment. Shortly after their hospital admission, the participants completed the Hope Scale (Snyder et al., 1991) and the Functional Independence Measure (FIM, a measure of self-sufficiency; Linacre et al., 1994), among other scales. Three months after discharge, they again completed the FIM and the Craig Hospital Assessment and Reporting Technique (CHART, which assesses areas of potential handicapped behavior; Whiteneck et al., 1992). The investigators found that elevated levels of hope during the early phases of rehabilitation predicted higher functional skill and participation levels later on as recovery proceeded postdischarge.

How and why did hope, an individual level personality trait, enhance rehabilitation and recovery? Kortte and colleagues (2012) offered two possible reasons this positive psychological construct proved to be effective during and after rehabilitation.

First, higher levels of hope likely promoted determination and prompted a search for pathways (i.e., means, methods) to achieve desired goals during rehabilitation. Second, hopefulness helped to diminish the perceived magnitude of the difficulties the PWDs faced. Put another way, as a positive psychological variable, hope gave the PWDs "a sense of possibility to overcome barriers encountered by persons with significant impairments" (Kortte et al., 2012, p. 253).

Psychological variables linked to one of the three levels of analysis of positive psychology, then, hold some promise for psychosocial interventions linked to disability and rehabilitation (for additional examples of disability-related research, see Dunn & Dougherty, 2005; Kortte et al., 2012). Approaches using constructs and variables drawn from or otherwise linked to positive psychology have the advantage of fostering a focus on good rather than poor predictive outcomes (e.g., higher levels of depressive symptoms or depression). Adopting proactive approaches that highlight positive factors (e.g., assets, strengths) can be useful in shaping positive recovery trajectories after injury and disability (Bonanno, 2004; Seligman, 2002a). We now turn to the study of resilience or how some people rally when confronted with life challenges, including disability.

Resilience and Disability

The term *resilience* refers to people's adaptive reactions to trauma or other adverse circumstances and life events. Interestingly, much of the original theoretical work on resilience is based on research with children and adolescents facing seemingly untenable situations (for reviews see Masten, 2007; Masten et al., 2009). The psychological crux of resilience is twofold: People cope with adversity and then become stronger because of it. Resilient behaviors are often described using synonyms such as endurance, resoluteness, hardiness, stamina, robustness, and durability of spirit (Craig, 2012). Where psychological qualities are concerned, resilient people are presumed to display high levels of self-esteem, possess good problem-solving skills, show self-efficacy, and maintain a positive outlook when facing daunting situations (Craig, 2012; Masten, Best, & Garmezy, 1990; Rutter, 1979; Werner & Smith, 1982).

Given the variety of synonymous terms, resilience is often easier to demonstrate through a behavioral example than a definition. One recent study had participants disclose their personal history of lifetime adversity prior to immersing their hands in an ice water bath (the classic cold-pressor task from experimental psychology; Seerey et al., 2013). People reporting moderate levels of life stress showed a less negative response to the ice bath than did those reporting low or high levels of life adversity. Perhaps earlier exposure to ultimately manageable hardships inoculates individuals—makes them resilient—against future adversity.

There are concrete steps individuals can take to cultivate resilience (American Psychological Association, 2012b; see also Gill, 1995; Longmore, 1985):

- Accepting that change is a part of life.
- Being decisive and relying on problem-focused and task-focused coping strategies.
- Holding on to a hopeful outlook.
- Framing events—particularly stressful ones—by keeping them in a balanced perspective.
- Connecting to family, friends, and people in the community.

All of these are reasonable approaches that make good sense but may be more difficult to rely upon when faced with a challenge such as disability onset or some other trauma. Although they are no doubt helpful, steps such as these also must be considered through the filter of people's personalities and experiences; one resilient response that works for one person may not work for another.

As a psychological construct, resilience should be treated as distinct from—but related to—adjustment and coping (Fergus & Zimmerman, 2005). Adjustment to some stressor (e.g., disability onset) represents a favorable outcome that could be linked to resilient responses. Similarly, when PWDs cope favorably with the disruptive aspects of daily life with a disability (e.g., reliance on others with self-care, limited mobility), their adaptive responses and positive attitude might illustrate a resilient personality. Coping responses contribute to resilience and, in turn, likely emerge from resilience.

At present, there is not much research directly associating resilience with disability, particularly physical disability (Craig, 2012). However, we have already discussed some constructs and concepts drawn from Wright's (1983) theorizing that serve as evidence for the value of promoting resilience among PWDs. These include the following:

- Emphasizing the assets PWDs already have or can acquire in lieu of focusing on lost or never realized abilities (see Chapter 2)
- The link between self-esteem and acceptance of the reality of disability, in which higher levels of the former result when the latter occurs (see Chapter 2); denying disability or attempting to hide or mask it is linked to lower levels of self-esteem and poorer adjustment
- The psychosocial benefits of adopting a coping rather than a succumbing framework (see Chapter 5)

We have also discussed psychological concepts in the context of disability and rehabilitation that are representative of resilient responses, including self-acceptance (see Chapter 2), personal growth (Chapter 7), finding meaning and purpose in life (Chapter 5), and having positive connections to other people (see the discussion below of the good life following disability onset). When present, these concepts point to resilience and mental health (Ryff & Singer, 2003).

Dunn, Uswatte, and Elliott (2009) suggested that the cultivation of positive emotions in PWDs could also be an avenue for exploring resilience. Positive affect is routinely recognized as an effective coping resource (Aspinwall, 2001), for example, and Barbara Fredrickson's research indicates that resilient people are more likely to both experience and benefit from positive emotions than their less resilient counterparts. Based on the broaden-and-build model of positive emotions, positive affect neutralizes the lingering effects of negative emotional states (Tugade & Fredrickson, 2002, 2004). (This positive psychological model posits that positive emotions *broaden* individuals' outlooks, allowing them to *build on* subsequent learning to develop future emotional and mental resources; Fredrickson, 1998.) Tugade and Fredrickson (2004) found that when positive emotions are linked to resilience, the emotions promote a return to baseline levels of physiological and psychological function. This result was found in a prospective field project that gathered responses before and after the September 11, 2001 terror attacks. College students identified as resilient were found to show lower depression levels and greater postevent psychological growth than a group of less resilient peers (Fredrickson, Tugade, Waugh, & Larkin, 2003).

What sorts of factors enhance or reduce people's resilience? Craig (2012) suggested that Wright's (1983) theoretical and empirical work highlights roles for protective and risk factors in understanding resilient responses. Protective factors are those qualities (i.e., environmental, social/interpersonal, psychological/physical) that enable people to face and withstand adversity. The upper-half of Table 7.3 illustrates some protective factors that can promote a coping framework that contributes to resilience. In contrast, risk factors are those qualities whose presence reduces people's abilities to confront harsh conditions. These factors jeopardize people's abilities to respond in resilient ways, which means they are vulnerable to whatever stressors are present. The lower half of Table 7.3 lists some representative risk factors. Note that the respective lists in Table 7.3 are by no means exhaustive, as a wide variety of variables can qualify as protective or risk factors linked to resilience (or its absence; for longer lists of protective and risk factors, see Craig, 2012; Masten et al., 2009).

Space constraints preclude further discussion of resilience research, but readers are encouraged to consult a review by Craig (2012), who discusses studies of several types of physical disability (e.g., burns, chronic pain, diabetes, traumatic brain injury, spinal

TABLE 7.3

SELECTED PROTECTIVE FACTORS CONTRIBUTING TO AND RISK FACTORS
UNDERMINING RESILIENCE

Environmental	Social/Interpersonal	Psychological/Physical
Protective Factors		
Community resources	Stable family support	Healthy self-esteem
Safe housing	Employment	Physical health
Secure income/finances	Social support/friends	Problem-solving skills
Risk Factors		
No community resources	No family support	Anxiety, stress
Unsafe, unsecured housing	Unemployment	Compromised physical health
Unstable income/finances	Limited or no social support	Poor communication skills

Source: Adapted from Craig (2012, Tables 26.1 and 26.2, p. 478).

cord injury, multiple sclerosis) that incorporated concepts that could be construed as resilience or models that explicitly entailed resilience. Ultimately, then, resilience refers to a category of factors that help to restore psychosocial balance in the face of threatening events. In other words, resilience enables people to maintain or regain good lives. What other activities can PWDs perform that will allow them to live good lives and provide satisfaction? And in the sense of positive psychology, what is meant by "the good life"?

Living "the Good Life" with Disability

> The widespread assumption that disability means suffering feeds a fear of indifference and a social order that doesn't know what to do with us if it can't fit its ideal of normal. When we seek what we need to live good lives as we are, we come against that wall... We need to bear witness to our pleasures.
> HARRIETT MCBRYDE JOHNSON (2005, p. 253)

One of the major themes of positive psychology is encouraging people to lead the *good life*. Since antiquity, philosophers, social commentators, and ordinary people have sought to define and live the good life. Is the good life found in love of family? Is it found in a focus on purpose or meaning, such as that encountered in work or creative acts? Positive psychology defines the good life as one that is personally satisfying, fulfilling, and meaningful, which means it is partially idiosyncratic but also tied to shared perspectives regarding what is reinforcing in human experience (e.g., Dunn & Brody, 2008).

In the context of a theory of authentic happiness, Seligman (2002b) identified three approaches to "the good life": the pleasant life, the good life, and the meaningful life. A pleasant life is marked by the frequent presence of positive emotions (e.g., euphoria, contentment, joy, happiness), whereas a good life is one in which people use their character strengths to exercise their efficacy in the world (e.g., Table 7.1), thereby remaining true to themselves. This form of the good life is focused on continual personal growth and development. The meaningful life, in turn, builds on the good life so that a person's character strengths and virtues are channeled to help others and the community—in other words, to do the greater good, an outcome relevant to positive psychology's third level of analysis. There are advantages associated with each of these *lives*, but the latter two resonate to the traditional notion that the good life is more than mere pleasure or self-focused hedonism (e.g., Waterman, 2013).

What is the nature of the good life where disability is concerned? Does that life differ from that of the not-yet-disabled person? Paraphrasing Aristotle (1984), who noted that "the active life will be the best" (p. 1325b), Dunn and Brody (2008) argued that the good life with physical disability, for example, entails PWDs making the "right" choices and then essentially acting on them. These authors relied upon the three dimensions identified by positive psychologists as characterizing the good life: *positive connections to other people, positive personal qualities,* and *life regulation qualities* (e.g., Compton, 2004; Lopez & Snyder, 2009; Seligman, 2002b). We will define each of these dimensions and consider how related activities undertaken by PWDs could help them to live good lives. One important note: When engaging in activities representing each dimension, Dunn and Brody (2008) advocated that PWDs seek a favorable balance between their own independence (i.e., personal agency) and interdependence (i.e., communion with others; Helgeson, 1994); an imbalance in either direction frequently leads to psychosocial difficulties (Helgeson & Fritz, 1999, 2000).

Positive connections to other people. Beneficial relations with others include loving people, forgiving wrongdoings great and small, maintaining close ties with family members, as well as having basic skills at forming and retaining friendships. No doubt, too, the quality of people's interpersonal relationships matter to their well-being. The types of actions encompassed by this dimension are not unique to PWDs.

Socializing with other people by being a part of larger, even multiple, social networks, for example, represents elected sources of social pleasure and reflects leading a good life (Lyubomirsky, Sheldon, & Schkade, 2005). How individuals share and receive good news regarding positive events has intrapersonal as well as

interpersonal effects (Gable, Reis, Impett, & Asher, 2004). *Capitalizing* or responding with enthusiasm, sincere interest, and attentive listening generates positive emotions and forges closer relationships with others (whereas selfishly sharing one's own
triumphs without attending to those of others does not).

Another straightforward way to live a good life is by offering *help* to others, which
occurs when people perform "random acts of kindness" or offer assistance when and
where it is needed (Lyubomirsky et al., 2005). The working assumption, which is yet
to be definitively empirically demonstrated, is that doing things for other people not
only feels good (i.e., generates positive emotions, maintains positive moods) but also
has psychological benefits for the helper (Salovey, Mayer, & Rosenhan, 1991). We need
not exhaust the possibilities for establishing positive connections with other people
here. Suffice it to say that with moderate vigilance and diligence, PWDs can identify
opportunities in the course of daily living to foster positive associations with family,
friends, acquaintances, co-workers, and even strangers met in the course of daily life.

Positive personal qualities. As previously discussed, character strengths and virtues represent positive personal qualities that people already have or can develop.
A person with a new disability, for example, may need to learn some new social skills
to counter common outsider expectations (e.g., use of a wheelchair does not indicate that you are intellectually dull). Finding meaning in disability and responding
with resilience, too, represent positive personal qualities linked with the good life.
Dunn and Brody (2008) identified some other qualities that PWDs should enact in
order to lead a good life. *Expressing gratitude* to other people for their kindness and
good will, for example, is associated with higher levels of well-being (e.g., Watkins,
Woodward, Stone, & Russell, 2003), and it is an easy thing for anyone to do. Being
thankful for what you already have or counting your proverbial blessings, too, fos-
ters close connections with others, extends the life of positive emotional experiences, and slows down adjustments to positive events (Larsen & Prizmic, 2008).

Displaying a good sense of *humor* by laughing at life's ups and downs is a mature
coping response and a good way to adjust to life's challenges (e.g., Gill, 1995; Vaillant,
1995), just as it can magnify positive emotions (Kuiper & Martin, 1998) and diminish stress (e.g., Taylor, Kemeny, Reed, Bower, & Gruenewald, 2000). Rehabilitation
researchers believe that humor promotes both coping with and adapting to disability (Burkhead, Deborah, & Marini, 1996); indeed, humor can serve as a skill that
PWDs can acquire as a foil for anxiety associated with typical, sometimes awkward,
social encounters with nondisabled persons (Callahan, 1990; Marini, 1992).

Grit is a recently coined, promising positive personal quality that should be
examined in the context of disability and rehabilitation. Treated as a noncognitive
trait, grit refers to a passion for achieving long-term goals and having the necessary perseverance to meet them (Duckworth, Peterson, Matthews, & Kelly, 2007).

Grit enables some people to try harder than others to succeed at challenges, and those who have higher levels of grit do demonstrate necessary amounts of effort and attention to obtain desired outcomes despite adversity and setbacks. Gritty people are, in a word, tenacious. Grit, which can be learned, is assessed with a brief scale (Duckworth et al., 2007) and heretofore has been examined in academic-related settings; however, the construct seems to be a potentially fruitful one to examine following disability onset in order to predict short-term and long-term rehabilitation outcomes (see also MacCann & Roberts, 2010; Maddi et al., 2012).

Life-regulation qualities. Life-regulation qualities are abilities that enable people to maintain autonomy and to exercise self-control as they develop interests, pursue goals, and affect the lives of those close to them. Persistence at important tasks, fulfilling everyday responsibilities (e.g., studying, being punctual, carrying out chores), and delaying gratification represent important and beneficial life-regulation qualities. Life-regulation qualities should enable PWDs to maintain positive outlooks, mental and physical health, and well-being. Dunn and Brody (2008) suggested these qualities should add a necessary balance to life following the onset of disability.

Taking part in some regular *exercise* regimen is important for all people, including PWDs. Just as good health is linked to well-being, so is physical exercise. A particular concern for PWDs is the degree to which their activities may be restricted. Williamson and colleagues (Williamson, 1998; Williamson, Schulz, Bridges, & Behan, 1994) find that PWDs are at risk for depressive symptoms when they cannot perform familiar actions (e.g., self-grooming, visiting friends and family, preparing meals, performing household responsibilities), thus pursuing regular exercise qualifies as one of these routine behaviors (e.g., Fleig, Pomp, Schwarzer, & Lippke, 2013; Ginis et al., 2003).

Attending to *creature comforts* and *special pleasures* also helps to regulate daily life by relieving stress and fostering positive anticipation in giving PWDs. Although the accompanying recommendations might seem obvious, the hectic nature of daily life often prevents people from experiencing them as often as they might wish. According to Dunn and Brody (2008), creature comforts include pursuing hobbies, eating enjoyable, healthful, and satisfying meals, taking occasional naps, or just relaxing. Intimacy and sexuality, too, can be added to this list, as PWDs are sexual beings (Juergens & Smedema, 2009). As for special pleasures, the late Harriett McBryde Johnson (2005) noted that they "are so bound up with our disabilities that we wouldn't experience them, or wouldn't experience them the same way, without our disabilities" (p. 254). Johnson, for example, enjoyed the "great sensual pleasure to zoom by power chair" (p. 2). Dunn and Brody (2008) noted that rehabilitation researchers have largely overlooked the special pleasures linked to disability, which is unfortunate, given that pleasurable events reduce negative emotions (Fichman,

Koestner, Zuroff, & Gordon, 1999) and self-rewards are apt to enhance emotional well-being (Larsen & Prizmic, 2008).

Arguably, one of the most important life-regulation qualities, one linked with disability identity (see Chapter 6), is the ability to give back by being generative. *Generativity* is a key milestone in Erikson's (1963, 1968) developmental theory, and positive psychology views such "giving back" to others, including the community (Putnam, 2001), as evidence of wisdom, a virtue, as well as a life-regulation quality in its own right (e.g., Baltes, Gluck, & Kunzman, 2002; Peterson & Seligman, 2004). PWDs could be generative by serving as a mentor, a sponsor, or a counselor to other PWDs (especially those who are in the early phase of rehabilitation therapy) or even following disability onset, as well as working to improve institutions that help the disability community. As Dunn and Brody (2008) suggested, "Being generative while living a good life with disability could entail providing informal counseling to peers with disabilities, accepting participatory or leadership roles in clubs or social organizations, organizing community events, among many other possibilities" (p. 420).

Seeking to lead the good life with disability involves mindfully making choices and taking actions whose aims are to promote well-being, not mere happiness or good feelings. Regulating life-qualities, creating positive connections to others, and displaying positive personal qualities are valuable activities in their own respective rights, but it is likely that the benefits with each dimension wash over, as it were, into the others, thereby enhancing our overall quality of life. We now turn from more concrete behaviors that can promote a good life to the domain of people's beliefs about themselves and what matters to them—their values—following disability.

A Broader View: Value Changes after Disability

The fundamental purpose of positive psychology is to help people remember what matters in life, to highlight those qualities that make life enjoyable and worth living. As we learned in Chapter 2, an important focus of rehabilitation psychology is to help PWDs accept the losses associated with their disabilities and to help them ultimately accommodate themselves to them. Both situations involve a recognizable shift in people's perspective from things and situations that are less than ideal to those things that bolster and even broaden self-understanding and satisfaction. In this last section, we discuss issues of value change or how the perceived relative worth of particular qualities linked to the self can be altered in order to promote and maintain a positive self-image.

Dembo, Leviton, and Wright (1975) and Wright (1983), among others (e.g., Livneh, 1980; Marinelli & Dell Orto, 1984; Shontz, 1975), argued that PWDs adjust more fully to disability when they accept whatever loss the disability entails and align their values accordingly—that is, constructively alter their beliefs about what is important—to meet the demands and the various changes disability brings. Meaningful value change or modification is theorized to occur when the accompanying changes are not devalued, that is, seen as threatening to a person's self-image. Changing one's values or adopting new ones is never an easy feat even in the best of times, and it is assuredly a greater challenge under stressful conditions. However, both insiders and outsiders (i.e., family, friends, caregivers, medical professionals) will experience value changes. Our interest is naturally in the former, but the latter, too, must accept (i.e., not devalue) the disabilities of those close to them so as not to undermine relationships or add to their psychosocial burdens (Wright, 1983).

Wright (1983) suggested that value change involved four interdependent activities:

- *Enlarging the scope of values.* The main goal here is to focus on, appreciate, and take interest in activities that can (still) be accomplished as being of higher value than those that cannot be performed. Being a "good father" remains a value, but the means of realizing it could shift from playing catch with a child to going to all the child's ballgames. Recognizing existing or potential assets is important here, as well.
- *Subordinating physical concerns relative to other values.* PWDs, particularly those with physical disabilities, generally benefit from focusing less on the importance of physical appearance and other aesthetic concerns and more on personality, skills, competencies, interests, and the like—in other words, on issues of psychosocial substance rather than form. This type of value change is admittedly challenging in a culture that celebrates youth and bodily perfection, but the overemphasis on how you look must be countered by the recognition of the myriad qualities of the whole person. Ideally, of course, individuals—both PWDs and nondisabled individuals—could broaden their conceptions of physical beauty. Keany and Glueckauf (1993) note that covert disabilities (e.g., diabetes, hearing impairment, emotional disabilities) also involve value loss and potential devaluation; thus, they also warn against overemphasis on visible disabilities.
- *Containing spread effects.* The issue here is how disability in one domain can wash over into others, creating the impression (usually false) of related problems (e.g., slowed speech is presumed to indicate compromised memory or cognition). Both insiders and outsiders must remind themselves of the person–environment relation (really, revelation) that disability produces certain constraints in some—not all—situations. In turn, the limits are both psychological and physical barriers created by the larger culture and its values, and not exclusively linked to ability changes attributable to disability.

As discussed earlier (see Chapter 1), the person-first approach can aid in limiting spread effects.

- *Transforming comparative-status values into asset values.* Social comparison may be an inevitable human activity (Festinger, 1954), but PWDs should strive to avoid comparing themselves to nondisabled people or even other PWDs on dimensions on which they are dissimilar. Making such comparisons can lower your self-perceived status relative to others ("I can't even move as easily as Ken can and his disability looks worse than mine; I'm just a lump") and create feelings of inadequacy in the process. Similarly, PWDs should not compare their current selves to their predisability selves, but rather to their early postonset selves. In effect, PWDs should focus on their own relative progress and goals and remember the assets encompassed by a wider scope of values.

Keany and Glueckauf (1993) reviewed the available research on value change linked to these four activities, suggesting that although the theory is sound, the approaches to measurement are too diffuse to capture real value change and to clearly demonstrate the hypothesized adjustment. To address the problem, the researchers recommended that rehabilitation psychologists rely on and adapt Rokeach's (1973) hierarchical analysis of values. In his general theory of values, Rokeach assumes that certain behaviors and states are more preferable than others, and can be categorized as either *terminal values* or *instrumental values.* Terminal values are idealized end states (e.g., the good life, a happy marriage, the perfect job), whereas instrumental values are idealized ways of behaving that promote attainment of the former (e.g., being a responsible person, being an attentive and loving spouse, being a hard worker). Within the model, each type of value is arranged hierarchically, so a terminal value will have an accompanying list of instrumental values subsumed under it. A given terminal value (e.g., being a happy person) and its instrumental values, in turn, can be subsumed under a higher terminal value in the value hierarchy (e.g., leading a meaningful life), and so on. Keany and Glueckauf (1993) claim that "Acceptance ... is a reorganization of instrumental and terminal values in a person's value system to accommodate life changes brought on by disability" (p. 207).

Keany and Glueckauf's (1993) critique is a good one, as it offers strategies to more effectively and properly test the role of value change in acceptance of loss and its impact on long-term adjustment to disability. Unfortunately, there have been few subsequent empirical investigations based on this hierarchical approach. At least two studies have examined the role of value changes since the Keany and Glueckauf critique, however. Weitzenkamp and colleagues (2000) explored quality of life issues and shifts in clients' ranked priorities (similar to values) following spinal cord injury (SCI). Compared to a similar nondisabled control group of men, those with SCI did not view health or work as central to their perceived quality of life. Instead, the severity of their disability and their own "abilities and accomplishments" influenced their rankings. Following the logic of Dembo, Wright, and Leviton (1975) and Wright (1983), the researchers suggested that the SCI clients appeared to devalue the now-less-attainable goals in favor of those areas of their lives in which they could be successful.

The second study, which examined cancer patients' value changes following their diagnosis, did rely on Rokeach's (1973) value analysis and its accompanying survey instrument. In a cross-sectional design, Greszta and Sieminska (2011) had cancer patients compare their current values with their recollections of their past values, finding that 27 out of 36 values changed in degree of perceived importance (i.e., 16 values increased and 11 decreased; the rest remained stable). Value clusters that increased in importance included personal orientation (e.g., happiness, self-respect), religious morality (e.g., forgiving, helpful), and delayed gratification (e.g., wisdom, inner harmony). In contrast, clusters that declined included immediate gratification (e.g., pleasure, a comfortable life), self-expansion (e.g., ambitious, capable), and competence (e.g., a sense of accomplishment, intellectual). Although based on retrospection rather than a longitudinal assessment, these results, too, indicate that what matters to people typically changes—their values appear to shift in predicted directions—following health threats and disability. Again, more solid support for this position will require an investigator to conduct a prospective longitudinal study assessing the proposed hierarchical model and linking the value changes closely to the experience of disability.

Both positive psychology and rehabilitation psychology, respectively, posit that changes in world views can have a favorable impact on people's outlooks about themselves and their lives. These perceptual adjustments are not ways to deny reality or disability; rather, a better way to think of the process is one in which certain aspects of people's lives are brought into sharper focus so that their relative value is enhanced. Put another way, the shift in emphasis is from negative characteristics to more positive qualities. Contradictions that become apparent in people's value systems (e.g., a value once deemed critically important has lost its urgency or relevance), too, can help to shift values in new and constructive directions. As was noted at the chapter's outset, the shift from a pathology orientation to one focused on human strengths is something of a sea change in the discipline of psychology (although rehabilitation psychology can legitimately claim to have been prescient in this regard), and it is no less challenging in any individual's life.

Conclusions

Positive psychology is providing new principles and practices for investigators and clinicians interested in what keeps people hale, hearty, happy, and healthy. Yet this orientation is not really new to rehabilitation psychology or the social psychology of disability. As we have seen in the first seven chapters of this book, the social psychology of disability developed in positive directions from the outset in order to help PWDs lead the most fulfilling and meaningful lives possible. As we turn to the final chapter, which explores the ecology of disability—the wider world of social, political, and other issues in which PWDs must make their ways—it will be critical to keep the social psychology of disability and its conceptual fruits in mind.

Questions

1. Define positive psychology and explains its relevance to disability and rehabilitation issues. Is it possible to argue that rehabilitation psychology has always been concerned with what are known as positive psychological issues? Why?

2. Discuss some of the perspectives shared by positive psychology and rehabilitation psychology. Can you identify any others?

3. Define positive psychology's three levels of analysis. Create novel examples of disability-related research to represent each level of analysis.

4. What is resilience? What factors enhance or reduce resilience? How can PWDs display resilience in daily life? Provide some examples of resilient behaviors linked to disability and rehabilitation.

5. What is the good life? What is the good life for PWDs? Are both the same? Provide some activities that PWDs can perform as they seek the good life.

6. Why are value changes linked to the acceptance of loss and disability acceptance? Describe some of the ways PWDs are hypothesized to shift their values so as to promote adjustment.

7. What changes in the approach to the study of value changes do Keany and Glueckauf (1993) advocate? Outline a longitudinal study aimed at demonstrating the benefits of value changes following the onset of disability. What values would you assess? How frequently? What population of PWDs would you recruit?

The positive context consists of two major parts. One refers to the assets and abilities of the person with a disability, the other to the hidden resources and forces in society which are there to be tapped and strengthened in the effort to bring about needed change.

BEATRICE A. WRIGHT (1983, p. 480)

8 The Ecology of Disability

THE OVERARCHING MESSAGE of this concluding chapter is that the social psychology of disability must move beyond a largely exclusive emphasis on the person to embrace multiple and relevant environmental factors—in other words, the experience of disability must be understood as the Lewinian analysis intended (Dembo, 1982; Dunn, 2010, 2011; Wright, 1983), as being based on *the person in the environment.* The challenge, of course, is that curious social perceivers focus on the people and their disabilities while routinely neglecting or at least minimizing the impact of the environments they inhabit. This social-psychological fact poses problems for properly understanding disability, the forces people with disabilities (PWDs) encounter in daily life, and the ways in which rehabilitation psychologists can effectively intervene.

Wright and Lopez (2009) eloquently compared the person and environment to the classic figure–ground relation in psychology. Gestalt psychology posited that two visual components are required for people to actually see an object in proper perspective: a *figure* (the object itself) and the *ground* (the background on which the object is overlaid). Visually, then, any object appears to stand out against the ground, and that is Wright and Lopez's point. Try as people (lay or professional) might attempt to be objective, the person is always perceived to be an active figure, which is why attributes such as race, gender, appearance, emotionality, disability, and age capture so much attention. Our perceptual systems attend to either the figure or the ground but not both simultaneously; attention is usually drawn to the former, and in the case of PWDs, the eye tends to be drawn to a single feature—the disability itself. As noted in Chapter 2, this selective focus often results in labeling, nullifying the role of the environment, so that its impact appears to be vague when its real influence is apt to be quite powerful. Thus, clients are highlighted perceptually and attributionally over the context provided by clinics, rehabilitation settings, hospital wards, or their homes; teachers over the schools in which they teach; and so on.

What social perceivers overlook is that the ground, the environment, is the medium that affords the figure—the person—the opportunity to behave (Heider, 1926), but may also pose limits on certain behavioral expressions. Indeed, the environment influences the very nature of the behavior. However, unless there is some reason for the environment and the things present in it—structures, calamities, other people—to stand out, viewers tend to ignore it and focus on the person (but see Nisbett, 2004). To advance the social psychology of disability, in which the treatment, adjustment, and welfare of PWDs are concerned, attention needs to shift from the figure to the ground, from exclusively focusing on the person to the wider situation and its constraints and opportunities.

This chapter discusses areas in which a shift is already underway as well as areas in which more research and social policy advances will be welcome. Social support is presumed to be an important resource for PWDs, yet the specific dynamics of how reliance on others promotes well-being remains elusive. As we will see, there are costs and some benefits for caregivers and families who provide ongoing social support to PWDs. We then consider how PWDs can serve as advocates and experts in clinical settings prior to our discussion of how perspectives from disability studies and activism can inform psychological research on disability, including the social psychology of disability. We begin by discussing the dynamics of life for PWDs in the United States since the passage of the Americans with Disabilities Act (ADA) and related legislation, and then return to a basic problem posed by the social psychology of disability. How can outsiders become more comfortable and understanding when interacting with insiders?

Macrocosm: Life in Brief in Post-ADA America

Following over 60 years of activism and gradual social and legal progress, as well as some setbacks (Nielsen, 2012), disability rights came of age in the late twentieth century. The ADA was signed into law in July 1990, and in 2008, the ADA Amendments Act (ADAAA) was passed in order to broaden the definition of disability and to further determine who has a disability. The ADA has five titles covering issues of employment and employment accommodations (Title 1); availability of public services at the local, state, and national levels (Title 2); public accommodations for new construction and modifications to existing venues rendering them more accessible (Title 3); telecommunications accessibility (Title 4); and miscellaneous concerns, chiefly that reprisals, threats, and coercion aimed at PWDs seeking legal recourse in the ADA are prohibited (Title 5).

It would be naive to claim that the ADA has leveled the proverbial playing field in the United States for PWDs or that the legislation eliminated all forms of unequal treatment or social and economic discrimination linked to disability. There is progress and some good news, however. Passage of the ADA has dramatically increased both the presence and inclusion of PWDs in daily life. Though appropriately restrained, a National Council on Disability (2007) report noted the following advances attributable to the ADA:

- Increased accessibility for PWDs on public transit systems, particularly for wheelchair users. However, accessibility tends to be greater in metropolitan areas compared to rural ones.
- Public venues, such as museums, government offices, restaurants, stores, and theaters, are increasingly (if inconsistently) more accessible for PWDs with physical disabilities.
- Curb ramps have been installed in many sidewalks around the country, which makes mobility easier for wheelchair users, older adults, and other PWDs.
- More PWDs than ever before are voting.
- Telecommunication technology has improved for PWDs, including TTY technology for the Deaf (and no doubt the ubiquity of the internet has had positive influences).
- More PWDs are furthering their education, particularly at the postsecondary level. Educational support is increasingly available at colleges and universities.
- Many PWDs attribute quality of life advances to the ADA and polling data suggest that public attitudes toward disability are more favorable than in the past.

At the same time, serious problems remain:

- Employment discrimination for PWDs has declined somewhat, but not enough. Individuals with visible or severe disabilities continue to encounter discriminatory policies and hiring challenges.
- For most PWDs, the goal of economic self-sufficiency remains elusive.

In many ways, the post-ADA world is both a different and a better one for PWDs and their allies. As the disability historian Kim Nielsen (2012) wrote:

> The inclusion of people with disabilities into higher education, employment, popular culture, and all venues of pubic life has enriched society greatly. The reality of the ADA, however, is that like all civil rights legislation, it has been consistently tested and eroded in the courts, and sometimes ignored in practice. (p. 181)

To some extent, then, attention to implementing changes to the environment in which PWDs live and work has helped; the quality of their life in the macrocosm of disability is improving, if only gradually.

How can the lessons and tools of social psychology contribute to these advances? Attending to the environment, that is improving the nature of the situation, is obviously one way. Another is to return to the microcosm and constructively address the one-on-one interactions between PWDs and nondisabled people.

Microcosm: Unfamiliarity with Disability as an Ongoing Challenge

One of the simplest but most enduring concerns of well-intentioned nondisabled people is how to interact with PWDs. As we learned in Chapter 4, meaningful exchanges between nondisabled persons and PWDs occur when individuals enjoy equal status and where sustained contact promotes positive intergroup relations, enhanced understanding, reduced stereotyped thinking and behavior, and broadened attitudes. Until PWDs are still better integrated into employment, educational, and community settings, however, their frequency of contact with many nondisabled persons will likely remain low, a reality that can lead to misunderstanding, awkwardness, or worse outcomes in daily life.

Citing White, Wright, and Dembo (1948), Wright (1983) listed some helpful guidelines for nondisabled people to follow in initial encounters with PWDs (see also Millington, 2012). The main message is to treat any PWD as a person first and to respect his or her privacy and integrity. PWDs should decide how, when, and whether any discussion concerning their disability will occur, how it will proceed, and how much they wish to disclose about the onset, nature, and consequences of their disability. In general, then, nondisabled people should follow the lead and honor the wishes of PWDs. Some basic guidelines for achieving these modest but important goals are presented in Table 8.1, and implementing change at the microcosm level is a way to work for broader understanding in the larger macrocosm. More detailed suggestions regarding ways to enhance interactions with

TABLE 8.1

SOME GENERAL RECOMMENDATIONS FOR INITIAL INTERACTIONS WITH PWDS

Curiosity is normal, but don't ask about a disability unless the PWD brings it up in conversation.

Don't talk about the disability unless the PWD wishes to do so.

Don't ask questions about a person's disability immediately.

Take into account the mood of the PWD.

Don't dwell on a disability; focus on the person.

Similarly, don't try to steer the person away from the subject of disability if he or she has a need to discuss it with you.

Avoid being solicitous; offer help only when asked or if the situation truly demands it.

Trying to "move things along" by expediting or assisting without being asked is usually not helpful.

Address a PWD directly; don't ask an attendant or family member about the PWD's needs.

Be polite and exercise common courtesy; treat PWDs as you prefer to be treated.

Source: Adapted from Wright (1983, p. 306).

PWDs, including within professional settings, are available from the American Psychological Association (2000, 2010b).

Reducing uncertainty in social discourse is an important goal. Fortunately, many PWDs have caregivers, family members, and friends who provide ongoing support. Such social support is an important environmental resource that is believed to provide ongoing benefits to PWDs. One caveat should be kept in mind, however; providers (or would-be providers) of social support need to develop a clear understanding of what support to provide, when, and how much, being careful to avoid sabotaging the efforts of PWDs themselves.

The Presumed Importance of Social Support

Help usually comes from the people around us. By definition, then, social support is a characteristic that is either present or absent within the environment portion of the person–environment relation. *Social support* refers to various forms of physical, informational, emotional, and other aid provided by members of an individual's social network (e.g., family, friends or peers, co-workers, professionals). Numerous studies in psychology demonstrate that the presence of social support has a decidedly favorable impact on physical health and well-being (e.g., Dickerson & Zoccola, 2009; Taylor, 2007; Wills & Fegan, 2001). A main benefit of social support is that during stressful times, tangible or intangible aid from others acts as a buffer against pressure and anxiety. Social support probably maintains well-being in several ways, such as by reducing the intensity of physiological reactions to stressors, guiding people to make constructive appraisals of challenging events, encouraging preventive behaviors (e.g., routine exercise), and discouraging health-compromising activities (e.g., smoking). Being a source of social support, too, can provide psychological and physical benefits to individuals who aid others (e.g., Brown, Nesse, Vinokur, & Smith, 2003).

Two categories of social support—assistance based on structural components and assistance based on functional components—appear with some frequency in the social support literature (Cohen & Syme, 1985; Cohen & Wills, 1985). *Structural components* involve the number of and interconnections among social ties and social relationships (e.g., marital status, number of friendships, degree of overlap among friendships). Social integration, a structural indicator, is assessed by examining roles (e.g., partner, spouse, parent, neighbor, club or church member), social activities (e.g., volunteering, solo or group memberships in community organizations or clubs), and the degree to which individuals feel embedded within a stable social structure (e.g., Brissette, Cohen, & Seeman, 2000).

In contrast, the *functional components* of social support refer to supportive exchanges between an individual and those in his or her social network of relationships. The word "exchange" is key here; support is given by one person to another with the implicit understanding of reciprocity—that is, an "in kind" return deed may occur in the future. The nature of these functional exchanges can be informational, emotional, or instrumental (i.e., material; help with completing tasks, financial assistance) (e.g., Cohen, 1988; Cohen & Wills, 1985).

Social support is presumed to be an important factor in helping people adjust to the onset and consequences of disability (for reviews see Chronister, 2009; Chwalisz & Vaux, 2000). During rehabilitation, for example, support from family members has a decided positive impact beyond that tied to the PWD's personality or other psychological qualities (Kendell, Saxby, Farrow, & Naisby, 2001). Although individuals with extraverted or resilient personalities might be expected to be strong advocates for their own needs (see Chapter 7), other PWDs with less assertive personal styles will likely rely more on social support to navigate healthcare and treatment issues (Johnson-Greene & Touradji, 2010). Of course, even highly assertive people can act less so when recovering from illnesses or accidents, or when they are constrained by the rules or routines found in medical settings. A meta-analysis (essentially a statistical summary study of similar studies) also revealed a connection between PWD's functional support and the quality of their rehabilitation outcomes (Chronister, Chou, Frain, & Cardoso, 2008). Perceptions of social support (i.e., belief in its presence and availability) and the PWD's satisfaction with the support were positively linked to psychological health; however, actual (received) support had a more pronounced influence on the PWD's adjustment to disability than on their psychological health. As we have witnessed previously, people's perceptions of disability experiences can be as important as what actually happens to them.

Despite such evidence, Livneh and Martz (2012) point out that within the broad context of chronic illness and disability, the specific mechanisms promoting the benefits of social support are still uncertain (see also Chwalisz & Vaux, 2000). Does the source of support matter (i.e., family vs. friends vs. a rehabilitation team), for example, or the nature of the support (e.g., informational, emotional, financial)? Perhaps the duration of the support, its intensity, and even whether the support is unidirectional or bidirectional (i.e., mutually supportive) are key factors. Livneh and Martz (2012) suggest that future research on social support and disability should address and seek to clarify these issues.

Following the lead of positive psychology (recall Chapter 7) and disability studies (discussed below), researchers should also attend to the impact of social support in the absence of disability duress, that is, when PWDs are enjoying their familiar routine lives and benefiting from their close relationships. Traditionally, social support is studied when people's lives are in upheaval, but one can well imagine that the presence of others and the connection to others have ongoing benefits beyond the reduction of stress, such as the maintenance of health and pursuit of leisure time interests. Examining this possibility in the lives of PWDs who have chronic but manageable disabilities might provide further insight into identifying who fares well and why across time. Social support comes from various sources, but most often comes from caregivers who are apt to be family members.

Support and Its Consequences for Caregivers and Families

The family is an obvious and important source of social support for PWDs. Yet the onset of disability poses challenges for the well-being of the designated caregiver or caregivers within the family unit. Family members who struggle with the broader changes wrought by disability (e.g., care responsibilities, increased household demands, financial issues, time off from work) often display more distress than the individual who acquired the disability (Elliott & Shewchuk, 2004). The attitudes and actions of family members as caregivers can also have pronounced influence on both the physical and psychological adjustment of PWDs. Decreased acceptance of disability was found among PWDs leaving a rehabilitation facility when their caregivers were impulsive and careless about solving problems related to their care-giving responsibilities (Elliott, Shewchuk, & Richards, 1999). Thus, caregivers' reactions (and perhaps that of the larger family) to disability onset has consequences for the PWD's adaptation to and possibly outlook on their conditions.

For some family members, providing ongoing care is seen as a major burden, one that triggers stress, leads to social isolation due to ongoing duties, and negatively affects thoughts, feelings, personality, and behavior (Florian, Katz, & Lahav, 1989). Beyond the social and emotional consequences of caring for a PWD, there is usually a financial impact (e.g., income loss or change) as well (e.g., Kozloff, 1987). For those individuals who have cared for a PWD for an extended period of time, caregiver burnout is also a risk (e.g., Stav & Florian, 1986; Ursprung, 1986). Rehabilitation staff members who have fewer sources of social support demonstrate greater susceptibility to burnout (Clanton, Rude, & Taylor, 1992), so it is logical to assume that family-based caregivers would be similarly at risk, with their vulnerability perhaps increasing over time.

On the other hand, some research indicates that positive changes for families and caregivers occur following disability onset. Crewe (1993) observes that the shared concern represented by disability can bring family members closer together. Olkin (1999) suggests that disability compels families to deal meaningfully with the reality of mortality, and to examine their values and trust with one another, which can lead to stronger levels of commitment and solidify marital and familial bonds. More detailed discussion concerning how families adapt to disability and caregiving issues can be found in Glover-Graf (2012), Rivera (2012), Rosenthal, Kosciulek, Lee, Frain, and Ditchman (2009), and Shewchuk and Elliott (2000).

We now return to the important relationship between PWDs and the professionals who counsel and treat them, a situation usually entailing both support from and involvement of families.

Clinical Connection: Clients as Co-Managers

One seemingly obvious (but easily overlooked) lesson of the insider–outside distinction is that no one knows the experience of disability better than an insider—and a given group of insiders really knows only its own disability experience, not necessarily that of other PWDs. Outsiders—even experts in rehabilitation, physical or occupational therapy, medicine, nursing, whatever area of health or psychological care—are still outsiders (although there are some clinical and research professionals who are insiders with respect to disability). Their expertise and training are admittedly very important, even essential, to providing care for and improving the lives of PWDs. But their knowledge of a given person's disability is still indirect and incomplete, which means they need to consult with the person and *enjoin him or her to be a part of the healthcare team* (thereby striving to implement the rehabilitation principle that the patient is an important team member).

More than three decades ago, Wright (1983) suggested that clients act as co-managers of their own care and treatment during the rehabilitation process. That recommendation remains a critically important one. And as noted in Chapter 1, whether they are referred to as clients, co-managers, consumers, or participants, their role should be active, not passive. Two of Wright's (1983) value-laden beliefs (Principles 6 and 7) emphasize this message. Principle 6 urges that PWDs who receive medicorehabilitation services should be actively engaged in related decision making because it directly affects their lives and because they have insights and impressions about their conditions that are simply not available to others. As Wright wrote, clients ". . . not only contribute data to their case but also help to evaluate the data and to work toward solutions . . ." (p. 418).

Principle 7 expands the focus from the individual with the disability to a larger group including, not surprisingly, family members and those directly involved in the welfare of the PWD. Thus, caregivers, spouses, children, and significant others should be a part of the rehabilitation process to share perspectives, to be collaborators, and, as already noted, to provide social support.

An important caveat here for both the PWD and the professionals who provide care is that co-management entails active discussion, give and take, perhaps even debate (and some compromise) about treatment and related care issues. Active participation on the part of PWDs and their groups should not be mistaken by the rehabilitation team as merely a "cooperative attitude" (Wright, 1983, p. 417). PWDs must avoid playing the part of the "good patient" or the "good client," and the professionals who counsel them must not expect undue deference or enthusiastic agreement with all recommendations. In most circumstances, PWDs should retain control over their destinies. This observation is also germane to conducting research on the social psychology of disability or rehabilitation psychology more generally.

Disability Studies, Activism, and Rehabilitation Research: Toward Collaboration

Disability studies, a relatively new field of scholarship, and the discipline of psychology approach the study of disability from different vantage points and with distinct missions. As a result, there has been tension, not all of it constructive, between the perspectives and approaches individuals in each field use to explore the experience of disability. We begin by characterizing the focus and critiques of disability studies and disability activism and then consider the resulting implications for work in psychology concerning disability.

Disability Studies and Activism

The main goal of disability studies is to counter perspectives that disability is tragic and that PWDs are unfortunates who are to be pitied or, worse still, patronized, infantilized, and excluded aside from mainstream culture. As Siebers (2011) cogently stated:

> Disability studies does not treat disease or disability, hoping to cure or avoid them; it studies the social meanings, symbols, and stigmas attached to disability identity and asks how they relate to enforced systems of exclusion and oppression, attacking the widespread belief that having an able body and mind determines whether one is a quality human being. (pp. 3–4)

As a concept and construct, *disability* becomes a problem of and for society at large and not any particular individual with a disability (for overviews, see Goodley, 2011; Siebers, 2011).

The field of disability studies generally rejects the idea that a given disability can or even should be cured, which means that traditional medical approaches that have influenced the sciences—and to a considerable extent rehabilitation psychology—are routinely criticized for being too narrow in their focus, overpathologizing, resulting in unintended prejudice toward and objectification of PWDs. Siebers (2011), for example, notes that the field of disability studies not only fights oppression aimed at PWDs, but also argues that disability changes the tenor of discussions about societal rights and social policy. Thus, the field of disability studies engages in serious and often protracted debates about controversial issues linked to disability and PWDs, including assisted suicide (see also Olkin, 2005), genetic research, technologies designed to redress particular disabilities (e.g., cochlear implants), and abortion. As Siebers (2011) and others in the disability studies community suggest, policy issues that appear clear-cut to outsiders can become complex and nuanced when issues of power, civil rights, individual fates, and disability are considered.

Yet the responsibility of coping with the attendant consequences of disability is routinely placed on individual PWDs who must somehow "adjust" or "adapt" to their circumstances. Individual rather than societal responsibility (i.e., the person, not the situation) means that, in general, disability remains a personal problem; this represents the main point of contention the field of disability studies has with contemporary psychology (including rehabilitation psychology in particular; see below) and its approach to treating PWDs. Change or adaptation should not be goals exclusively required of the individual; rather, the field of disability studies argues for systemic change at all levels of society (e.g., laws, culture, politics, accessibility).

Disability activism, in turn, builds on the polemical arguments made by disability studies, hoping that structural changes are possible. Longmore (2003), for example, highlights key features of the disability rights movement, including the following:

- Seeing disability as a rallying point for collective empowerment and self-determination
- Changing the emphasis from correcting individuals to reforming society
- Contesting power held by policy professionals and bureaucrats
- Framing disability as a social and, in part, political problem, not a medical, rehabilitative, or individual problem
- Viewing social participation, integration, and the availability of services, access, accommodations, and ameliorative devices as a matter of civil rights, not charity or public expense.

At the same time that activists and theoreticians from disability studies are asserting the rights for PWDs to have greater independence in daily life, they are also seeking more meaningful levels of interdependence within society. These critical observations triggered some debate about the nature of research on disability issues in psychology.

Revisiting and Revising Psychological Research on Disability

Olkin and Pledger (2003) expressed concern that research on disability issues would remain limited for several reasons, chief among them that PWDs themselves rarely act as investigators but are primarily participants. These authors note that in contrast, scholarship in disability studies is very often conceived and executed by PWDs. Thus, their concern about progress in rehabilitation psychology (and, for present purposes, the social psychology of disability) can be summarized by the disability activist slogan "nothing about us without us."

More specifically, Olkin and Pledger (2003) point to research challenges such as the following:

- *Disability research is one of the few areas dealing with minority experience that has few minorities (i.e., PWDs) taking a lead in the research effort.*

Researchers who study race, ethnicity, women's issues, ageism, and sexual orientation, for example, are often representatives of the groups they study. In effect, the underrepresentation of researchers with disabilities creates genuine conceptual and structural problems for psychological research (e.g., insider–outsider issues, perceived legitimacy).

- *The current state of research efforts perpetuates a we–they divide.* Most investigators are not disabled whereas most or all research participants have disabilities. As Olkin and Pledger (2003) noted with more than a touch of irony, "Disability research is mostly 'outsider' research—by people without disabilities about people with disabilities" (p. 300). The social-psychological dynamics of the ingroup–outgroup processes should not be ignored here (recall Chapter 1), nor should the related issue of co-management of disability (recall the discussion in the previous section). At the same time, we must acknowledge that nondisabled investigators and practitioners make important contributions in rehabilitation psychology and related fields. The issue is one for which perhaps more balance on research teams is desirable.

- *Most disability and rehabilitation research does not incorporate issues of disability history and culture; rather, it tends to focus on issues of treatment (usually acute), adjustment, and adaptation.* Concerns emanating from medical models or linked to pathology linger in spite of scholarly advances focusing on a social model in which disability is viewed from a societal, chronic, life-span-oriented perspective or theories and insights from positive psychology (recall Chapter 7).

- *Despite the Lewinian focus on person–environment relations, existing research approaches do not fully embrace disability as a problem of civil rights, and social, legal, and economic concerns.* Although common, disability is still usually conceived of as a state or condition affecting an individual, not a group of people. In essence, the figure is still the focus and not the ground, the complex social environment or milieu that affects all PWDs.

Olkin and Pledger were also reiterating and extending observations about disability research made by Olkin (1997, 1999). In effect, research in rehabilitation psychology, including that focused on social-psychological factors, can be said to follow practices linked to traditional moral and medical models of disability (often referred to as Paradigm 1), whereas a newer approach, Paradigm 2, focuses on issues of social action, civil rights, and a more group-level of analysis. The two paradigms are summarized in Table 8.2.

To be sure, there were critical replies to Olkin and Pledger's (2003) concerns and to related views expressed by Pledger (2003) and Tate and Pledger (2003) regarding the content of and implications resulting from comparing the paradigms. Critiques of the approach used to study the experience of disability had appeared before. Fine and Asch (1988), for example, offered criticisms of primarily social-psychological

TABLE 8.2

TWO PARADIGMS FOR PSYCHOLOGICAL RESEARCH ON DISABILITY

Paradigm 1	Paradigm 2
Based on a Medical Model	Based on a Social Model
Pathology-orientation	Societal, systemic-orientation
Views differences as deficits or aberrations	Adopts a lifespan approach
Is typically cross-sectional	Uses the concept of "response" to disability as a fluid process
Sees PWDs and their families as at high risk for difficulties	Promotes health and resilience
Focused predominantly on intrapsychic, personal characteristics or intrapersonal variables	Usually focuses on the chronic phases of disability
Tends to focus on acute phases of disability onset or exacerbation	Values disability history and culture as well as interpersonal relationships
Is more likely to be conducted in inpatient or treatment settings	Incorporates those being researched into the research process
Uses the concept of "adjustment" or "adaptation" to disability	Sees the major problems of disability as social, political, economic, and legal
Uses norms based on able-bodied individuals for comparison	Is grounded in the belief that PWDs have been denied their civil rights
Is about, but rarely by, PWDs	Seeks remedies in public policy, legislation, and systemic programmatic changes
Perpetuates a we–they model	It usually not just about, but by, PWDs

Source: Adapted from Olkin and Pledger (2003, Table 2, p. 301).

approaches to disability that ignore person–environment relations and sometimes adopted a tragic or victimization perspective 15 years earlier. In a retort to the claimed advances of Paradigm 2, Thomas (2004), for example, noted that the new perspective was really neither particularly new nor revolutionary, that rehabilitation researchers had "long recognized the importance of the psychosocial aspects of disability and the interaction between persons and their environments" (p. 275). More recently, McCarthy (2014), too, claimed that much of Paradigm 2 is a logical extension of Paradigm 1 or, put another way, the person–environment approach of rehabilitation psychology is entirely compatible with the social model advanced by disability studies and psychologists who are aligned with its perspectives. Indeed, McCarthy reminds us that much of the early research in the social psychology of disability by Lewinian researchers such as Barker, Wright, and Gonick (1946) and Barker (1948) explored what is now known as the minority model of disability (see McCarthy, 2014).

Professional quarrels about which approach for studying the social psychology of disability is the "right" one are unnecessary and divisive. Instead, interested, committed researchers and practitioners should heed the observations and criticisms about the direction of psychosocial research on disability. No doubt that there is sufficient justification for expressing concern that the study of the experience of disability is often too focused at the level of factors that affect the *individual with a disability* (e.g., Olkin & Pledger, 2003). Perhaps we need a social psychology of disability that is more *social* or *societal*, one that combines the strengths of rehabilitation psychology and disability studies and examines disability more broadly—how it affects the lives of those close to PWDs as well as the PWDs themselves and the larger community in which both reside. In other words, a wider perspective on the person—or better still, persons—in situations and the role of disabilities therein.

Perhaps a more sophisticated approach to the social psychology of disability can forge a reasonable compromise between at least some aspects of Paradigms 1 and 2. Certainly, the focus on acute phases of disability onset and accompanying medical and psychological complications requires emphasis on individualized treatment and rehabilitation. Concerns with issues of adjustment gradually become useful in the short to medium term timeframe following disability onset. As individuals stabilize and adapt to the effects of disability, a longer term perspective focused on the context in which PWDs live and work will become more important. This arena entails the focus on social support from family and friends, available community resources, and related social, economic, legal, and political issues connected to disability.

Quality of life issues for PWDs assuredly entail health and well-being, but of greater concern should be access to assistive technologies for mobility, communication, and employment; education and (re)training; and supportive living environments, among other shared concerns (e.g., Olkin & Pledger, 2003). Recognition of cultural influences broadly defined (i.e., race, age, ethnicity, sexual orientation, gender, religion), folkways, and the structure of communities, too, should be considered (see Chronister & Johnson, 2009; Mpofu, Chronister, Johnson, & Denham, 2012).

There is a final concern regarding research involving PWDs: accessibility. Olkin (2004) discussed the fact that PWDs are routinely precluded from taking part in research aimed at understanding or ameliorating disability (and we must assume psychological research more generally) because of accessibility issues. PWDs are not recruited effectively, for example, nor are research materials (e.g., survey content, question phrasing, person first language) developed with different categories of disability in mind. These concerns are magnified when the matter of diversity within the disability community is considered; disabilities are heterogeneous. For research on the experience of disability to be generalizable and to address issues of importance, participant samples should be more representative. Olkin (2004) provides some helpful observations and suggestions that researchers and practitioners should consider when designing research projects about PWDs. Beyond issues of research participation, psychology should also work harder to recruit PWDs to pursue graduate education and careers in the discipline and profession of psychology (e.g., Andrews et al., 2013).

Looking Back, Looking Ahead

> Research that produces nothing but books will not suffice.
> KURT A. LEWIN (1948, p. 144)

The closing epigraph from Lewin (1948) serves as an important reminder. For the social psychology of disability to be useful, its observations, concepts, and insights must actually be used to improve the lives of PWDs and to promote understanding among those who have, do not have, or will develop a disability. In other words, constructs such as the insider–outsider distinction or coping versus succumbing frameworks must move from the classroom or library to the clinic and community where they will have practical and positive effects. Readers have a responsibility to share the implications of the person–environment relation in order to promote constructive views of life with disability and to counter naive, usually negative orambivalent, attitudes about disability. For their part, PWDs must remain active and adamant about their civil rights; they must continue to take charge of their lives and advocate for appropriate care and treatment, as well as complete community integration and access. Following Wright (1983), we must always remember that "The extent of limitations is as much a function of physical and social environmental barriers, if not more so, than of personal disability" (p. 479).

Questions

1. Why is the figure–ground metaphor from Gestalt psychology relevant to the person–environment relation? Why should the environment become a greater concern for research on the social psychology of disability?

2. Given the societal impact of the ADA, what is the macrocosm view of disability where advances are concerned? What work remains? Now consider the microcosm: Describe an ideal encounter between an outsider who is unfamiliar with disability and an insider.

3. Define social support and outline some of its guises. Why is social support presumed to be an important resource for PWDs? What would researchers and practitioners like to know about the social support and disability?

4. Describe some of the social support-related risks for caregivers and families of PWDs. Does the onset of disability provide any benefits?

5. Explain the role of PWDs as co-managers in the treatment and rehabilitation process. How does this role reflect the dynamic of the insider–outsider distinction in the social psychology of disability?

6. Among researchers who work in various subfields of psychology, what makes those who pursue rehabilitation psychology and the social psychology of disability stand out? Why do critics from, for example, disability studies raise this difference as a concern?

7. Compare and contrast the empirical perspectives associated with the so-called Paradigms 1 and 2. Are these two approaches truly dichotomous? Are there reasonable ways to compromise so as to approach practice and research for and with PWDs in ways that play to the strengths of both approaches?

8. What have you learned about the social psychology of disability? How will you advance the social psychology of disability in the future?

Notes

CHAPTER 1

1. Clinically, this view is embodied in the biopsychosocial model, which posits that physical and mental health are due to interactions among biological, psychological, and social factors (e.g., Rath & Elliott, 2011).

2. The issue of institutionalization is politically and socially charged, as there is evidence that most PWDs living in these settings could be cared for more humanely and cheaply at home (see Johnson, 2003; Shapiro, 1994).

CHAPTER 2

1. However, in rehabilitation psychology, the term *secondary gain* is pejorative, as it describes advantages a person gains by adopting or maintaining a sick role. Here and elsewhere in this book, secondary gains are used in the positive and adaptive social-psychological sense.

CHAPTER 3

1. People can also display a fundamental positive bias in their relations with others. This occurs when something perceived as salient, positive, and found in a vague context serves as a primary influence in channeling an individual's future perceptions, thoughts, and affect in a positive direction (Wright, 1988).

CHAPTER 5

1. A friend who is a rehabilitation psychologist told me of watching his graduate mentor promote a coping framework while working with a young man who had recently sustained a spinal cord injury. The mentor asked the young man, "Aren't you more than someone who walks?"

References

Abroms, K. I., & Kodera, T. L. (1979). Acceptance hierarchy of handicaps: Validation of Kirk's statement "Special education often begins where medicine stops." *Journal of Learning Disabilities, 12*, 15–20. doi: 10.1177/002221947901200104

Adcock, R. J., Goldberg, M. L., Patterson, D. R., & Brown, P. B. (2000). *Rehabilitation Psychology, 45*, 179–192. doi: 10.1037/0090-5550.45.2.179

Adler, A. B., Wright, B. A., & Ulicny, G. R. (1991). Fundraising portrayals of people with disabilities: Donations and attitudes. *Rehabilitation Psychology, 36*, 231–240. doi: 10.1037/h0079085

Adorno, T. W., Frenkel-Brunswik, E., Levinson, D. J., & Sanford, R. N. (1950). *The authoritarian personality*. New York, NY: Harper.

Albarracin, D., Johnson, B. T., & Zanna, M. P. (Eds.). (2005). *The handbook of attitudes*. Mahwah, NJ: Erlbaum.

Albrecht, G. L. (1996). Using subjective health assessments in practice and policy making. *Health Care Analysis, 4*, 284–292.

Albrecht, G. L., & Devlieger, P. J. (1999). The disability paradox: High quality of life against all odds. *Social Science & Medicine, 48*, 977–988. doi: 10.1016/S0277-9536(98)00411-0

Alloy, L. B., Albright, J. S., Abramson, L. Y., & Dykman, B. M. (1990). Depressive realism and nondepressive optimistic illusions: The role of the self. In R. E. Ingram (Ed.), *Contemporary psychological approaches to depression: Theory, research, and treatment*. New York, NY: Plenum. doi: 10.1007/978-1-4613-0649-8_6

Allport, F. H. (1924). *Social psychology*. Boston, MA: Houghton Mifflin.

Allport, G. W. (1954a). *The nature of prejudice*. Reading, MA: Addison-Wesley.

Allport, G. W. (1954b). The historical background of modern social psychology. In G. Lindzey (Ed.), *Handbook of social psychology* (Vol. 1, pp. 3–56). Cambridge, MA: Addison-Wesley.

Allport, G. W. (1985). The historical background of social psychology. In G. Lindzey & E. Aronson (Eds.), *Handbook of social psychology: Vol. 1. Theory & methods* (3rd ed., pp. 1–46). New York, NY: Random House.

Altermatt, T. W., & DeWall, C. N. (2003). Agency and virtue: Dimensions underlying subgroups of women. *Sex Roles, 49,* 631–641. doi: 10.1023/B:SERS.0000003133.90488.71

Altman, B. M. (1981). Studies of attitudes toward the handicapped: The need for new direction. *Social Problems, 28,* 321–337. doi: 10.2307/800306

Americans With Disabilities Act of 1990, Pub. L. No. 101–336, 104 Stat. 327 (1991).

American Psychological Association. (1994). *Publication manual of the American Psychological Association* (4th ed.). Washington, DC: Author.

American Psychological Association. (2000). *Enhancing your interactions with people with disabilities.* Retrieved from http://www.apa.org/pi/disability/resources/publications/enhancing.aspx?item=1

American Psychological Association. (2010a). *Publication manual of the American Psychological Association* (6th ed.). Washington, DC: Author.

American Psychological Association. (2010b). *Interacting with our members who have disabilities.* Retrieved from http://www.apa.org/pi/disability/resources/interacting-disabilities.aspx

American Psychological Association. (2012a). Guidelines for assessment of and intervention with persons with disabilities. *American Psychologist, 67,* 43–62. doi: 10.1037/a0025892

American Psychological Association. (2012b). *The road to resilience: 10 ways to build resilience.* Retrieved from http://www.apa.org/helpcenter/road-resilience.aspx

Amsel, R., & Fichten, C. S. (1988). Effects of contact on thoughts about interaction with students who have a physical disability. *Journal of Rehabilitation, 54,* 61–65.

Anderson, K. J. (2010). *Benign bigotry: The psychology of subtle prejudice.* New York, NY: Cambridge University Press.

Andrews, E. E., Kuemmel, A., Williams, J. L., Pilarski, C. R., Dunn, M., & Land, E. M. (2013). Providing culturally competent supervision to trainees with disabilities in rehabilitation settings. *Rehabilitation Psychology, 58,* 233–244. doi: 10.1037/a0033338

Antonak, R. F. (1979). An ordering-theoretic analysis of attitudes toward disabled persons. *Rehabilitation Psychology, 26,* 136–144. doi: 10.1037/h0090918

Antonak, R. F. (1981). Psychometric analysis of the Attitude Toward Disabled Persons Scale, Form-O. *Rehabilitation Counseling Bulletin, 23,* 169–176.

Antonak, R. F. (1982). Development and psychometric analysis of the Scale of Attitudes Toward Disabled Persons. *The Journal of Applied Rehabilitation Counseling, 13,* 22–29.

Antonak, R. F., & Livneh, H. (1988). *Measurement of attitudes toward people with disabilities: Methods, psychometrics and scales.* Springfield, IL: Charles C Thomas.

Antonak, R. F., & Livneh, H. (2000). Measurement of attitudes toward persons with disabilities. *Disability and Rehabilitation: An International, Multidisciplinary Journal, 22,* 211–224.

Antonovsky, A. (1987). *Unraveling the mystery of health: How people manage stress and stay well.* San Francisco, CA: Jossey-Bass.

Aristotle. (1984). *Complete works. Revised Oxford translation in 2 volumes* (J. Barnes, Ed.). Princeton, NJ: Princeton University Press.

Arkes, H. R., & Tetlock, P. E. (2004). Attributions of implicit prejudice, or "Would Jesse Jackson "fail" the Implicit Association Test." *Psychological Inquiry, 15,* 257–278. doi: 10.1207/s15327965pli1504_01

Aronson, J., Lustina, M. J., Good, C., Keough, K., Steele, C. M., & Brown, J. (1999). White men can't do math: Necessary and sufficient factors in stereotype threat. *Journal of Experimental Social Psychology, 35*, 29–46. doi: 10.1006/jesp.1998.1371

Asch, S. E. (1946). Forming impressions of personality. *Journal of Abnormal and Social Psychology, 41*, 258–290. doi: 10.1037/h0055756

Aspinwall, L. G. (2001). Dealing with adversity: Self-regulation, coping, adaptation, and health. In A. Tesser & N. Schwartz (Eds.), *The Blackwell handbook of social psychology: Vol. 1. Intraindividual processes* (pp. 591–614). Malden, MA: Blackwell.

Aspinwall, L. G., & Staudinger, U. M. (Eds.). (2003). *A psychology of human strengths: Fundamental questions and future directions for a positive psychology*. Washington, DC: American Psychological Association.

Bachelder, J. (1989). Effectiveness of a simulation activity to promote positive attitudes and perceptions of the elderly. *Educational Gerontology, 15*, 363–375. doi: 10.1080/0380127890150404

Ballard, M., Corman, L., Gottlieb, J., & Kaufman, M. J. (1977). Improving the social status of mainstreamed retarded children. *Journal of Educational Psychology, 69*, 605–611. doi: 10.1037/0022-0663.69.5.605

Baltes, P. B., Gluck, J., & Kunzman, U. (2002). Wisdom: Its structure and function in regulating successful life span development. In C. R. Snyder & S. J. Lopez (Eds.), *Handbook of positive psychology* (pp. 327–347). New York, NY: Oxford University Press.

Banaji, M. R., & Heiphetz, L. (2010). Attitudes. In S. T. Fiske, D. Gilbert, & G. Lindzey (Eds.), *Handbook of social psychology* (5th ed., Vol. 1, pp. 353–393). Hoboken, NJ: Wiley.

Bandura, A. (1978). The self system in reciprocal determinism. *American Psychologist, 33*, 344–358. doi: 10.1037/0003-066X.33.4.344

Bargh, J. A., Chaiken, S., Raymond, P., & Hymes, C. (1996). The automatic evaluation effect: Unconditional automatic attitude activation with a pronunciation task. *Journal of Experimental Social Psychology, 32*, 104–128. doi: 10.1006/jesp.1996.0005

Barker, R. G. (1947). The somatopsychologic problem. *Psychosomatic Medicine, 9*, 192–196.

Barker, R. G. (1948). The social psychology of physical disability. *Journal of Social Issues, 4*(4), 28–37. doi: 10.1111/j.1540-4560.1948.tb01516.x

Barker, R. G., Wright, B. A., & Gonick, M. R. (1946). *Adjustment to physical handicap and illness: A survey of the social psychology of physique and disability (Bulletin No. 55)*. New York, NY: Social Science Research Council. doi: 10.1037/11780-000

Barker, R. G., Wright, B. A., Meyerson, L., & Gonick, M. R. (1953). *Adjustment to physical handicap and illness: A survey of the social psychology of physique and disability* (2nd ed.). New York, NY: Social Science Research Council.

Baumeister, R. F. (2011). The self. In R. F. Baumeister & E. J. Finkel (Eds.), *Advanced social psychology: The state of the science* (pp. 139–175). New York, NY: Oxford University Press.

Baumeister, R. F., Bratslavsky, E., Finkenauer, C., & Vohs, K. D. (2001). Bad is stronger than good. *Review of General Psychology, 5*, 323–370. doi: 10.1037/1089-2680.5.4.323

Baumeister, R. F., & Finkel, E. J. (2010). *Advanced social psychology: The state of the science*. New York, NY: Oxford University Press.

Baumeister, R. F., & Vohs, K. D. (2002). The pursuit of meaningfulness in life. In C. R. Snyder & S. J. Lopez (Eds.), *Handbook of positive psychology* (pp. 608–618). New York, NY: Oxford University Press.

Belgrave, F. Z. (1991). Psychosocial predictors of adjustment to disability in African Americans. *Journal of Rehabilitation, 57*, 37–40.

Bem, D. J. (1970). *Beliefs, attitudes, and human affairs*. Belmont, CA: Brooks/Cole.

Benham, P. K. (1988). Attitudes of occupational therapy personnel toward people with disabilities. *American Journal of Occupational Therapy, 42*, 305–311. doi: 10.5014/ajot.42.5.305

Berscheid, E., & Walster, E. (1974). Physical attractiveness. In L. Berkowitz (Ed.), *Advances in experimental social psychology* (Vol. 7, pp. 157–215). New York, NY: Academic Press.

Biswas-Diener, R. (2013, April 6). *One myth of positive psychology clearly explained: How science is spun into myth*. Retrieved from http://www.psychologytoday.com/blog/significant-results/201304/one-myth-positive-psychology-clearly-explained

Bloom, P. (2010). *How pleasure works: The new science of why we like what we like*. New York, NY: Norton.

Bodenhamer, E., Achterberg-Lawlis, J., Kevorkian, G., Belanus, A., & Cofer, J. (1983). Staff and patient perceptions of the psychosocial concerns of spinal cord injured persons. *American Journal of Physical Medicine, 62*, 182–193.

Bogart, K. R. (2014). The role of disability self-concepts in adaptation to congenital or acquired disability. *Rehabilitation Psychology, 59*, 107–115. doi: 10.1037/a0035800

Bonanno, G. A. (2004). Loss, trauma, and human resilience: Have we underestimated the human capacity to thrive after extremely aversive events? *American Psychologist, 59*, 20–28. doi: 10.1037/0003-066X.59.1.20

Bower, J. E., Kemeny, M. E., Taylor, S. E., & Fahey, J. L. (1998). Cognitive processing, discovery of meaning, CD 4 decline, and AIDS-related mortality among bereaved HIV-seropositive men. *Journal of Consulting and Clinical Psychology, 66*, 979–986. doi: 10.1037/0022-006X.66.6.979

Boyce, W. (1998). Participation of disability advocates in research partnerships with health professionals. *Canadian Journal of Rehabilitation, 12*, 85–93.

Boyd, N. F., Sutherland, H. J., Heasman, K. Z., Tritchler, D. L., & Cummings, B. J. (1990). Whose utilities for decision analysis? *Medical Decision Making, 10*, 58–67. doi: 10.1177/0272989X9001000109

Brault, M. W. (2012). *Americans with Disabilities: 2010. Current Population Reports, P70–131*. Washington, DC: U. S. Census Bureau.

Breckler, S. J. (1984). Empirical validation of affect, behavior, and cognition as distinct components of attitude. *Journal of Personality and Social Psychology, 37*, 917–927.

Brehm, J. W. (1966). *A theory of psychological reactance*. New York, NY: Academic Press.

Brehm, S. S., & Brehm, J. W. (1981). *Psychological reactance*. New York, NY: Wiley.

Brendl, C. M., Markman, A. B., & Messner, C. (2001). How do indirect measures of evaluation work? Evaluating the inference of prejudice in the Implicit Association test. *Journal of Personality and Social Psychology, 81*, 760–773. doi: 10.1037/0022-3514.81.5.760

Brewer, M. B., & Brown, R. J. (1998). Intergroup relations. In D. T. Gilbert, S. T. Fiske, & G. Lindzey (Eds.), *The handbook of social psychology* (4th ed., Vol. 2). New York, NY: McGraw-Hill.

Brickman, P., & Campbell, D. T. (1971). Hedonic relativism and planning the good society. In M. H. Appley (Ed.), *Adaptation level theory: A symposium* (pp. 287–302). New York, NY: Academic Press.

Brickman, P., Coates, D., & Janoff-Bulman, R. (1978). Lottery winners and accident victims: Is happiness relative? *Journal of Personality and Social Psychology, 36*(8), 917–927. doi: 10.1037/0022-3514.36.8.917

Brissette, I., Cohen, S., & Seeman, T. E. (2000). Measuring social integration and social network. In S. Cohen, L. Underwood, & B. H. Gottlieb (Eds.), *Social support measurement and intervention* (pp. 53–85). New York, NY: Oxford University Press.

Brodwin, M. G., & Orange, L. M. (2002). Attitudes toward disability. In J. D. Andrew & C. W. Faubion (Eds.), *Rehabilitation services: An introduction for the human service professional* (pp. 174–197). Osage Beach, MO: Aspen Professional Services.

Brown, S. L., Nesse, R. M., Vinokur, A. D., & Smith, D. M. (2003). Providing social support may be more beneficial than receiving it: Results from a prospective study of mortality. *Psychological Science, 14,* 320–327. doi: 10.1111/1467-9280.14461

Bruyère, S. M., & O'Keefe, J. (1994). *Implications of the Americans With Disabilities Act for psychology.* Washington, DC: American Psychological Association.

Bruyère, S. M., & Peterson, D. B. (2005). Introduction to the special section on the International Classification of Functioning, Disability, and Health (ICF): Implications for rehabilitation psychology. *Rehabilitation Psychology, 50,* 103–104. doi: 10.1037/0090-5550.50.2.103

Buckingham, J. T., & Alicke, M. D. (2002). The influence of individual versus aggregate social comparison and the presence of others on self-evaluations. *Journal of Personality and Social Psychology, 83,* 1117–1130. doi: 10.1037/0022-3514.83.5.1117

Bulman, R. J., & Wortman, C. B. (1977). Attributions of blame and coping in the "real world": Severe accident victims react to their lot. *Journal of Personality and Social Psychology, 35,* 351–363. doi: 10.1037/0022-3514.35.5.351

Burgstahler, S., & Doe, T. (2004). Disability-related simulations: If, when, and how to use them. *Review of Disability Studies, 1*(2), 4–17.

Burkhead, E. J., Deborah, J., & Marini, I. (1996). Humor, coping, and adaptation to disability. *Journal of Applied Rehabilitation Counseling, 27,* 50–53.

Byrd, E. K., & Elliott, T. R. (1988). Media and disability: A discussion of research. In H. E. Yuker (Ed.), *Attitudes toward persons with disabilities* (pp. 82–95). New York, NY: Springer.

Cacioppo, J. T., Gardener, W. L., & Bernston, G. G. (1997). Beyond bipolar conceptualizations and measures: The case of attitudes and evaluative space. *Personality and Social Psychology Review, 1,* 3–25. doi: 10.1207/s15327957pspr0101_2

Callahan, J. (1990). *Don't worry, he won't get far on foot.* New York, NY: Vintage.

Calhoun, L., & Tedeschi, R. (Eds.). (2006). *Handbook on posttraumatic growth: Research and practice.* Mahwah, NJ: Erlbaum.

Cameron, L., Rutland, A., Turner, R., Holman-Nicolas, R., & Powell, C. (2011). "Changing attitudes with a little imagination": Imagined contact effects on young children's intergroup bias. *Anales de Psicologia, 27*(3), 708–717.

Campbell, J. D., Assanand, S., & DiPaula, A. (2000). Structural features of the self-concept and adjustment. In A. Tesser, R. B. Felson, & J. M. Suls (Eds.), *Psychological perspectives on self and identity* (pp. 67–87). Washington, DC: American Psychological Association. doi: 10.1037/10357-003

Caplan, B. (1995). Choose your words! *Rehabilitation Psychology, 40,* 233–240.

Caplan, B., & Shechter, J. (1987). Depression and denial in disabling illness. In B. Caplan (Ed.), *Rehabilitation psychology desk reference* (pp. 133–170). Rockville, MD: Aspen Systems Corporation.

Caplan, B., & Shechter, J. (1993). Reflections on the "depressed," "unrealistic," "inappropriate," "manipulative," "unmotivated," "noncompliant," "denying," "maladjusted," "regressed," etc. patient. *Archives of Physical Medicine and Rehabilitation, 74,* 1123–1124.

Carver, C. S., Scheier, M. F., Miller, C. J., & Fulford, D. (2009). Optimism. In S. J. Lopez & C. R. Snyder (Eds.), *The Oxford handbook of positive psychology* (pp. 303–311). New York, NY: Oxford University Press. doi: 10.1093/oxfordhb/9780195187243.013.0028

Chan, C. C., Lee, T. M. C., Yuen, H. K., & Chan, F. (2002). Attitudes towards people with disabilities between Chinese rehabilitation and business students: An implication for practice. *Rehabilitation Psychology, 47*, 324–338. doi: 10.1037/0090-5550.47.3.324

Chan, F., da Silva Cordoso, E., & Chronister, J. A. (Eds.). (2009). *Understanding psychosocial adjustment to chronic illness and disability: A handbook for evidence-based practitioners in rehabilitation.* New York, NY: Springer.

Chan, F., Livneh, H., Pruett, S., Wang, C.-C., & Zheng, L. X. (2009a). Societal attitudes toward disability: Concepts, measurements, and interventions. In F. Chan, E. da Silva Cordoso, & J. A. Chronister (Eds.), *Understanding psychosocial adjustment to chronic illness and disability: A handbook for evidence-based practitioners in rehabilitation* (pp. 333–367). New York, NY: Springer.

Chan, F., Tarvydas, V., Blalock, K., Strause, D., & Atkins, B. (2009b). Unifying and elevating rehabilitation counseling through model-driven, diversity-sensitive evidence-based practice. *Rehabilitation Counseling Bulletin, 52*, 114–119. doi: 10.1177/0034355208323947

Charlton, J. I. (1998). *Nothing about us without us: Disability oppression and empowerment.* Berkeley, CA: University of California Press. doi: 10.1525/california/9780520207950.001.0001

Chen, R., Brodwin, M. G., Cardoso, E., & Chan, F. (2002). Attitudes toward people with disabilities in the social context of dating and marriage: A comparison of American, Taiwanese, and Singaporean college students. *Journal of Rehabilitation, 68*, 5–11.

Chou, C.-C., Lee, E.-J., Catalano, D. E., Ditchman, N., & Wilson, L. M. (2009). Positive psychology and psychosocial adjustment to chronic illness and disability. In F. Chan, E. Da Silva Cardoso, & J. A. Chronister (Eds.), *Understanding psychosocial adjustment to chronic illness and disability: A handbook for evidence-based practitioners in rehabilitation* (pp. 207–241). New York, NY: Springer.

Chronister, J. (2009). Social support and rehabilitation: Theory, research, and measurement. In F. Chan, E. Da Silva Cardoso, & J. A. Chronister (Eds.), *Understanding psychosocial adjustment to chronic illness and disability: A handbook for evidence-based practitioners in rehabilitation* (pp. 149–183). New York, NY: Springer.

Chronister, J. A., Chou, C. C., Frain, M., & Cardoso, E. (2008). The relationship between social support and rehabilitation related outcomes: A meta-analysis. *Journal of Rehabilitation, 74*, 16–32.

Chronister, J., & Johnson, E. (2009). Multiculturalism and adjustment to disability. In F. Chan, E. Da Silva Cardoso, & J. A. Chronister (Eds.), *Understanding psychosocial adjustment to chronic illness and disability: A handbook for evidence-based practitioners in rehabilitation* (pp. 479–518). New York, NY: Springer.

Chwalisz, K., & Vaux, A. (2000). Social support and adjustment to disability. In R. G. Frank & T. R. Elliott (Eds.), *Handbook of rehabilitation psychology* (pp. 537–563). Washington, DC: American Psychological Association. doi: 10.1037/10361-025

Clanton, L. D., Rude, S., & Taylor, C. (1992). Learned resourcefulness as a moderator of burnout in a sample of rehabilitation providers. *Rehabilitation Psychology, 37*, 131–140. doi: 10.1037/h0079105

Clunies-Ross, G., & O'Meara, K. (1989). Changing the attitudes of students toward peers with disabilities. *Australian Psychologist, 24*, 273–284. doi: 10.1080/00050068908259566

Cohen, S. (1988). Psychosocial models of social support in the etiology of physical disease. *Health Psychology, 7*, 269–297. doi: 10.1037/0278-6133.7.3.269

Cohen, S., & Syme, S. L. (Eds.). (1985). *Social support and health.* San Diego, CA: Academic Press. doi: 10.1037/0033-2909.98.2.310

Cohen, S., & Wills, T. A. (1985). Social support, stress, and the buffering hypothesis. *Psychological Bulletin, 98*, 310–357.

Cohler, B. J. (2007). *Writing desire: Sixty years of gay autobiography.* Madison, WI: University of Wisconsin Press.

Cole, J. (2004). *Still lives: Narratives of spinal cord injury.* London, England: Bradford Books.

Collins, R. L., Taylor, S. E., & Skokan, L. A. (1990). A better world or a shattered vision? Changes in life perspective following victimization. *Social Cognition, 8*, 263–285. doi: 10.1521/soco.1990.8.3.263

Comer, R. J., & Piliavin, J. A. (1972). The effects of physical deviance upon face to face interaction: The other side. *Journal of Personality and Social Psychology, 23*, 33–39. doi: 10.1037/h0032922

Compton, W. C. (2004). *An introduction to positive psychology.* Belmont, CA: Thompson-Wadsworth.

Corrigan, P. W. (Ed.). (2014). *The stigma of disease and disability: Understanding causes and overcoming injustices.* Washington, DC: American Psychological Association.

Corrigan, P. W., & Watson, A. C. (2002). Understanding the impact of stigma on people with mental illness. *World Psychiatry, 1*(1), 16–20.

Corrigan, P. W., River, L. P., Lundin, R. K., Uphoff Wasowski, K., Campion, J., Mathisen, J., et al. (2000). Stigmatizing attributions about mental illness. *Journal of Community Psychology, 28*(1), 91–102. doi: 10.1002/(SICI)1520-6629(200001)28:1<91::AID-JCOP9>3.0.CO;2-M

Craig, A. (2012). Resilience in people with physical disabilities. In P. Kennedy (Ed.), *Oxford handbook of rehabilitation psychology* (pp. 474–491). New York, NY: Oxford University Press. doi: 10.1093/oxfordhb/9780199733989.013.0026

Crewe, N. (1993). Spousal relationships and disability. In F. P. Haseltine, S. Cole, & D. Gray (Eds.), *Reproductive issues for persons with physical disabilities* (pp. 141–151). Baltimore, MD: Paul H. Brookes.

Crisp, R. J., & Turner, R. N. (2009). Can imagined interactions produce positive perceptions? Reducing prejudice through simulated social contact. *American Psychologist, 64*, 231–240. doi: 10.1037/a0014718

Crisp, R. J., & Turner, R. N. (2013). Imagined group contact: Refinements, debates, and clarifications. In G. Hodson & M. Hewstone (Eds.), *Advances in intergroup contact* (pp. 135–151). New York, NY: Psychology Press.

Crocker, J., Major, B., & Steele, C. (1998). Social stigma. In D. T. Gilbert, S. T. Fiske, & G. Lindzey (Eds.), *The handbook of social psychology* (4th ed., Vol. 2, pp. 504–553). New York, NY: McGraw-Hill.

Csikszentmihalyi, M. (1990). *Flow: The psychology of optimal experience.* New York, NY: Harper & Row.

Cuddy, A. J. C., Fiske, S. T., & Glick, P. (2007). The BIAS map: Behaviors from intergroup affect and stereotypes. *Journal of Personality and Social Psychology, 92*, 631–648. doi: 10.1037/0022-3514.92.4.631

Cuddy, A. J. C., Fiske, S. T., & Glick, P. (2008). Warmth and competence as universal dimensions of social perception: The stereotype content model and the BIAS map. In M. P. Zanna (Ed.), *Advances in Experimental Social Psychology* (Vol. 40, pp. 61–149). New York, NY: Academic Press.

Cushman, L. A., & Dijkers, M. (1990). Depressed mood in spinal cord injured patients: Staff perceptions and patient realities. *Archives of Physical Medicine and Rehabilitation*, *71*, 191–196.

Darling, R. B. (2013). *Disability and identity: Negotiating self in a changing society*. Boulder, CO: Lynne Rienner Publishers.

Deal, M. (2007). Aversive disablism: Subtle prejudice toward disabled people. *Disability and Society*, *22*, 93–107. doi: 10.1080/09687590601056667

Delle Fave, A. (2006). The impact of subjective experiences on the quality of life: A central issue for health professionals. In M. Csikszentmihalyi & I. S. Csikszentmihalyi (Eds.), *A life worth living: Contributions to positive psychology* (pp. 165–181). New York, NY: Oxford University Press.

Dembo, T. (1964). Sensitivity of one person to another. *Rehabilitation Literature*, *25*, 231–235.

Dembo, T. (1969). Rehabilitation psychology and its immediate future: A problem of utilization of psychological knowledge. *Rehabilitation Psychology*, *16*, 63–72.

Dembo, T. (1970). The utilization of psychological knowledge in rehabilitation. *Welfare Review*, *8*, 1–7.

Dembo, T. (1982). Some problems in rehabilitation as seen by a Lewinan. *Journal of Social Issues*, *38*, 131–139. doi: 10.1111/j.1540-4560.1982.tb00848.x

Dembo, T., Leviton, G. L., & Wright, B. A. (1975). Adjustment to misfortune: A problem of social-psychological rehabilitation. *Rehabilitation Psychology*, *22*(1), 1–100. doi: 10.1037/h0090832

Dembo, T., Leviton, G., & Wright, B. A. (1956). Adjustment to misfortune—a problem of social-psychological rehabilitation. *Artificial Limbs*, *3*(2), 4–62.

de Montaigne, M. (1991). *The complete essays* (M. A. Screech, Trans.). New York, NY: Penguin. (Original work published 1580)

de N Abrantes-Pais, F., Friedman, J. K., Lovallo, W. R., & Ross, E. D. (2007). Psychological or physiological: Why are tetraplegic patients content? *Neurology*, *49*, 261–267.

Dickerson, S. S., & Zoccola, P. M. (2009). Toward a biology of social support. In S. J. Lopez & C. R. Snyder (Eds.), *Oxford handbook of positive psychology* (2nd ed., pp. 519–526). New York, NY: Oxford University Press. doi: 10.1093/oxfordhb/9780195187243.013.0049

Diener, E. (1980). Deindividuation: The absence of self-awareness and self-regulation in group members. In P. B. Paulus (Ed.), *Psychology of group influence* (pp. 209–242). Hillsdale, NJ: Erlbaum.

Diener, E. (1984). Subjective well-being. *Psychological Bulletin*, *95*, 542–575. doi: 10.1037/0033-2909.95.3.542

Diener, E. (2008). Myths in the science of happiness, and directions for future research. In M. Eid & R. J. Larsen (Eds.), *The science of subjective well-being* (pp. 493–514). New York, NY: Guilford Press.

Diener, E., & Biswas-Diener, R. (2008). *Happiness: Unlocking the mysteries of psychological wealth*. Malden, MA: Wiley-Blackwell.

Diener, E., Fraser, S. C., Beaman, A. L., & Kelem, R. T. (1976). Effects of deindividuation variables on stealing among Halloween trick-or-treaters. *Journal of Personality and Social Psychology, 33*, 178–183. doi: 10.1037/0022-3514.33.2.178

Diener, E., Lucas, R. E., & Scollon, C. N. (2006). Beyond the hedonic treadmill: Revising the adaptation theory of well-being. *American Psychologist, 61*, 305–314. doi: 10.1037/0003-066X.61.4.305

Diener, E., Oishi, S., & Lucas, R. E. (2003). Personality, culture, and subjective well-being: Emotional and cognitive evaluations of life. *Annual Review of Psychology, 54*, 403–425. doi: 10.1146/annurev.psych.54.101601.145056

Diener, E., & Suh, E. M. (Eds.). (2000). *Culture and subjective well-being.* Cambridge, MA: MIT Press.

Diener, E., Suh, E. M., Lucas, R. E., & Smith, H. L. (1999). Subjective well-being: Three decades of progress. *Psychological Bulletin, 125*, 276–302. doi: 10.1037/0033-2909.125.2.276

Dijkers, M. (1997). Quality of life after spinal cord injury: A meta-analysis of the effects of the disablement components. *Spinal Cord, 35*, 829–840. doi: 10.1038/sj.sc.3100571

Dijkers, M. P. J. M. (2005). Quality of life of individuals with spinal cord injury: A review of conceptualization, measurement, and research findings. *Journal of Rehabilitation Research and Development, 42*, 87–110. doi: 10.1682/JRRD.2004.08.0100

Dijkers, M., & Cushman, L. A. (1990). Differences between rehabilitation disciplines in views of depression in spinal cord injury patients. *Paraplegia, 28*, 380–391. doi: 10.1038/sc.1990.51

Dion, K. K., Berscheid, E., & Walster, E. (1972). What is beautiful is good. *Journal of Personality and Social Psychology, 24*, 285–290. doi: 10.1037/h0033731

Dovidio, J. F., & Fazio, R. F. (1992). New technologies for direct and indirect assessment of attitudes. In J. Tanur (Ed.), *Questions about survey questions: Meaning, memory, attitudes, and social interaction* (pp. 204–237). New York, NY: Russell Sage Foundation.

Dovidio, J. F., & Gaertner, S. L. (2004). Aversive racism. In M. P. Zanna (Ed.), *Advances in experimental social psychology* (Vol. 36, pp. 1–51). San Diego, CA: Academic Press.

Dovidio, J. F., & Gaertner, S. L. (2010). Intergroup bias. In S. T. Fiske, D. Gilbert, & G. Lindzey (Eds.), *Handbook of social psychology* (5th ed., Vol. 2, pp. 1084–1121). Hoboken, NJ: Wiley.

Dovidio, J. F., Glick, P., & Rudman, L. A. (Eds.). (2005). *On the nature of prejudice: Fifty years after Allport.* Malden, MA: Blackwell. doi: 10.1002/9780470773963

Dovidio, J. F., Kawakami, K., Johnson, C., Johnson, B., & Howard, A. (1997). On the nature of prejudice: Automatic and controlled processes. *Journal of Experimental Social Psychology, 33*, 510–540. doi: 10.1006/jesp.1997.1331

Dovidio, J. F., Major, B., & Crocker, J. (2000). Stigma: Introduction and overview. In T. F. Heatherton, R. E. Kleck, M. R. Hebl, & J. G. Hull (Eds.), *The social psychology of stigma* (pp. 1–28). New York, NY: Guilford.

Dovidio, J. F., Pagotto, L., & Hebl, M. R. (2011). Implicit attitudes and discrimination against people with physical disabilities. In R. L. Wiener & S. L. Wilborn (Eds.), *Disability and age discrimination: Perspectives in law and psychology* (pp. 157–184). New York, NY: Springer. doi: 10.1007/978-1-4419-6293-5_9

Drolsbaugh, M. (1996). *What is deaf pride?* Retrieved from http://www.ldpride.net/deafpride.htm

Duckworth, A. L., Peterson, C., Matthews, M. D., & Kelly, D. R. (2007). Grit: Perseverance and passion for long-term goals. *Journal of Personality and Social Psychology, 92*(6), 1087–1101. doi: 10.1037/0022-3514.92.6.1087

Duggan, C. H., & Dijkers, M. (2001). Quality of life after spinal cord injury: A qualitative study. *Rehabilitation Psychology, 46*, 3–27. doi: 10.1037/0090-5550.46.1.3

Dunn, D. S. (1994). Positive meaning and illusions following disability: Reality negotiation, normative interpretation, and value change. *Journal of Social Behavior and Personality, 9*(5), 123–138.

Dunn, D. S. (1996). Well-being following amputation: Salutary effects of positive meaning, optimism, and control. *Rehabilitation Psychology, 41*, 285–302. doi: 10.1037/0090-5550.41.4.285

Dunn, D. S. (2005). Negotiating realities to understand others: Teaching about meaning and well-being. *Journal of Social and Clinical Psychology, 24*, 30–40. doi: 10.1521/jscp.24.1.30.59176

Dunn, D. S. (2010). The social psychology of disability. In R. G. Frank, B. Caplan, & M. Rosenthal (Eds.), *Handbook of rehabilitation psychology* (2nd ed., pp. 379–390). Washington, DC: American Psychological Association.

Dunn, D. S. (2011). Situations matter: Teaching the Lewinian link between social psychology and rehabilitation psychology. *Journal of the History of Psychology, 14*(4), 405–411. doi: 10.1037/a0023919

Dunn, D. S. (2013). *Research methods for social psychology* (2nd ed.). Hoboken, NJ: Wiley.

Dunn, D. S., & Brody, C. (2008). Defining the good life following acquired physical disability. *Rehabilitation Psychology, 53*(4), 413–425. doi: 10.1037/a0013749

Dunn, D. S., & Burcaw, S. (2013). Disability identity: Exploring first person accounts of disability experience. *Rehabilitation Psychology, 58*, 148–157. doi: 10.1037/a0031691

Dunn, D. S., & Dougherty, S. B. (2005). Prospects for a positive psychology of rehabilitation. *Rehabilitation Psychology, 50*, 305–311.

Dunn, D. S., & Elliott, T. R. (2005). Revisiting a constructive classic: Wright's *Physical Disability: A Psychosocial Approach. Rehabilitation Psychology, 50*, 183–189. doi: 10.1037/0090-5550.50.2.183

Dunn, D. S., & Elliott, T. R. (2008). The place and promise of theory in rehabilitation psychology research. *Rehabilitation Psychology, 53*, 254–267. doi: 10.1037/a0012962

Dunn, D. S., Fisher, D. J., & Beard, B. M. (2012). Revisiting the mine-thine problem: A sensitizing exercise for clinic, classroom, and attributional research. *Rehabilitation Psychology, 57*, 113–123. doi: 10.1037/a0027967

Dunn, D. S., Fisher, D., & Beard, B. (2013). Disability as diversity rather than (in)difference: Understanding others' experiences through one's own. In D. S. Dunn, R. A. R. Gurung, K. Naufel, & J. H. Wilson (Eds.), *Controversy in the psychology classroom: Using hot topics to foster critical thinking* (pp. 209–223). Washington, DC: American Psychological Association. doi: 10.1037/14038-013

Dunn, D. S., & Hammer, E. (2014). On teaching multicultural psychology. In F.T. L. Leong, L. Comas-Diaz, G. Nagayama Hall, & J. Trimble (Eds.), *APA handbook of multicultural psychology: Vol. 1: Theory and Research* (pp. 43–58). Washington, DC: American Psychological Association. doi: 10.1037/14189-003

Dunn, D. S., Uswatte, G., & Elliott, T. R. (2009). Happiness, resilience and positive growth following physical disability: Issues for understanding, research, and therapeutic intervention. In

S. J. Lopez & C. R. Snyder (Eds.), *Oxford handbook of positive psychology* (2nd ed., pp. 651–664). New York: Oxford University Press. doi: 10.1093/oxfordhb/9780195187243.013.0062

Dunning, D., Heath, C., & Suls, J. M. (2004). Flawed self-assessment: Implications for health, education, and the workplace. *Psychological Science in the Public Interest, 5*(3), 69–106. doi: 10.1111/j.1529-1006.2004.00018.x

Eagly, A. H., Ashmore, R. D., Makhijani, M. G., & Longo, L. C. (1991). What is beautiful is good, but . . .: A meta-analytic review of research on the physical attractiveness stereotype. *Psychological Bulletin, 110,* 107–128. doi: 10.1037/0033-2909.110.1.109

Eagly, A. H., & Chaiken, S. (1993). *The psychology of attitudes.* Fort Worth, TX: Harcourt.

Ehde, D. M. (2010). Application of positive psychology to rehabilitation psychology. In R. Frank, M. Rosenthal, & B. Caplan (Eds.), *Handbook of rehabilitation psychology* (2nd ed., pp. 417–424). Washington, DC: American Psychological Association.

Eid, M., & Larsen, R. J. (Eds.). (2008). *The science of subjective well-being.* New York, NY: Guilford Press.

Elliott, T. R. (2002). Psychological explanations of personal journeys: Hope for a positive psychology in theory, practice, and policy. *Psychological Inquiry, 13,* 295–298.

Elliott, T. R., Herrick, S. M., & Witty, T. E. (1992). Problem-solving appraisal and the effects of social support among college students and persons with disabilities. *Journal of Counseling Psychology, 39,* 219–226. doi: 10.1037/0022-0167.39.2.219

Elliott, T. R., & Kennedy, P. (2004). Treatment of depression following spinal cord injury: An evidence-based review. *Rehabilitation Psychology, 49,* 134–139. doi: 10.1037/0090-5550.49.2.134

Elliott, T. R., & Kurylo, M. (2000). Hope over disability: Lessons from one young woman's triumph. In C. R. Snyder (Ed.), *The handbook of hope: Theory, measurement, and interventions* (pp. 373–386). New York, NY: Academic Press. doi: 10.1016/B978-012654050-5/50022-1

Elliott, T. R., Kurylo, M., & Rivera, P. (2002). Positive growth following acquired physical disability. In C. R. Snyder & S. J. Lopez (Eds.), *Handbook of positive psychology* (pp. 687–699). New York, NY: Oxford University Press.

Elliott, T. R., MacNair, R. R., Yoder, B., & Byrne, C. A. (1991). Interpersonal behavior moderates "kindness norm" effects on cognitive and affective reactions to physical disability. *Rehabilitation Psychology, 36*(1), 57–66. doi: 10.1037/h0079071

Elliott, T. R., & Shewchuk, R. M. (2004). Family adaptation in illness, disease, and disability. In J. M. Raczynski & L. C. Leviton (Eds.), *Handbook of clinical health psychology: Volume 2. Disorders of behavior and health* (pp. 379–403). Washington, DC: American Psychological Association.

Elliott, T. R., Shewchuk, R. M., & Richards, J. S. (1999). Caregiver social problem-solving abilities and family member adjustment to recent-onset physical disability. *Rehabilitation Psychology, 44,* 104–123. doi: 10.1037/0090-5550.44.1.104

Epstein, R. A., Heinemann, A. W., & McFarland, L. V. (2010). Quality of life in veterans and service members with major traumatic limb loss from Vietnam and OIF/OEF conflicts. *Journal of Rehabilitation Research and Development, 47,* 373–385. doi: 10.1682/JRRD.2009.03.0023

Erikson, E. H. (1963). *Childhood and society.* New York, NY: Norton.

Erikson, E. H. (1968). *Identity: Youth and crisis.* New York, NY: Norton.

Ernst, F. A. (1987). Contrasting perceptions of distress by research personnel and their spinal cord injured subjects. *American Journal of Physical Medicine, 66,* 12–15.

Fein, S., & Spencer, S. J. (1997). Prejudice as self-image maintenance: Affirming the self though derogating others. *Journal of Personality and Social Psychology, 73*, 31–44. doi: 10.1037/0022-3514.73.1.31

Feingold, A. (1992). Good-looking people are not what we think. *Psychological Bulletin, 111*, 304–341. doi: 10.1037/0033-2909.111.2.304

Fenrick, N. J., & Petersen, T. K. (1984). Developing positive attitude changes in attitudes towards moderately/severely handicapped students through a peer tutoring program. *Education and Training of the Mentally Retarded, 19*, 83–90.

Fergus, S., & Zimmerman, M. A. (2005). Adolescent resilience: A framework for understanding healthy development in the face of risk. *Annual Review of Public Health, 26*, 399–419. doi: 10.1146/annurev.publhealth.26.021304.144357

Festinger, L. (1954). A theory of social comparison processes. *Human Relations, 7*, 117–140. doi: 10.1177/001872675400700202

Festinger, L. (1957). *A theory of cognitive dissonance.* Stanford, CA: Stanford University Press.

Fichman, L., Koestner, R., Zuroff, D. C., & Gordon, L. (1999). Depressive styles and the regulation of negative affect: A daily experience study. *Cognitive Therapy and Research, 23*, 483–495. doi: 10.1023/A:1018768320680

Fichten, C. S., Amsel, R., Bourdon, C. V., & Creti, L. (1988). Interaction between college students with physical disabilities and their professors. *Journal of Applied Rehabilitation Counseling, 19*, 13–20. doi: 10.1037/h0079074

Fichten, C. S., Robillard, K., Tagalakis, V., & Amsel, R. (1991). Casual interaction between college students with various disabilities and their nondisabled peers: The internal dialogue. *Rehabilitation Psychology, 32*, 3–20.

Findler, L., Vilchinsky, N., & Werner, S. (2007). The Multidimensional Attitude Scale toward persons with disabilities (MAS): Construction and validation. *Rehabilitation Counseling Bulletin, 50*(3), 166–176. doi: 10.1177/0034355207050030401

Fine, M., & Asch, A. (1988). Disability beyond stigma: Social interaction, discrimination, and activism. *Journal of Social Issues, 44*, 3–21. doi: 10.1111/j.1540-4560.1988.tb02045.x

Fiske, S. T. (2005). Social cognition and the normality of prejudgment. In J. F. Dovidio, P. Glick, & L. A. Rudman (Eds.), *On the nature of prejudice: Fifty years after Allport* (pp. 36–53). Malden, MA: Blackwell. doi: 10.1002/9780470773963.ch3

Fiske, S. T. (2011). *Envy up, scorn down: How status divides us.* New York, NY: Russell Sage Foundation.

Fiske, S. T., Cuddy, A. J. C., Glick, P., & Xu, J. (2002). A model of (often mixed) stereotype content: Competence and warmth respectively follow from perceived status and competition. *Journal of Personality and Social Psychology, 82*, 878–902. doi: 10.1037/0022-3514.82.6.878

Fiske, S. T., & Taylor, S. E. (2008). *Social cognition: From brains to culture.* New York, NY: McGraw-Hill.

Fleig, L., Pomp, S., Schwarzer, R., & Lippke, S. (2013). Promoting exercise maintenance: How interventions with booster sessions improve long-term rehabilitation outcomes. *Rehabilitation Psychology, 58*(4), 323–333. doi: 10.1037/a0033885

Florian, V., Katz, S., & Lahav, V. (1989). Impact of traumatic brain damage on family dynamics and functioning: A review. *Brain Injury, 3*, 219–233. doi: 10.3109/02699058909029637

Ford, A. B., Liske, R. E., & Ort, R. S. (1962). Reactions of physicians and medical students to chronic illness. *Journal of Chronic Diseases, 15*, 785–794. doi: 10.1016/0021-9681(62)90049-8

Frank, R. G., & Elliott, T. (1987). Life stress and psychological adjustment to spinal cord injury. *Archives of Physical Medicine and Rehabilitation, 68,* 344–347.

Frank, R. G., Rosenthal, M., & Caplan, B. (Eds.). (2010). *Handbook of rehabilitation psychology* (2nd ed.). Washington, DC: American Psychological Association.

Frankl, V. E. (1985). *Man's search for meaning* (Rev. & updated). New York, NY: Washington Square Press.

Fredrickson, B. L. (1998). What good are positive emotions? *Review of General Psychology, 2,* 300–319. doi: 10.1037/1089-2680.2.3.300

Fredrickson, B. L., Tugade, M. M., Waugh, C. E., & Larkin, G. (2003). What good are positive emotions in crises?: A prospective student of resilience and emotions following the terrorist attacks in the United States on September 11, 2001. *Journal of Personality and Social Psychology, 84,* 365–376. doi: 10.1037/0022-3514.84.2.365

Freedman, V. A. (2012). Disability, participation, and subjective well-being in older couples. *Social Science and Medicine, 74,* 588–596. doi: 10.1016/j.socscimed.2011.10.018

Frost, N. (2011). *Qualitative research methods in psychology.* Berkshire, England: Open University Press.

Gable, S. L., Reis, H. T., Impett, E. A., & Asher, E. R. (2004). What do you do when things go right? The intrapersonal and interpersonal benefits of sharing positive events. *Journal of Personality and Social Psychology, 87,* 228–245. doi: 10.1037/0022-3514.87.2.228

Gaertner, S. L., & Dovidio, J. F. (1986). The aversive form of racism. In J. F. Dovidio & S. L. Gaertner (Eds.), *Prejudice, discrimination, and racism* (pp. 61–89). Orlando, FL: Academic Press.

Gaertner, S. L., Dovidio, J. F., & Houlette, M. A. (2010). Social categorization. In J. F. Dovidio, M. Hewstone, P. Glick, & V. M. Esses (Eds.), *Handbook of prejudice, stereotyping, and discrimination* (pp. 526–543). London, England: Sage. doi: 10.4135/9781446200919.n32

Gibson, J. (2009). Navigating social norms: The psychological implications of living in the United States with a disability. In C. A. Marshall, E. Kendall, M. E. Banks, & R. M. S. Gover (Eds.), *Disabilities: Insights from across fields and around the world* (Vol. 2, pp. 139–150). Westport, CT: Praeger.

Gilbert, D. T. (2006). *Stumbling on happiness.* New York, NY: Knopf.

Gilbert, D. T., & Hixon, J. G. (1991). The trouble of thinking: Activation and application of stereotypic beliefs. *Journal of Personality and Social Psychology, 60,* 509–517. doi: 10.1037/0022-3514.60.4.509

Gilbert, D. T., Lieberman, M. D., Morewedge, C., & Wilson, T. D. (2004). The peculiar longevity of things not so bad. *Psychological Science, 15,* 14–19. doi: 10.1111/j.0963-7214.2004.01501003.x

Gilbert, D. T., & Malone, P. S. (1995). The correspondence bias. *Psychological Bulletin, 117,* 21–38. doi: 10.1037/0033-2909.117.1.21

Gilbert, D. T., Pinel, E. C., Wilson, T. D., Blumberg, S. J., & Wheatley, T. P. (1998). Immune neglect: A source of durability bias in affective forecasting. *Journal of Personality and Social Psychology, 75,* 617–638. doi: 10.1037/0022-3514.75.3.617

Gill, C. J. (1995). A psychological view of disability culture. *Disabilities Studies Quarterly, 15*(4), 15–19.

Gill, C. J. (1997). Four types of integration in disability identity development. *Journal of Vocational Rehabilitation, 9,* 39–46. doi: 10.1016/S1052-2263(97)00020-2

Gillham, J. E., & Seligman, M. E. P. (1999). Footsteps on the road to a positive psychology. *Behaviour Research and Therapy, 37*, S163–S173. doi: 10.1016/S0005-7967(99)00055-8

Gilovich, T. (1991). *How we know what isn't so.* New York, NY: Free Press.

Gilovich, T., Griffin, D. W., & Kahneman, D. (Eds.). (2002). *Heuristics and biases: The psychology of intuitive judgment.* New York, NY: Cambridge University Press. doi: 10.1017/CBO9780511808098

Ginis, K., Latimer, A. E., McKechnie, K., Ditor, D. S., McCartney, N., Hicks, A. L., &. . . Craven, B. (2003). Using exercise to enhance subjective well-being among people with spinal cord injury: The mediating influences of stress and pain. *Rehabilitation Psychology, 48*(3), 157–164. doi: 10.1037/0090-5550.48.3.157

Glover-Graf, N. M. (2012). Family adaptation across cultures toward a loved one who is disabled. In I. Marini, N. M. Glover-Graf, & M. J. Millington (Eds.), *Psychosocial aspects of disability: New perspectives and counseling strategies* (pp. 169–189). New York, NY: Springer.

Goffman, E. (1963). *Stigma: Notes on the management of spoiled identity.* Englewood Cliffs, NJ: Prentice-Hall.

Goodley, D. (2011). *Disability studies: An interdisciplinary introduction.* Thousand Oaks, CA: Sage.

Gottlieb, J., Corman, L., & Curci, R. (1984). Attitudes toward mentally retarded children. In R. L. Jones (Ed.), *Attitude and attitude change in special education: Theory and practice* (pp. 143–156). Reston, VA: Council for Exceptional Children.

Gouvier, W. D., Coon, R. C., Todd, M. E., & Fuller, K. H. (1994). Verbal interaction with individuals presenting with or without physical disabilities. *Rehabilitation Psychology, 39*, 263–268. doi: 10.1037/h0080322

Greenwald, A. G., & Banaji, M. R. (1995). Implicit social cognition: Attitudes, self-esteem, and stereotypes. *Psychological Review, 102*, 4–27. doi: 10.1037/0033-295X.102.1.4

Greenwald, A. G., McGhee, D. E., & Schwartz, J. K. L. (1998). Measuring individual differences in implicit cognition: The implicit association test. *Journal of Personality and Social Psychology, 74*, 1464–1480. doi: 10.1037/0022-3514.74.6.1464

Greenwald, A. G., Poehlman, T. A., Uhlmann, E. L., & Banaji, M. R. (2009). Understanding and using the Implicit Association Test: III. Meta-analysis of predictive validity. *Journal of Personality and Social Psychology, 97*, 17–41. doi: 10.1037/a0015575

Greszta, E., & Sieminska, M. J. (2011). Patient-perceived changes in the system of values after cancer diagnosis. *Journal of Clinical Psychology in Medical Settings, 18*, 55–64. doi: 10.1007/s10880-011-9221-z

Groomes, D. A. G., & Linkowski, D. C. (2007). Examining the structure of the revised Acceptance of Disability Scale. *Journal of Rehabilitation, 73*(3), 3–9.

Hahn, H. (1988). The politics of physical differences: Disability and discrimination. *Journal of Social Issues, 44*, 39–48. doi: 10.1111/j.1540-4560.1988.tb02047.x

Hahn, H. D., & Belt, T. L. (2004). Disability identity and attitudes toward cure in a sample of disabled activists. *Journal of Health and Social Behavior, 45*, 453–464. doi: 10.1177/002214650404500407

Haidt, J. (2005). *The happiness hypothesis: Finding modern truth in ancient wisdom.* New York, NY: Basic Books.

Hamera, E. K., & Shontz, F. C. (1978). Perceived positive and negative effects of life-threatening illness. *Journal of Psychosomatic Research, 22*, 419–424. doi: 10.1016/0022-3999(78)90064-8

Hammell, K. W. (2004). Exploring quality of life following high spinal cord injury: A review and critique. *Spinal Cord, 42*, 491–502. doi: 10.1038/sj.sc.3101636

Harris, R. M., & Harris, A. C. (1977). Devaluation of the disabled in fund raising appeals. *Rehabilitation Psychology, 24*, 69–78. doi: 10.1037/h0090915

Hastorf, A. H., Northcraft, G., & Picciotto, S. (1979). Helping the handicapped: How realistic is the performance feedback received by the physically handicapped? *Personality and Social Psychology Bulletin, 5*, 373–376. doi: 10.1177/014616727900500321

Hebl, M., & Kleck, R. E. (2000). The social consequences of physical disability. In T. F. Heatherton, R. E. Kleck, M. R. Hebl, & J. G. Hull (Eds.), *Stigma: Social psychological perspectives* (pp. 419–440). New York, NY: Guilford.

Heider, F. (1926). Ding und medium. *Symposium, 1*, 109–157.

Heider, F. (1958). *The psychology of interpersonal relations*. New York, NY: Wiley. doi: 10.1037/10628-000

Heinemann, A. W., Bulka, M., & Smetak, S. (1988). Attributions and disability acceptance following traumatic injury: A replication and extension. *Rehabilitation Psychology, 33*, 195–206.

Heinemann, A. W., & Shontz, F. C. (1982). Acceptance of disability, self-esteem, sex role identity, and reading aptitude in deaf adolescents. *Rehabilitation Counseling Bulletin, 25*, 197–203.

Helgeson, V. S. (1994). Relation of agency and communion to well-being: Evidence and potential explanations. *Psychological Bulletin, 116*, 421–428. doi: 10.1037/0033-2909.116.3.412

Helgeson, V. S., & Fritz, H. L. (1999). Unmitigated agency and unmitigated communion: Distinctions from agency and communion. *Journal of Research in Personality, 33*, 131–158. doi: 10.1006/jrpe.1999.2241

Helgeson, V. S., & Fritz, H. L. (2000). The implications of unmitigated agency and unmitigated communion for domains of problem behavior. *Journal of Personality, 68*, 1031–1057. doi: 10.1111/1467-6494.00125

Helson, H. (1964). *Adaptation-level theory*. New York, NY: Harper & Row.

Hevern, V. W. (2008). Why narrative psychology can't afford to ignore the body. Special Issue: Proceedings of the 2nd Annual Meeting of the Northeastern Evolutionary Psychology Society. *Journal of Social, Evolutionary, and Cultural Psychology, 2*(4), 217–233.

Higgins, R. L., & Gallagher, M. W. (2009). Reality negotiation. In S. J. Lopez & C. R. Snyder (Eds.), *Oxford handbook of positive psychology* (pp. 475–482). New York, NY: Oxford University Press. doi: 10.1093/oxfordhb/9780195187243.013.0045

Hirschberger, G., Florian, V., & Mikulincer, M. (2005). Fear and compassion: A terror management analysis of emotional reactions to physical disability. *Rehabilitation Psychology, 50*, 246–257. doi: 10.1037/0090-5550.50.3.246

Hochschild, A. R. (2012). *The managed heart: Commercialization of human feeling* (Rev. ed.). Berkeley, CA: University of California Press.

Holland, J. C., & Lewis, S. (2000). *The human side of cancer: Living with hope and coping with uncertainty*. New York, NY: Harper Collins.

Hollingsworth, D. K., Johnson, W. C., Jr., & Cook, S. W. (1989). Beatrice A. Wright: Broad lens, sharp focus. *Journal of Counseling and Development, 67*, 384–393. doi: 10.1002/j.1556-6676.1989.tb02098.x

Hurst, N. P., Jobanputra, P., Hunter, M., Lambert, M., Lochhead, A., & Brown, H. (1994). Validity of Euroqol—a generic health status instrument—in patients with rheumatoid arthritis. *British Journal of Rheumatology, 33*, 655–662. doi: 10.1093/rheumatology/33.7.655

Image Center Blog. (2011, March 11). The halo effect. Retrieved on March 12, 2013 from http://www.imagemd.org/blog/archives/29

Jahoda, M. (1958). *Current concepts of positive mental health.* New York, NY: Basic Books. doi: 10.1037/11258-000

Janoff-Bulman, R. (1992). *Shattered assumptions: Towards a new psychology of trauma.* New York, NY: Free Press.

Janoff-Bulman, R., & Frieze, I. H. (1983). A theoretical perspective for understanding reactions to victimization. *Journal of Social Issues, 39,* 1–17. doi: 10.1111/j.1540-4560.1983.tb00138.x

Johnson, H. B. (2003a, February 16). Unspeakable conversations. *The New York Times Magazine, 152,* 74–79.

Johnson, H. B. (2003b, November 23). The disability gulag. *The New York Times Magazine, 153,* 58–64.

Johnson, H. B. (2005). *Too late to die young: Nearly true tales from a life.* New York, NY: Henry Holt.

Johnson, H. B. (2006). *Accidents of nature:* New York, NY: Henry Holt.

Johnson, M. (2003). *Make them go away: Clint Eastwood, Christopher Reeve, and the case against disability rights.* Louisville, KY: The Avocado Press.

Johnson-Greene, D., & Touradji, P. (2010). Assessment of personality and psychopathology. In R. G. Frank, M. Rosenthal, & B. Caplan (Eds.), *Handbook of rehabilitation psychology* (2nd ed., pp. 195–211). Washington, DC: American Psychological Association.

Jones, E. E. (1998). Major developments in five decades of social psychology. In D. T. Gilbert, S. T. Fiske, & G. Lindzey (Eds.), *The handbook of social psychology* (4th ed., Vol. 1, pp. 3–57). New York, NY: McGraw-Hill.

Jones, E. E., Farina, A., Hastorf, A. H., Markus, H., Miller, D. T., & Scott, R. A. (1984). *Social stigma: The psychology of marked relationships.* New York, NY: Freeman and Company.

Jones, E. E., & Nisbett, R. E. (1971). The actor and the observer: Divergent perceptions of the causes of behavior. In E. E. Jones, D. E. Kanouse, H. H. Kelley, R. E. Nisbett, S. Valins, & B. Weiner (Eds.), *Attribution: Perceiving the causes of behavior* (pp. 79–94). Morristown, NJ: General Learning Press.

Jones, E. E., & Sigall, H. (1971). The bogus pipeline technique: A new paradigm for measuring affect and attitude. *Psychological Bulletin, 76,* 349–364. doi: 10.1037/h0031617

Josselson, R., & Harway, M. (Eds.). (2012). *Navigating multiple identities: Race, gender, culture and roles.* New York, NY: Oxford University Press. doi: 10.1093/acprof:oso/9780199732074.001.0001

Juergens, M., & Smedema, S. (2009). Sexuality and disability. In F. Chan, E. Da Silva Cardoso, & J. A. Chronister (Eds.), *Understanding psychosocial adjustment to chronic illness and disability: A handbook for evidence-based practitioners in rehabilitation* (pp. 443–478). New York, NY: Springer.

Kahneman, D. (2000). Experienced utility and objective happiness: A moment-based approach. In D. Kahneman & A. Tversky (Eds.), *Choices, values, and frames* (pp. 673–692). New York, NY: Russell Sage Foundation and Cambridge University Press.

Kahneman, D. (2011). *Thinking, fast and slow.* New York, NY: Farrar, Straus, and Giroux.

Kasser, T. (2002). *The high price of materialism.* Cambridge, MA: MIT Press.

Katz, D. (1960). The functional approach to the study of attitudes. *Public Opinion Quarterly, 24*(2), 163–205. doi: 10.1086/266945

Katz, I. (1981). *Stigma: A social psychological analysis.* Hillsdale, NJ: Erlbaum.

Katz, I., Glass, D. C., Lucidio, D., & Farber, J. (1977). Ambivalence, guilt, and denigration of a physically handicapped victim. *Journal of Personality, 47,* 419–429. doi: 10.1111/j.1467-6494.1979.tb00207.x

Katz, I., Glass, D. C., Lucidio, D., & Farber, J. (1979). Harm-doing and victim's racial or orthopedic stigma as determinants of helping behavior. *Journal of Personality, 47,* 340–364. doi: 10.1111/j.1467-6494.1979.tb00207.x

Katz, I., Hass, R. G., & Bailey, J. (1988). Attitudinal ambivalence and behavior toward people with disabilities. In H. E. Yuker (Ed.), *Attitudes toward persons with disabilities* (pp. 47–57). New York, NY: Springer.

Katz, I., Wackenhut, J., & Haas, R. G. (1986). Racial ambivalence, value duality, and behavior. In J. F. Dovidio & S. L. Gaertner (Eds.), *Prejudice, discrimination, and racism* (pp. 35–59). Orlando, FL: Academic Press.

Keany, K. C. M-H., & Glueckauf, R. L. (1993). Disability and value change: An overview and reanalysis of acceptance of loss theory. *Rehabilitation Psychology, 38,* 199–210. doi: 10.1037/h0080297

Kelley, H. H. (1950). The warm-cold variable in the first impressions of persons. *Journal of Personality, 18,* 431–439. doi: 10.1111/j.1467-6494.1950.tb01260.x

Kelley, H. H. (1967). Attribution theory in social psychology. In D. Levine (Ed.), *Nebraska symposium on motivation* (Vol. 15, pp. 192–238). Lincoln, NE: University of Nebraska Press.

Kelley, H. H. (1973). Process of causal attribution. *American Psychologist, 28,* 107–128. doi: 10.1037/h0034225

Kendell, K., Saxby, B., Farrow, M., & Naisby, C. (2001). Psychological factors associated with short-term recovery from total knee replacement. *British Journal of Health Psychology, 6,* 41–52. doi: 10.1348/135910701169043

Kenworthy, J. B., Turner, R. N., Hewstone, M., & Voci, A. (2005). Intergroup contact: When does it work, and why? In J. F. Dovidio, P. Glick, & L. A. Rudman (Eds.), *On the nature of prejudice: Fifty years after Allport* (pp. 278–292). Malden, MA: Blackwell. doi: 10.1002/9780470773963.ch17

Kerr, N. (1961). Understanding the process of adjustment to disability. *Journal of Rehabilitation, 27*(6), 16–18.

Keyes, C. L. M., & Haidt, J. (Eds.). (2003). *Flourishing: Positive psychology and the life well-lived.* Washington, DC: American Psychological Association. doi: 10.1037/10594-000

Kleck, R. E. (1968). Physical stigma and nonverbal cues emitted in face to face interactions. *Human Relations, 21,* 19–28. doi: 10.1177/001872676802100102

Kleck, R. E. (1969). Physical stigma and task oriented interactions. *Human Relations, 22,* 53–60. doi: 10.1177/001872676902200103

Kleck, R. E., Ono, H., & Hastorf, A. (1966). The effects of physical deviance upon face-to-face interaction. *Human Relations, 19,* 425–436. doi: 10.1177/001872676601900406

Knowles, D. (2013, April 22). Dance teacher who lost foot in Boston Marathon bombing vows to dance again and run in next year's marathon. *New York Daily News.* Retrieved from http://www.nydailynews.com/news/national/boston-amputee-vows-dance-article-1.1324519

Koch, T. (2004). The difference that difference makes: Bioethics and the challenge of "disability." *Journal of Medicine and Philosophy, 29*(6), 697–716. doi: 10.1080/03605310490882975

Kortte, K. B., Stevenson, J. E., Hosey, M. H., Castillo, R., & Wegener, S. T. (2012). Hope predicts positive functional role outcomes in acute rehabilitation populations. *Rehabilitation Psychology, 57,* 248–255. doi: 10.1037/a0029004

Kozloff, R. (1987). Networks of social support and the outcome from severe head injury. *Journal of Head Trauma and Rehabilitation, 2,* 14–23. doi: 10.1097/00001199-198709000-00004

Kravetz, S., Katz, S., & Albez, D. (1994). Attitudes toward Israeli war veterans with disabilities: Combat versus noncombat military service and responsibility for disability. *Rehabilitation Counseling Bulletin, 37,* 371–379.

Kuiper, N. A., & Martin, R. A. (1998). Laughter and stress in daily life: Relation to positive and negative affect. *Motivation And Emotion, 22*(2), 133–153. doi: 10.1023/A:1021392305352

Kuyper, H., & Dijkstra, P. (2009). Better-than-average effects in secondary education: A 3-year follow-up. *Educational Research and Evaluation, 15,* 167–184. doi: 10.1080/13803610902804416

Langer, E. J., Fiske, S., Taylor, S. E., & Chanowitz, B. (1976). Stigma, staring, and discomfort: A novel-stimulus hypothesis. *Journal of Experimental Social Psychology, 12,* 451–463. doi : 10.1016/0022-1031(76)90077-9

LaPiere, R. T. (1934). Attitudes vs. actions. *Social Forces, 13,* 230–237. doi: 10.2307/2570339

Larsen, R. J., & Prizmic, Z. (2008). Regulation of emotional well-being: Overcoming the hedonic treadmill. In M. Eid & R. J. Larsen (Eds.), *The science of subjective well-being* (pp. 258–289). New York, NY: Guilford.

Lazarus, R. S., & Folkman, S. (1984). *Stress, appraisal, and coping.* New York, NY: Springer.

Lea, M., Spears, R., & de Groot, D. (2001). Knowing me, knowing you: Anonymity effects on social identity processes within groups. *Personality and Social Psychology Bulletin, 27,* 526–537. doi: 10.1177/0146167201275002

Lechner, S. C., Tennen, H., & Affleck, G. (2009). Benefit-finding and growth. In S. J. Lopez & C. R. Snyder (Eds.), *Oxford handbook of positive psychology* (2nd ed., pp. 633–640). New York, NY: Oxford University Press. doi: 10.1093/oxfordhb/9780195187243.013.0060

Leek, D. F. (1966). *Formation of impressions of persons with a disability.* Unpublished master's thesis, University of Kansas, Lawrence.

Lehman, D. R., Wortman, C. B., & Williams, A. F. (1987). Long-term effects of losing a spouse or child in a motor vehicle crash. *Journal of Personality and Social Psychology, 52,* 218–231. doi: 10.1037/0022-3514.52.1.218

Lerner, M. J. (1980). *The belief in a just world: A fundamental delusion.* New York, NY: Plenum Press.

Levinskas, A. (1997). Prevalence of mine/thine phenomenon across dissimilar individuals. *Dissertation Abstracts International Section A: Humanities and Social Sciences, 58*(3-A), 0738.

Levy, J. M., Jessop, D. J., Rimmerman, A., & Levy, P. H. (1993). Attitudes of executives in Fortune 500 corporations toward the employability of persons with severe disabilities: Industrial and service corporations. *Journal of Applied Rehabilitation Counseling, 24,* 19–31.

Lewin, K. A. (1935). *A dynamic theory of personality.* New York, NY: McGraw-Hill.

Lewin, K. A. (1948/1997). *Resolving social conflicts: Field theory in social science.* Washington, DC: American Psychological Association.

Lewinsohn, P. M., Clarke, G. N., & Hops, H. (1990). Cognitive-behavioral treatment for depressed adolescents. *Behavior Therapy, 21,* 385–401. doi 10.1016/S0005-7894(05)80353-3

Li, L., & Moore, D. (1998). Acceptance of disability and its correlates. *The Journal of Social Psychology, 138*(1), 13–25. doi: 10.1080/00224549809600349

Liesener, J. J., & Mills, J. (1999). An experimental study of disability spread: Talking to an adult in a wheelchair like a child. *Journal of Applied Social Psychology, 29,* 2083–2092. doi: 10.1111/j.1559-1816.1999.tb02296.x

Linacre, J., Heinemann, A. W., Wright, B. D., Granger, C. V., & Hamilton, B. B. (1994). The structure and stability of the Functional Independence Measure. *Archives of Physical Medicine and Rehabilitation, 75,* 127–132.

Lincoln, Y. S., & Guba, E. G. (1985). *Naturalistic inquiry.* Newbury Park, CA: Sage.

Linkowski, D. C. (1971). A scale to measure acceptance of disability. *Rehabilitation Counseling Bulletin, 14,* 236–244.

Linton, S. (2007). *My body politic: A memoir.* Ann Arbor, MI: University of Michigan Press.

Linville, P. W. (1985). Self-complexity and affective extremity: Don't put all of your eggs in one cognitive basket. *Social Cognition, 3*(1), 94–120. doi: 10.1521/soco.1985.3.1.94

Linville, P. W. (1987). Self-complexity as a cognitive buffer against stress-related illness and depression. *Journal of Personality and Social Psychology, 52*(4), 663–676. doi: 10.1037/0022-3514.52.4.663

Linville, P. W., & Jones, E. E. (1980). Polarized appraisals of outgroup members. *Journal of Personality and Social Psychology, 38,* 689–703. doi: 10.1037/0022-3514.38.5.689

Livneh, H. (1980). The process of adjustment to disability: Feelings, behaviors, and counseling strategies. *Psychosocial Rehabilitation Journal, 4,* 26–35.

Livneh, H. (1982). On the origin of negative attitudes toward people with disabilities. *Rehabilitation Literature, 43,* 338–347.

Livneh, H. (1987). Person-environment congruence: A rehabilitation perspective. *International Journal of Rehabilitation Research, 10,* 3–19. doi: 10.1097/00004356-198703000-00001

Livneh, H. (1988). A dimensional perspective on the origin of negative attitudes toward persons with disabilities. In H. E. Yuker (Ed.), *Attitudes toward persons with disabilities* (pp. 35–46). New York, NY: Springer.

Livneh, H., & Antonak, R. F. (1997). *Psychosocial adaptation to chronic illness and disability.* Gaithersburg, MD: Aspen.

Locksley, A., Ortiz, V., & Hepburn, C. (1980). Social categorization and discriminatory behavior: Extinguishing the minimal intergroup discrimination effect. *Journal of Personality and Social Psychology, 39*(5), 773–783. doi: 10.1037/0022-3514.39.5.773

Loewenstein, G., O'Donoghue, T., & Rabin, M. (2003). Projection bias in predicting future utility. *Quarterly Journal of Economics, 118,* 1209–1248. doi: 10.1162/003355303322552784

Longmore, P. K. (1985). A note on language and the social identity of disabled people. *American Behavioral Scientist, 28,* 419–423. doi: 10.1177/000276485028003009

Lopez, S. J., & Snyder, C. R. (Eds.). (2003). *Positive psychological assessment: A handbook of models and measures.* Washington, DC: American Psychological Association. doi: 10.1037/10612-000

Lopez, S. J., & Snyder, C. R. (Eds.). (2009). *Oxford handbook of positive psychology* (2nd ed.). New York, NY: Oxford University Press. doi: 10.1093/oxfordhb/9780195187243.001.0001

Lucas, R. (2007a). Adaptation and the set-point model of subjective well-being: Does happiness change after major life events. *Current Directions in Psychological Science, 16,* 75–79. doi: 10.1111/j.1467-8721.2007.00479.x

Lucas, R. (2007b). Long-term disability is associated with lasting changes in subjective-well being: Evidence from two nationally representative longitudinal studies. *Journal of Personality and Social Psychology, 92,* 717–730. doi: 10.1037/0022-3514.92.4.717

Lucas, R. E., Dyrenforth, P. S., & Diener, E. (2008). Four myths about subjective well-being. *Social and Personality Psychology Compass, 2*, 2001–2015. doi: 10.1111/j.1751-9004.2008.001 40.x

Luthans, F., & Youssef, C. M. (2009). Positive workplaces. In S. J. Lopez & C. R. Snyder (Eds.), *Oxford handbook of positive psychology* (2nd ed., pp. 579–588). New York, NY: Oxford University Press. doi: 10.1093/oxfordhb/9780195187243.013.0055

Lyubomirsky, S. (2008). *The how of happiness: A new approach to getting the life you want.* New York, NY: Penguin.

Lyubomirsky, S. (2013). *The myths of happiness: What should make you happy, but doesn't, what shouldn't make you happy, but does.* New York, NY: Penguin.

Lyubomirsky, S., Sheldon, K. M., & Schkade, D. (2005). Pursuing happiness: The architecture of sustainable change. *Review of General Psychology, 9*, 111–131. doi: 10.1037/1089-2680.9.2.111

MacCann, C., & Roberts, R. D. (2010). Do time management, grit, and self-control relate to academic achievement independently of conscientiousness? In R. E. Hicks (Ed.), *Personality and individual differences: Current directions* (pp. 79–90). Bowen Hills, QLD Australia: Australian Academic Press.

MacMillan, D. L., & Morrison, G. M. (1984). Sociometric research in special education. In R. L. Jones (Ed.), *Attitude and attitude change in special education: Theory and research* (pp. 70–92). Reston, VA: Council for Exceptional Children.

Macrae, C. N., & Bodenhausen, G. V. (2001). Social cognition: Categorical person perception. *British Journal of Social Psychology, 92*, 239–255.

Maddi, S. R., Matthews, M. D., Kelly, D. R., Villarreal, B., & White, M. (2012). The role of hardiness and grit in predicting performance and retention of USMA cadets. *Military Psychology, 24*(1), 19–28. doi: 10.1080/08995605.2012.639672

Maggio, R. (1991). *The bias-free word finder: A dictionary of nondiscriminatory language.* Boston, MA: Beacon Press.

Major, B., & Crocker, J. (1993). Social stigma: The affective consequences of attributional ambiguity. In D. M. Mackie & D. L. Hamilton (Eds.), *Affect, cognition, and stereotyping: Interactive processes in intergroup perception* (pp. 345–370). New York, NY: Academic Press.

Maras, P., & Brown, R. (1996). Effects of contact on children's attitudes toward disability: A longitudinal study. *Journal of Applied Social Psychology, 94*, 265–277.

Marinelli, R. P., & Dell Orto, A. E. (1984). *The psychological and social impact of disability.* New York, NY: Springer.

Marini, L. (1992). The use of humor in counseling as a social skill for clients who are disabled. *Journal of Applied Rehabilitation Counseling, 23*, 30–36.

Markus, H., & Wurf, E. (1987). The dynamic self-concept: A social psychological perspective. *Annual Review of Psychology, 38*, 299–337. doi: 101146/annurev.ps.38.020187.001503

Marrow, A. J. (1977). *The practical theorist: The life and work of Kurt Lewin.* New York, NY: Teachers College Press.

Mason, A., Pratt H. D., Patel, D. R., Greydanus, D. E., & Yahya, K. Z. (2004). Prejudice toward people with disabilities. In J. L. Chin (Ed.), *The psychology of prejudice and discrimination: Disability, religion, physique, and other traits* (Vol. 4, pp. 52–93). Westport, CT: Praeger.

Mason, L., & Muhlenkamp, A. (1976). Patients' self-reported affective states following loss and caregivers' expectations of patients' affective states. *Rehabilitation Psychology, 23*, 72–76. doi: 10.1037/h0090904

Massimini, F., & Delle Fave, A. (2000). Individual development in a bio-cultural perspective. *American Psychologist, 55,* 24–33. doi: 10.1037/0003-066X.55.1.24

Masten, A. S. (2007). Resilience in developing systems: Progress and promise as the fourth wave rises. *Development and Psychopathology, 2,* 425–444. doi: 10.1017/S0954579400005812

Masten, A. S., Best, K. M., & Garmezy, N. (1990). Resilience and development: Contributions from the study of children who overcame adversity. *Development and Psychopathology, 2,* 425–444. doi: 10.1017/S0954579400005812

Masten, A. S., Cutuli, J. J., Herbers, J. E., & Reed, M.-G. J. (2009). Resilience in development. In S. J. Lopez & C. R. Snyder (Eds.), *Oxford handbook of positive psychology* (pp. 117–131). New York, NY: Oxford University Press. doi: 10.1093/oxfordhb/9780195187243.013.0012

McAdams, D. P. (1993). *The stories we live by: Personal myths and the making of the self.* New York, NY: Morrow.

McAdams, D. P. (2001). The psychology of life stories. *Review of General Psychology, 5,* 100–122. doi: 10.1037/1089-2680.5.2.100

McAdams, D. P. (2006). *The person: A new introduction to personality psychology.* Hoboken, NJ: Wiley.

McAdams, D. P., Josselson, R., & Lieblich, A. (Eds.). (2006). *Identity and story: Creating self in narrative.* Washington, DC: American Psychological Association. doi: 10.1037/11414-000

McAdams, D. P., & McLean, K. C. (2013). Narrative identity. *Current Directions in Psychological Science, 22,* 233–238. doi: 10.1177/0963721413475622

McCarthy, H. (2011). A modest festschrift and insider perspective on Beatrice Wright's contributions to rehabilitation theory and practice. *Rehabilitation Counseling Bulletin, 54*(2), 67–81. doi: 10.1177/0034355210386971

McCarthy, H. (2014). Cultivating our roots and extending our branches: Appreciating and marketing rehabilitation theory and research. *Rehabilitation Counseling Bulletin, 53*(2), 67–79.

McGuire, W. J., McGuire, C. V., Child, P., & Fujioka, T. (1978). Salience of ethnicity in the spontaneous self-concept as a function of one's ethnic distinctiveness in the social environment. *Journal of Personality and Social Psychology, 36,* 511–520. doi: 10.1037/0022-3514.36.5.511

McMillen, J. C., & Cook, C. L. (2003). The positive by-products of spinal cord injury and their correlates. *Rehabilitation Psychology, 48,* 77–85. doi: 10.1037/0090-5550.48.2.77

McMillen, J. C., Smith, E. M., & Fisher, R. H. (1997). Perceived benefit and mental health after three types of disaster. *Journal of Consulting and Clinical Psychology, 65,* 733–739. doi: 10.1037/0022-006X.65.5.733

Mellers, B. A., & McGraw, A. P. (2001). Anticipated emotions as guides to choice. *Current Directions in Psychological Science, 10,* 210–214. doi: 10.1111/1467-8721.00151

Meyerson, L. (1948). Physical disability as a social psychological problem. *Journal of Social Issues, 4,* 2–10. doi: 10.1111/j.1540-4560.1948.tb01513.x

Milgram, S. (1963). Behavioral study of obedience. *Journal of Abnormal and Social Psychology, 67,* 371–378. doi: 10.1037/h0040525

Millington, M. J. (2012). Basic do's and don'ts in counseling persons with disabilities. In I. Marini, N. M. Glover-Graf, & M. J. Millington (Eds.), *Psychosocial aspects of disability: Insider perspectives and counseling strategies* (pp. 465–480). New York, NY: Springer.

Minkler, M., & Wallerstein, N. (Eds.). (2003). *Community-based participatory research for health.* San Francisco, CA: Jossey-Bass.

Monteith, M. J., Arthur, S. A., & Flynn, S. M. (2010). Self-regulation and bias. In J. F. Dovidio, M. Hewstone, P. Glick, & V. M. Esses (Eds.), *Handbook of prejudice, stereotyping, and discrimination* (pp. 493–507). Los Angeles, CA: Sage. doi: 10.4135/9781446200919.n30

Mpofu, E., Chronister, J., Johnson, E. T., & Denham, G. (2012). Aspects of culture influencing rehabilitation and persons with disabilities. In P. Kennedy (Ed.), *Oxford handbook of rehabilitation psychology* (pp. 543–553). New York, NY: Oxford University Press. doi: 10.1093/oxfordhb/9780199733989.013.0030

Murphy, R. F. (1990). *The body silent*. New York, NY: W. W. Norton & Co.

Myers, D. G. (1980). *Inflated self: Human illusions and the biblical call to hope*. New York, NY: Seabury Press.

Myers, D. G., & Diener, E. (1995). Who is happy? *Psychological Science, 6*, 10–19. doi: 10.1111/j.1467-9280.1995.tb00298.x

National Council on Disability. (2007). *The impact of the Americans with Disabilities Act: Assessing the progress toward achieving the goals of the Americans with Disabilities Act*. Retrieved from http://www.ncd.gov/publications/2007/07262007

Nelson, T. D. (Ed.). (2009). *Handbook of prejudice, stereotyping, and discrimination*. New York, NY: Psychology Press.

Nielsen, K. E. (2012). *A disability history of the United States*. Boston, MA: Beacon Press.

Niemiec, R. M. (2013). VIA character strengths: Research and practice (the first 10 years). In H. Knoop & A. Fave (Eds.), *Well-being and cultures: Perspectives from positive psychology* (pp. 11–29). New York, NY: Springer Science + Business Media. doi: 10.1007/978-94-007-4611-4_2

Nisbett, R. E. (1980). The trait construct in lay and professional psychology. In L. Festinger (Ed.), *Retrospections on social psychology* (pp. 109–130). New York: Oxford University Press.

Nisbett, R. E. (2004). *The geography of thought: How Asians and Westerners think differently. . . and why*. New York, NY: Free Press.

Nisbett, R. E., Caputo, C., Legant, P., & Maracek, J. (1973). Behavior as seen by the actor and as seen by the observer. *Journal of Personality and Social Psychology, 27*, 154–164. doi: 10.1037/h0034779

Nisbett, R. E., & Ross, L. (1980). *Human inference: Strategies and shortcomings of social judgment*. Englewood Cliffs, NJ: Prentice-Hall.

Nisbett, R. E., & Wilson, T. D. (1977). Telling more than we can know: Verbal reports on mental processes. *Psychological Review, 84*, 231–259. doi: 10.1037/0033-295X.84.3.231

Nosek, B. A., Greenwald, A. G., & Banaji, M. R. (2007). The Implicit Association Test at age 7: A methodological and conceptual review. In J. A. Bargh (Ed.), *Automatic processes in social thinking and behavior* (pp. 265–292). Philadelphia, PA: Psychology Press.

Oakes, P. (2001). The root of all evil in intergroup relations? Unearthing the categorization process. In R. Brown & S. L. Gaertner (Eds.), *Blackwell handbook of social psychology: Intergroup processes* (pp. 3–21). London, England: Blackwell.

Olkin, R. (1997). Five models of research on disability: Shifting the paradigm from pathology to policy. *Newsletter of the American Family Therapy Academy, 67*, 27–32.

Olkin, R. (1999). *What psychotherapists should know about disability*. New York, NY: Guilford.

Olkin, R. (2004). Making research accessible to participants with disabilities. *Journal of Multicultural Counseling and Development, 32*, 332–343.

Olkin, R. (2005). Why I changed my mind about physician-assisted suicide: How Stanford University made a radical out of me. *Journal of Disability Policy Studies, 16,* 68–71. doi: 10.11 77/10442073050160011101

Olkin, R., & Pledger, C. (2003). Can disability studies and psychology join hands? *American Psychologist, 58*(4), 296–304. doi: 10.1037/0003-066X.58.4.296

Oyserman, D., Elmore, K., & Smith, G. (2012). Self, self-concept, and identity. In M. R. Leary & J. P. Tangney (Eds.), *Handbook of self and identity* (2nd ed., pp. 69–104). New York: Guilford.

Park, C. L., Lechner, S. C., Antoni, M. H., & Stanton, A. L. (Eds.). (2009). *Medical illness and positive life change: Can crisis lead to personal transformation?* Washington, DC: American Psychological Association.

Park, J. H., Faulkner, J., & Schaller, M. (2003). Evolved disease-avoidance processes and contemporary anti-social behavior: Prejudicial attitudes and avoidance of people with physical disabilities. *Journal of Nonverbal Behavior, 27,* 65–87. doi: 10.1023/A:1023910408854

Pastalan, L. A. (1974). The simulation of age-related sensory losses: A new approach to the study of environmental barriers. *New Outlook for the Blind, 68,* 356–362.

Patterson, D. R., Everett, J. J., Bombardier, C. H., Questad, K. A., Lee, V. K., & Marvin, J. A. (1993). Psychological effects of severe burn injuries. *Psychological Bulletin, 113,* 362–378. doi: 10.1037/0033-2909.113.2.362

Pelka, F. (1997). *The ABC-CLIO companion to the disability rights movement.* Santa Barbara, CA: ABC-CLIO.

Pennebaker, J. W. (1997). *Opening up: The healing power of expressing emotions (rev. ed).* New York, NY: Guilford.

Pennebaker, J. W. (2004). *Writing to heal: A guided journal for recovering from trauma & emotional upheaval.* Oakland, CA: New Harbinger Publications.

Perry, R. B. (1935). *The thought and character of William James* (Vols. 1–2). Boston, MA: Little, Brown.

Peterson, C. (2006). *A primer in positive psychology.* New York, NY: Oxford University Press.

Peterson, C., & Park, N. (2011). Character strengths and virtues: Their role in well-being. In S. I. Donaldson, M. Csikszentmihalyi, & J. Nakamura (Eds.), *Applied positive psychology: Improving everyday life, health, schools, work, and society* (pp. 49–62). New York, NY: Routledge/Taylor & Francis Group.

Peterson, C., & Park, N. (2012). Character strengths and the life of meaning. In P. P. Wong (Ed.), *The human quest for meaning: Theories, research, and applications* (2nd ed., pp. 277–295). New York, NY: Routledge/Taylor & Francis Group.

Peterson, C., & Seligman, M. E. P. (2004). *Character strengths and virtues: A handbook and classification.* Washington, DC: American Psychological Association.

Peterson, D. B., & Rosenthal, D. R. (2005). The International Classification of Functioning, Disability and Health (ICF) as an allegory for history and systems in rehabilitation education. *Rehabilitation Education, 19,* 75–80.

Pettigrew, T. F. (1979). The ultimate attribution error: Extending Allport's cognitive analysis of prejudice. *Personality and Social Psychology Bulletin, 5,* 461–476. doi: 10.1177/014616727900500407

Pettigrew, T. F., & Tropp, L. R. (2000). Does intergroup contact reduce prejudice: Recent meta-analytic findings. In S. Oskamp (Ed.), *Reducing prejudice and discrimination: The Claremont Symposium on Applied Social Psychology* (pp. 93–114). Mahwah, NJ: Erlbaum.

Pettigrew, T. F., & Tropp, L. R. (2006). A meta-analytic test of intergroup contact theory. *Journal of Personality and Social Psychology, 90,* 751–783. doi: 10.1037/0022-3514.90.5.751

Pettigrew, T. F., & Tropp, L. R. (2008). How does intergroup contact reduce prejudice? Meta-analytic tests of three mediators. *European Journal of Social Psychology, 38,* 922–934. doi: 10.1002/ejsp.504

Pettigrew, T. F., & Tropp, L. R. (2011). *When groups meet: The dynamics of intergroup contact.* New York, NY: Psychology Press.

Philips, G. B. (1975). An exploration of employer attitudes concerning employment opportunities for deaf people. *Journal of Rehabilitation of the Deaf, 9,* 1–9.

Pinel, E. C. (1999). Stigma consciousness: The psychological legacy of social stereotypes. *Journal of Personality and Social Psychology, 76,* 114–128. doi: 10.1037/0022-3514.76.1.114

Pledger, C. (2003). Discourse on disability and rehabilitation issues: Opportunities for psychology. *American Psychologist, 58,* 279–284. doi: 10.1037/0003-066X.58.4.279

Postmes, T., & Spears, R. (1998). Deindividuation and antinormative behavior: A meta-analysis. *Psychological Bulletin, 123,* 238–259. doi: 10.1037/0033-2909.123.3.238

Pruett, S. R., & Chan, F. (2006). The development and psychometric validation of the Disability Attitude Implicit Association Test. *Rehabilitation Psychology, 51,* 202–213. doi: 10.1037/0090-5550.51.3.202

Putnam, M. (2005). Conceptualizing disability: Developing a framework for political disability identity. *Journal of Disability Policy Studies, 16,* 188–198. doi: 10.1177/10442073050160030601

Putnam, R. D. (2001). *Bowling alone: The collapse and revival of American community.* New York, NY: Simon & Schuster.

Quinn, D. M. (2006). Concealable versus conspicuous stigmatized identities. In S. Levin & C. van Laar (Eds.), *Stigma and group inequality: Social psychological perspectives* (pp. 83–103). Mahwah, NJ: Erlbaum.

Rand, K. L., & Cheavens, J. S. (2009). Hope theory. In S. J. Lopez & C. R. Snyder (Eds.), *Oxford handbook of positive psychology* (pp. 323–333). New York, NY: Oxford University Press. doi: 10.1093/oxfordhb/9780195187243.013.0030

Rath, J. F., & Elliott, T. R. (2011). Psychological models in rehabilitation psychology. In P. Kennedy (Ed.), *The Oxford handbook of rehabilitation psychology* (pp. 32–46). New York, NY: Oxford University Press.

Reeve, D. (2000). Oppression within the counseling room. *Disability and Society, 15,* 669–682. doi: 10.1080/09687590050058242

Richards, Z., & Hewstone, M. (2001). Subtyping and subgrouping: Processes for the prevention and promotion of stereotype change. *Personality and Social Psychology Review, 5,* 52–73. doi: 10.1207/S15327957PSPR0501_4

Riessman, C. K. (2008). *Narrative methods for the human sciences.* Thousand Oaks, CA: Sage.

Riis, J., Loewenstein, G., Baron, J., Jepson, C., Fagerlin, A., & Ubel, P. A. (2005). Ignorance of hedonic adaptation to hemodialysis: A study using ecological momentary assessment. *Journal of Experimental Psychology: General, 134,* 3–9. doi: 10.1037/0096-3445.134.1.3

Risen, J., & Gilovich, T. (2007). Informal logic fallacies. In R. J. Sternberg, H. L. Roediger III, & D. F. Halpern (Eds.), *Critical thinking in psychology* (pp. 110–130). New York, NY: Cambridge University Press.

Rivera, P. A. (2012). Families in rehabilitation. In P. Kennedy (Ed.), *Oxford handbook of rehabilitation psychology* (pp. 160–170). New York, NY: Oxford University Press. doi: 10.1093/oxfordhb/9780199733989.013.0009

Robey, K. L., Beckley, L., & Kirschner, M. (2006). Implicit infantilizing attitudes about disability. *Journal of Developmental and Physical Disabilities, 18*(4), 441–453. doi: 10.1007/s10882-006-9027-3

Roediger, R. (2004). What should they be called? *APS Observer, 17*(4), 5, 46–48.

Roessler, R., & Bolton, B. (1978). *Psychosocial adjustment to disability.* Baltimore, MD: University Park Press.

Rojahn, J., Komelasky, K. G., & Man, M. (2008). Implicit attitudes and explicit ratings of romantic attraction of college students toward opposite-sex peers with physical disabilities. *Journal of Developmental and Physical Disabilities, 20,* 389–397. doi: 10.1007/s10882-008-9108-6

Rokeach, M. (1973). *The nature of values.* New York, NY: Free Press.

Ronning, J. A., & Nabuzoka, D. (1993). Promoting social interaction and status of children with intellectual disabilities in Zambia. *Journal of Special Education, 27,* 277–305. doi: 10.1177/002246699302700302

Rosenthal, D. A., Kosciulek, J., Lee, G. K., Frain, M., & Ditchman, N. (2009). Family and adaptation to chronic illness. In F. Chan, E. Da Silva Cardoso, & J. A. Chronister (Eds.), *Understanding psychosocial adjustment to chronic illness and disability: A handbook for evidence-based practitioners in rehabilitation.* New York, NY: Springer.

Ross, L. (1977). The intuitive psychologist and his shortcomings: Distortions in the attribution process. In L. Berkowitz (Ed.), *Advances in experimental social psychology* (Vol. 10, pp. 174–221). New York, NY: Academic Press.

Ross, L., Amabile, T. M., & Steinmetz, J. L. (1977). Social roles, social control and biases in social perception. *Journal of Personality and Social Psychology, 35,* 485–494. doi: 10.1037/0022-3514.35.7.485

Ross, L., & Nisbett, R. E. (1991). *The person in the situation.* New York, NY: McGraw-Hill.

Rozin, R., & Royzman, P. B. (2001). Negativity bias, negativity dominance, and contagion. *Personality and Social Psychology Review, 5,* 296–320. doi: 10.1207/S15327957PSPR0504_2

Rudman, L. A. (2011). *Implicit measures for social and personality psychology.* Thousand Oaks, CA: Sage.

Rutter, M. (1979). Maternal deprivation, 1972–1978: New findings, new concepts, new approaches. *Child Development, 50,* 283–305. doi: 10.2307/1129404

Ryff, C. D., & Keyes. C. L. M. (1995). The structure of psychological well-being revisited. *Journal of Personality and Social Psychology, 69,* 719–727.

Ryff, C. D., & Singer, B. (2003). Flourishing under fire: Resilience as a prototype of challenged thriving. In C. L. M. Keyes & J. Haidt (Eds.), *Flourishing: Positive psychology and the life well-lived* (pp. 15–36). Washington, DC: American Psychological Association.

Sackett, D. L., & Torrance, G. W. (1978). The utility of different health states as perceived by the general public. *Journal of Chronic Diseases, 31,* 697–704. doi: 10.1016/0021-9681(78)90072-3

Salovey, P., Mayer, J. D., & Rosenhan, D. L. (1991). Mood and helping: Mood as a motivator of helping and helping as a regulator of mood. In M. S. Clark (Ed.), *Prosocial behavior* (pp. 215–237). Thousand Oaks, CA: Sage.

Samerotte, G. C., & Harris, M. B. (1976). Some factors influencing helping: The effects of handicap, responsibility, and requesting help. *Journal of Social Psychology, 98*, 39–45. doi: 10.1080/00224545.1976.9923363

Saperstein, J. A. (2010). *Atypical: Life with Asperger's in 20 1/3 chapters.* New York: NY: Penguin Group.

Sapir, E. (1951). *Selected writings in language, culture, and personality* (D. G. Mandelbaum, Ed.). Berkeley: University of California Press.

Schafer, W. (1996). *Stress management for wellness.* Orlando, FL: Harcourt Brace.

Scheier, M. F., Carver, C. S., & Bridges, M. W. (1994). Distinguishing optimism from neuroticism (and trait anxiety, self-mastery, and self-esteem): A reevaluation of the Life Orientation Test. *Journal of Personality and Social Psychology, 57*, 1024–1040. doi: 10.1037/0022-3514.57.6.1024

Scherer, M., Blair, K., Bost, R., Hanson, S., Hough, S., Kurylo, M., et al. (2010). Rehabilitation psychology. In I. B. Weiner & W. E. Craighead (Eds.), *The concise Corsini encyclopedia of psychology and behavioral science* (4th ed.). Hoboken, NJ: Wiley. doi: 10.1002/9780470479216.corpsy0785

Schneider, D. J. (2007). The belief machine. In R. J. Sternberg, H. L. Roediger III, & D. F. Halpern (Eds.), *Critical thinking in psychology* (pp. 251–270). New York, NY: Cambridge University Press.

Schulz, R., & Decker, S. (1985). Long-term adjustment to physical disability: The role of social support, perceived control, and self-blame. *Journal of Personality and Social Psychology, 48*, 1162–1172. doi: 10.1037/0022-3514.48.5.1162

Scotch, R. (1988). Disability as the basis for social movement: Advocacy and the politics of definition. *Journal of Social Issues, 1*, 159–172. doi: 10.1111/j.1540-4560.1988.tb02055.x

Sedikides, C., & Gregg, A. P. (2008). Self-enhancement: Food for thought. *Perspectives on Psychological Science, 3*(2), 102–116. doi: 10.1111/j.1745-6916.2008.00068.x

Seerey, M. D., Leo, R. J., Lupien, S. P., Knodrak, C. L., & Almonte, J. L. (2013). An upside to adversity? Moderate cumulative lifetime adversity is associated with resilient responses in the face of controlled stressors. *Psychological Science, 24*(7), 1181–1189. doi: 10.1177/0956797612469210

Seligman, M. E. P. (2002a). Positive psychology, positive prevention, and positive therapy. In C. R. Snyder & S. J. Lopez (Eds.), *Handbook of positive psychology* (pp. 3–9). New York, NY: Oxford University Press.

Seligman, M. E. P. (2002b). *Authentic happiness: Using the new positive psychology to realize your potential for lasting fulfillment.* New York, NY: Free Press.

Seligman, M. E. P., & Csikszentmihalyi, M. (2000). Positive psychology: An introduction. *American Psychologist, 55*, 5–14. doi: 10.1037/0003-066X.55.1.5

Seerey, M. D., Leo, R. J., Lupien, S. P., Knodrak, C. L., & Almonte, J. L. (2013). An upside to adversity? Moderate cumulative lifetime adversity is associated with resilient responses in the face of controlled stressors. *Psychological Science.* doi: 10.1177/0956797612469210

Shapiro, J. P. (1994). *No pity: People with disabilities forging a new civil rights movement.* New York, NY: Three Rivers Press.

Shaver, P. R., & Scheibe, E. (1967). Transformation of social identity: A study of chronic mental patients and college volunteers in a summer camp setting. *Journal of Psychology, 66*, 19–37. doi: 10.1080/00223980.1967.10544877

Shewchuk, R., & Elliott, T. R. (2000). Family caregiving in chronic disease and disability. In R. G. Frank & T. R. Elliott (Eds.), *Handbook of rehabilitation psychology* (pp. 553–563). Washington, DC: American Psychological Association. doi: 10.1037/10361-026

Shontz, F. C. (1975). *The psychological aspects of physical illness and disability*. New York, NY: Macmillan.

Shontz, F. C. (1982). Adaptation to chronic illness and disability. In T. Millon, C. Green, & R. Meagher (Eds.), *Handbook of clinical health psychology* (pp. 153–172). New York, NY: Plenum Press. doi: 10.1007/978-1-4613-3412-5_8

Shurka, E., Siller, J., & Dvonch, P. (1982). Coping behavior and personal responsibility as factors in the perception of disabled persons by the nondisabled. *Rehabilitation Psychology, 27*, 225–233. doi: 10.1037/h0091050

Siebers, T. (2011). *Disability theory*. Ann Arbor, MI: University of Michigan Press.

Sieff, E. M., Dawes, R. M., & Loewenstein, G. (1999). Anticipated versus actual responses to HIV test results. *American Journal of Psychology, 112*, 297–311. doi: 10.2307/1423355

Siller, J. (1984). Attitudes toward the physically disabled. In R. L. Jones (Ed.), *Attitudes and attitude change in special education: Theory and practice* (pp. 184–205). Reston, VA: Council for Exceptional Children.

Singer, J. A. (2004). Narrative identity and meaning-making across the adult lifespan: An introduction. *Journal of Personality, 72*, 437–459. doi: 10.1111/j.0022-3506.2004.00268.x

Singer, P. (2011). *Practical ethics*. New York, NY: Cambridge University Press. doi: 10.1017/CBO9780511975950

Smart, J. (2001). *Disability, society, and the individual*. Gaithersburg, MD: Aspen Publishers.

Smedema, S., Bakken-Gillen, S. K., & Dalton, J. (2009). Psychosocial adaptation to chronic illness and disability: Models and measurement. In F. Chan, E. Da Silva Cardoso, & J. A. Chronister (Eds.), *Understanding psychosocial adjustment to chronic illness and disability: A handbook for evidence-based practitioners in rehabilitation* (pp. 51–73). New York, NY: Springer.

Smith, D. M., Loewenstein, G., Jankovic, A., & Ubel, P. A. (2009). Happily hopeless: Adaptation to a permanent, but not a temporary, disability. *Health Psychology, 28*, 787–791. doi: 10.1037/a0016624

Smith, C. T., & Nosek, B. A. (2010). Implicit Association Test. In I. B. Weiner & W. E. Craighead (Eds.), *Corsini encyclopedia of psychology* (pp. 803–804). Hoboken, NJ: Wiley. doi: 10.1002/9780470479216.corpsy0433

Snyder, C. R. (1989). *Reality negotiation: From excuses to hope and beyond. Journal of Social and Clinical Psychology, 8*, 130–157. doi: 10.1521/jscp.1989.8.2.130

Snyder, C. R. (1994). *The psychology of hope: You can get there from here*. New York, NY: Free Press.

Snyder, C. R., Harris, C., Anderson, J., Holleran, S., Irving, L., Sigmon, S.,... & Harney, P. (1991). The will and the ways: Development and validation of an individual differences measure of hope. *Journal of Personality and Social Psychology, 60*, 570–585. doi: 10.1037/0022-3514.60.4.570

Snyder, C. R., & Higgins, R. L. (1988). Excuses: Their effective role in negotiating reality. *Psychological Bulletin, 104*, 23–35. doi: 10.1037/0033-2909.104.1.23

Snyder, C. R., & Higgins, R. L. (1997). Reality negotiation: Governing one's own self and being governed by others. *General Psychology Review, 4*, 336–350. doi: 10.1037/1089-2680.1.4.336

Snyder, C. R., Lopez, S. J., & Pedrotti, J. T. (2011). *Positive psychology: The scientific and practical exploration of human strengths (2nd ed.).* Thousand Oaks, CA: Sage.

Snyder, M., Tanke, E. D., & Berscheid, E. (1977). Social perception and interpersonal behavior: On the self-fulfilling nature of social stereotypes. *Journal of Personality and Social Psychology, 35,* 656–666. doi: 10.1037/0022-3514.35.9.656

Solomon, S., Greenberg, J., & Pyszczynski, T. (2004). The cultural animal: Twenty years of terror management theory and research. In J. Greenberg, S. L. Koole, & T. Pyszczynski (Eds.), *Handbook of experimental existential psychology* (pp. 13–34). New York, NY: Guilford.

Spencer, S. J., Steele, C. M., & Quinn, D. M. (1999). Stereotype threat and women's math performance. *Journal of Experimental Social Psychology, 35,* 4–28. doi: 10.1006/jesp.1998.1373

Stahi, S., & Crisp, R. J. (2008). Imagining intergroup contact promotes projection to outgroups. *Journal of Experimental Social Psychology, 44,* 943–957. doi: 10.1016/j.jesp.2008.02.003

Stapel, D. A., & Koomen, W. (2000). How far do we go beyond the information given? The impact of knowledge activation on interpretation and inference. *Journal of Personality and Social Psychology, 78,* 19–37. doi: 10.1037/0022-3514.78.1.19

Stav, A., & Florian, V. (1986). Burnout among social workers working with physically disabled persons and bereaved families. *Journal of Social Service Research, 10,* 81–94. doi: 10.1300/J079v10n01_08

Steele, C. M. (1997). A threat in the air: How stereotypes share intellectual identity and performance. *American Psychologist, 52,* 613–629. doi: 10.1037/0003-066X.52.6.613

Steele, C. M. (2011). *Whistling Vivaldi: How stereotypes affect us and what we can do.* New York, NY: Norton.

Svenson, O. (1981). Are we all less risky and more skillful than our fellow drivers? *Acta Psychologica, 47,* 143–148. doi: 10.1016/0001-6918(81)90005-6

Swain, J., & French, S. (2000). Towards an affirmation model of disability. *Disability and Society, 15,* 569–582. doi: 10.1080/09687590050058189

Tait, R., & Silver, R. C. (1989). Coming to terms with major negative events. In J. S. Uleman & J. A. Bargh (Eds.), *Unintended thought* (pp. 351–382). New York, NY: Guilford.

Tajfel, H. (Ed.). (1978). *Differentiation between social groups: Studies in the social psychology of intergroup relations. (European Monographs in Social Psychology 14.)* London, England: Academic Press.

Tajfel, H., Billig, M. G., Bundy, R. P., & Flament, C. (1971). Social categorization and intergroup behaviour. *European Journal of Social Psychology, 1*(2), 149–178. doi: 10.1002/ejsp.2420010202

Tate, D. G., & Pledger, C. (2003). An integrative conceptual framework of disability: New directions for research. *American Psychologist, 58,* 919–924. doi: 10.1037/0003-066X.58.4.289

Taylor, S. E. (1983). Adjustment to threatening events: A theory of cognitive adaptation. *American Psychologist, 38,* 1161–1173. doi: 10.1037/0003-066X.38.11.1161

Taylor, S. E. (2007). Social support. In H. S. Friedman & R. C. Silver (Eds.), *Foundations of health psychology* (pp. 145–171). New York, NY: Oxford University Press.

Taylor, S. E., & Brown, J. D. (1988). Illusions and well-being: A social psychological perspective on mental health. *Psychological Bulletin, 103,* 193–210. doi: 10.1037/0033-2909.103.2.193

Taylor, S. E., & Brown, J. D. (1994). Positive illusions and well-being revisited: Separating fact from fiction. *Psychological Bulletin, 116,* 21–27. doi: 10.1037/0033-2909.116.1.21

Taylor, S. E., Kemeny, M. E., Reed, G. M., Bower, J. E., & Gruenewald, T. L. (2000). Psychological resources, positive illusions, and health. *American Psychologist, 55,* 99–109. doi: 10.1037/0003-066X.55.1.99

Taylor, S. E., Lichtman, R. R., & Wood, J. V. (1984). Attributions, beliefs about control, and adjustment to breast cancer. *Journal of Personality and Social Psychology, 46,* 489–502. doi: 10.1037/0022-3514.46.3.489

Taylor, S. E., & Lobel, M. (1989). Social comparison activity under threat: Downward evaluation and upward contacts. *Psychological Review, 96,* 569–575. doi: 10.1037/0033-295X.96.4.569

Tedeschi, R. G., & Calhoun, L. G. (1995). *Trauma & transformation: Growth in the aftermath of suffering.* Thousand Oaks, CA: Sage.

Tennen, H., & Affleck, G. (2002). Benefit-finding and benefit-reminding. In C. R. Snyder & S. J. Lopez (Eds.), *Handbook of positive psychology* (pp. 584–597). New York, NY: Oxford University Press.

Terzi, L. (2004). The social model of disability: A philosophical critique. *Journal of Applied Philosophy, 21*(2), 141. doi: 10.1111/j.0264-3758.2004.00269.x

Terzi, L. (2009). Vagaries of the natural lottery: Human diversity, disability, and justice: A capability perspective. In K. Brownlee & A. Cureton (Eds.), *Disability and disadvantage* (pp. 86–111). New York, NY: Oxford University Press.

Thomas, A., Vaughn, D., & Doyle, A. (2007). Implementation of a computer based Implicit Association Test as a measure of attitudes toward individuals with disabilities. *Journal of Rehabilitation, 73,* 3–14.

Thomas, K. (2004). Old wine in a slightly cracked new bottle. *American Psychologist, 59,* 274–275. doi: 10.1037/0003-066X.59.4.274

Thompson, S. C. (1985). Finding positive meaning in a stressful event and coping. *Basic and Applied Social Psychology, 6,* 279–295. doi: 10.1207/s15324834basp0604_1

Thompson, S. C., & Janigian, A. S. (1988). Life schemes: A framework for understanding the search for meaning. *Journal of Social and Clinical Psychology, 7,* 260–280. doi: 10.1521/jscp.1988.7.2-3.260

Thurstone, J. R. (1959). A procedure for evaluating parental attitudes toward the handicapped. *American Journal of Mental Deficiency, 64,* 145–155.

Tollifson, J. (1997). Imperfection is a beautiful thing: On disability and meditation. In K. Fries (Ed.), *Staring back: The disability experience from the inside out* (pp. 105–114). New York: NY: Penguin Group.

Trieschmann, R. B. (1988). *Spinal cord injuries: Psychological, social, and vocational rehabilitation (2nd ed.).* New York, NY: Demos.

Tropp, L. R., & Mallett, R. K. (Eds.). (2011). *Moving beyond prejudice reduction: Pathways to positive intergroup relations.* Washington, DC: American Psychological Association. doi: 10.1037/12319-000

Tsang, H. H., Chan, F., & Chan, C. H. (2004). Factors influencing occupational therapy students' attitudes toward persons with disabilities: A conjoint analysis. *American Journal of Occupational Therapy, 58*(4), 426–434. doi: 10.5014/ajot.58.4.426

Tugade, M. M., & Fredrickson, B. L. (2002). Positive emotions and emotional intelligence. In L. Feldman-Barrett & P. Salovey (Eds.), *The wisdom of feelings: Psychological processes in emotional intelligence* (pp. 319–340). New York, NY: Guilford. doi: 10.1037/0022-3514.86.2.320

Tugade, M. M., & Fredrickson, B. L. (2004). Resilient individuals use positive emotion to bounce back from negative emotional arousal. *Journal of Personality and Social Psychology, 86*, 320–333.

Turner, R. N., & Crisp, R. J. (2010). Imagining intergroup contact reduces implicit prejudice. *British Journal of Social Psychology, 49*, 129–142. doi: 10.1348/014466609X419901

Turner, R. N., Crisp, R. J., & Lambert, E. (2007). Imagining intergroup contact can improve intergroup attitudes. *Group Processes and Intergroup Relations, 10*, 427–441. doi: 10.1177/1368430207081533

Ubel, P. A., Loewenstein, G., & Jepson, C. (2003). Whose quality of life? A commentary exploring discrepancies between health state evaluations of patients and the general public. *Quality of Life Research, 27*, 599–607. doi: 10.1023/A:1025119931010

Ubel, P. A., Lowenstein, G., & Jepson, C. (2005). Disability and sunshine: Can hedonic predictions be improved by drawing attention to focusing illusions or emotional adaptation. *Journal of Experimental Psychology: Applied, 11*, 111–123. doi: 10.1037/1076-898X.11.2.111

Ursprung, A. W. (1986). Burnout in the human services: A review of the literature. *Rehabilitation Counseling Bulletin, 29*, 190–199.

Vaillant, G. E. (1995). *Adaptation to life*. Cambridge, MA: Harvard University Press.

Vallacher, R. R., & Wegner, D. M. (1987). What do people think they're doing? Action identification and human behavior. *Psychological Review, 94*, 3–15. doi: 10.1037/0033-295X.94.1.3

Vash, C. (1978, April). *Avocational rehabilitation*. Keynote address presented at the Horizons West Therapeutic Recreation Conference, Handicapped Recreation Center, San Francisco, CA.

Vash, C. L., & Crewe, N. M. (2004). *Psychology of disability* (2nd ed.). New York, NY: Springer.

Vaughn, E., Thomas, A., & Doyle, A. L. (2011). The Multiple Disability Implicit Association Test: Psychometric analysis of a multiple administration IAT measure. *Rehabilitation Counseling Bulletin, 54*(4), 223–235. doi: 10.1177/0034355211403008

Vilchinsky, N., Findler, L., & Werner, S. (2010). Attitudes toward people with disabilities: The perspective of attachment theory. *Rehabilitation Psychology, 55*, 298–306. doi: 10.1037/a0020491

von Hentig, H. (1948). Physical desirability, mental conflict, and social crisis. *Journal of Social Issues, 4*(4), 21–27. doi: 10.1111/j.1540-4560.1948.tb01515.x

Vonofakou, C., Hewstone, M., & Voci, A. (2007). Contact with outgroup friends as a predictor of meta-attitudinal strength and accessibility of attitudes toward gay men. *Journal of Personality and Social Psychology, 92*, 804–820. doi: 10.1037/0022-3514.92.5.804

Wang, K., & Dovidio, J. F. (2011). Disability and autonomy: Priming alternative identities. *Rehabilitation Psychology, 56*, 123–127. doi: 10.1037/a0023039

Waterman, A. S. (Ed.). (2013). *The best within us: Positive psychology perspectives on eudaimonia*. Washington, DC: American Psychological Association. doi: 10.1037/14092-000

Watkins, P. C., Woodward, K., Stone, T., & Russell, L. (2003). Gratitude and happiness: Development of a measure of gratitude and relationships with subjective well-being. *Social Behavior and Personality, 31*, 431–452. doi: 10.2224/sbp.2003.31.5.431

Webb, E. J., Campbell, D. T., Schwartz, R. D., Sechrest, L., & Grove, J. B. (1981). *Nonreactive measures in the social sciences* (2nd ed.). Boston, MA: Houghton-Mifflin.

Wegner, D. M., & Gilbert, D. T. (2000). Social psychology—the science of human experience. In H. Bless & J. P. Forgas (Eds.), *The message within: The role of subjective experience in social cognition and behavior* (pp. 1–9). Philadelphia, PA: Psychology Press.

Weinberg, N. (1988). Another perspective: Attitudes of people with disabilities. In H. E. Yuker (Ed.), *Attitudes towards people with disabilities* (pp. 141–153). New York, NY: Springer.

Weiner, B. (1993). On sin versus sickness: A theory of perceived responsibility and social motivation. *American Psychologist, 48*, 957–965. doi: 10.1037/0003-066X.48.9.957

Weiner, B. (1995). *Judgments of responsibility: A foundation for a theory of social contact.* New York, NY: Guilford.

Weiner, B. (2006). *Social motivation, justice, and the moral emotions: An attributional approach.* Mahwah, NJ: Erlbaum.

Weitzenkamp. D. A., Gerhart, K. A., Charlifue, S. W., Whiteneck, G. G., Glass, C. A., & Kennedy, P. (2000). Ranking the criteria for assessing quality of life after disability: Evidence for priority shifting among long-term spinal cord injury survivors. *British Journal of Health Psychology, 5*(Part 1), 57–69. doi: 10.1348/135910700168766

Werner, E. E., & Smith, R. S. (1982). *Vulnerable but invincible: A study of resilient children.* New York, NY: McGraw-Hill.

Wheeler, L. (1966). Motivation as a determinant of upward comparison. *Journal of Experimental Social Psychology* (Suppl. 1), 27–31. doi: 10.1016/0022-1031(66)90062-X

White, R. K., Wright, B. A., & Dembo, T. (1948). Studies in adjustment to visible injuries: Evaluation of curiosity by the injured. *Journal of Abnormal and Social Psychology, 43*, 13–28. doi: 10.1037/h0057775

Whiteman, M., & Lukoff, I. F. (1965). Attitudes toward blindness and other physical handicaps. *Journal of Social Psychology, 66*, 133–145. doi: 10.1080/00224545.1965.9919629

Whiteneck, G. C., Brooks, C. A., Charlifue, S., Gerhart, K. A., Mellick, D., Overholser, D., & Richardson, G. N. (1992). *Guide for use of the Craig Handicap Assessment and Reporting Technique.* Englewood, CO: Craig Hospital.

Wilder, D. A. (1978). Perceiving persons as a group: Effects of attributions on causality and beliefs. *Social Psychology, 1*, 13–23. doi: 10.2307/3033593

Wilder, D. A. (1986). Social categorization: Implications for creation and reduction of intergroup bias. In L. Berkowitz (Ed.), *Advances in experimental social psychology* (Vol. 19, pp. 291–355). Orlando, FL: Academic Press.

Wiley, S., Philogène, G., & Revenson, T. A. (Eds.). (2012). *Social categories in everyday experience.* Washington, DC: American Psychological Association. doi: 10.1037/13488-000

Williamson, G. M. (1998). The central role of restricted normal activities in adjustment to illness and disability: A model of depressed affect. *Rehabilitation Psychology, 43*, 327–347. doi: 10.1037/0090-5550.43.4.327

Williamson, G. M., Schulz, R., Bridges, M. W., & Behan, A. M. (1994). Social and psychological factors in adjustment to limb amputation. *Journal of Social Behavior and Personality, 9*, 249–268.

Wills, T. A. (1981). Downward comparison principles in social psychology. *Psychological Bulletin, 90*, 245–271. doi: 10.1037/0033-2909.90.2.245

Wills, T. A. (1983). Social comparison in coping and help-seeking. In B. M. DePaulo, A. Nadler, & J. D. Fisher (Eds.), *New directions in helping* (Vol. 2, pp. 109–141). New York, NY: Academic Press.

Wills, T. A., & Fegan, M. (2001). Social networks and social support. In A. Baum, T. A. Revenson, & J. E. Singer (Eds.), *Handbook of health psychology* (pp. 209–234). Mahwah, NJ: Erlbaum.

Wilson, T. D. (2002). *Strangers to ourselves: Discovering the adaptive unconscious*. Cambridge, MA: Harvard University Press.

Wilson, T. D. (2005). The message is the method: Celebrating and exporting the experimental approach. *Psychological Inquiry, 16*, 185–193. doi: 10.1207/s15327965pli1604_09

Wilson, T. D. (2011). *Redirect: The surprising new science of psychological change*. New York, NY: Little, Brown and Company.

Wilson, T. D., Aronson, E., & Carlsmith, K. (2010). The art of laboratory experimentation. In S. T. Fiske, D. T. Gilbert, & G. Lindzey (Eds.), *Handbook of social psychology* (5th ed., Vol. 1, pp. 51–81). Hoboken, NJ: Wiley.

Wilson, T. D., & Dunn, E. W. (2004). Self-knowledge: Its limits, value, and potential for improvement. *Annual Review of Psychology, 55*, 493–518. doi: 10.1146/annurev.psych.55.090902.141954

Wilson, T. D., & Gilbert, D. T. (2003). Affective forecasting. In M. P. Zanna (Ed.), *Advances in experimental social psychology* (Vol. 35, pp. 345–411). San Diego, CA: Academic Press.

Wilson, T. D., & Gilbert, D. T. (2005). Affective forecasting: Knowing what to want. *Current Directions in Psychological Science, 14*, 131–134. doi: 10.1111/j.0963-7214.2005.00355.x

Wilson, T. D., Lindsey, S., & Schooler, T. Y. (2000). A model of dual attitudes. *Psychological Review, 107*, 101–126. doi: 10.1037/0033-295X.107.1.101

Wilson, T. D., Wheatley, T., Meyers, J. M., Gilbert, D. T., & Axsom, D. (2000). Focalism: A source of durability bias in affective forecasting. *Journal of Personality and Social Psychology, 78*, 821–836. doi: 10.1037/0022-3514.78.5.821

Wittenbrink, B., & Schwartz, N. (Eds.). (2007). *Implicit measures of attitudes*. New York, NY: Guilford Press.

Wong, P. T. P., & Weiner, B. (1981). When people ask "why" questions and the heuristics of attributional search. *Journal of Personality and Social Psychology, 40*, 650–663. doi: 10.1037/0022-3514.40.4.650

Wood, J. V., Taylor, S. E., & Lichtman, R. R. (1985). Social comparison in adjustment to breast cancer. *Journal of Personality and Social Psychology, 49*, 1169–1183. doi: 10.1037/0022-3514.49.5.1169

World Health Organization. (1980). *International classifications of impairments, disabilities, and handicaps: A manual of classifications relating to the consequences of disease*. Geneva, Switzerland: Author.

World Health Organization. (2001). *International classification of functioning, disability, and health*. Geneva, Switzerland: Author.

World Health Organization. (2011). *World report on disability: Summary*. Retrieved from http://www.who.int/disabilities/world_report/2011/report/en/

Wright, B. A. (1960). *Physical disability: A psychological approach*. New York, NY: Harper & Row. doi: 10.1037/10038-000

Wright, B. A. (1964). Spread in adjustment to disability. *Bulletin of the Menninger Clinic, 28*(4), 198–208.

Wright, B. A. (1972). Value-laden beliefs and principles for rehabilitation psychology. *Rehabilitation Psychology, 19*, 38–45. doi: 10.1037/h0090869

Wright, B. A. (1975). Sensitizing outsiders to the position of the insider. *Rehabilitation Psychology, 22*, 129–135. doi: 10.1037/h0090837

Wright, B. A. (1978). The coping framework and attitude change: A guide to constructive role-playing. *Rehabilitation Psychology, 25*, 177–183. doi: 10.1037/h0090957

Wright, B. A. (1983). *Physical disability: A psychosocial approach.* New York, NY: Harper & Row. doi: 10.1037/10589-000

Wright, B. A. (1987). Human dignity and professional self-monitoring. *Journal of Applied Rehabilitation Counseling, 18,* 12–14.

Wright, B. A. (1988). Attitudes and the fundamental negative bias. In H. E. Yuker (Ed.), *Attitudes toward persons with disabilities* (pp. 3–21). New York, NY: Springer.

Wright, B. A. (1989). Extension of Heider's ideas to rehabilitation psychology. *American Psychologist, 44,* 525–528. doi: 10.1037/0003-066X.44.3.525

Wright, B. A. (1991). Labeling: The need for greater person-environment individuation. In C. R. Snyder & D. R. Forsyth (Eds.), *Handbook of social and clinical psychology: The health perspective* (pp. 469–487). New York, NY: Pergamon Press.

Wright, B. A., & Fletcher, B. L. (1982). Uncovering hidden resources: A challenge in assessment. *Professional Psychology, 13,* 229–235. doi: 10.1037/0735-7028.13.2.229

Wright, B. A., & Lopez, S. J. (2009). Widening the diagnostic focus: A case for including human strengths and environmental resources. In C. R. Snyder & S. J. Lopez (Eds.), *Handbook of positive psychology* (2nd ed., pp. 71–88). New York, NY: Oxford University Press. doi: 10.1093/oxfordhb/9780195187243.013.0008

Wright, S. C., Aron, A., McLaughlin-Volpe, T., & Ropp, S. A. (1997). The extended contact effect: Knowledge of cross-group friendships and prejudice. *Journal of Personality and Social Psychology, 73,* 73–90. doi: 10.1037/0022-3514.73.1.73

Yuker, H. E. (1965). Attitudes as determinants of behavior. *Journal of Rehabilitation, 31,* 15–16.

Yuker, H. E. (Ed.). (1988). *Attitudes towards persons with disabilities.* New York, NY: Springer.

Yuker, H. E. (1994). Variables that influence attitudes toward people with disabilities: Conclusions from the data. *Journal of Social Behavior and Personality, 9,* 3–22.

Yuker, H. E., & Block, J. R. (1986). *Research with the Attitude Toward Disabled Persons Scales (ATDP): 1960–1985.* Hempstead, NY: Hofstra University.

Zimbardo, P. G. (1970). The human choice: Individuation, reason, and order versus deindividuation, impulse, and chaos. In W. J. Arnold & D. Levine (Eds.), *Nebraska Symposium on Motivation, 1969* (Vol. 17, pp. 237–307). Lincoln, NE: University of Nebraska Press.

Index

Note: Page numbers in *italics* denote table and charts.